IMAGES
of America

GERMAN MARIETTA AND WASHINGTON COUNTY

On the Cover: The Marietta Brewery, later named the Marietta Brewing Company, operated as the longest-lasting local brewing establishment in Marietta. German immigrants brewed beer and produced other beverages from 1898 to 1920 when Prohibition was enacted. The facility was capable of producing about 15,000 barrels of beer each year. At one time, the 20-man workforce produced about 500 bottles each day. (Courtesy of Washington County Historical Society.)

IMAGES
of America

German Marietta and Washington County

Jann Kuehn Adams

ARCADIA
PUBLISHING

ISBN 978-1-4671-1544-5

Published by Arcadia Publishing
Charleston, South Carolina

Printed in the United States of America

Library of Congress Control Number: 2015946385

For all general information, please contact Arcadia Publishing:
Telephone 843-853-2070
Fax 843-853-0044
E-mail sales@arcadiapublishing.com
For customer service and orders:
Toll-Free 1-888-313-2665

Visit us on the Internet at www.arcadiapublishing.com

Contents

ACKNOWLEDGMENTS

A publication that is a compilation of photographs, images, and historical information requires the assistance of many people. Contributors of photographs and images are noted in the courtesy lines. Thanks to them for sharing the photographs and giving their time in conversation. The following organizations and representative people significantly contributed to the collection of photographs, images, and information: Washington County Historical Society, Matamoras Historical Society, Marietta College Special Collections, Washington County Public Library, and the Oliver Tucker Museum. A special thank-you is due to Linda Showalter and Andrea Adkins for their scanning expertise and generous use of their time. Thank you to the following people for their special support: Cathy Schafer, Betsy Cook, John Miller, Phillip Crane, Jane Anne Rauch, Scott Britton, Ernest Thode, and Dona Cernus. Special gratitude is given to Linda Showalter for her encouragement to undertake this project.

INTRODUCTION

People of German heritage were among the earliest white settlers of Ohio. The German states were experiencing famines and political struggles, and people were eager to come to the land of plenty where men were allowed to participate in local government. Many migrated to the Eastern states during the late 1700s and in the early 1800s along Zane's Trace and the Ohio River. Marietta was one of the few settlements along the river for people to stop for a rest to exchange information, replenish supplies, and make the important decision to stay or look for livelihood on down the river.

The first pioneers of Marietta were officers and soldiers of the American Revolution who made the journey from Massachusetts to the Northwest Territory and were determined to make a new settlement in the likeness of a New England–style town. The Ohio Company of Associates, led by Gen. Rufus Putnam, initiated the settlement and surrounding lands. Their goal was to bestow a culture that would include a sense of stability, civil order, religious values, and the promotion of an educated community. In 1788, this was a tall order in a wilderness devoid of roads, common amenities, communication, and farmland. All obstacles demanded hard work, diligence, frugality, humility, and the fortitude to earn one's own way in the frontier.

Marietta, nestled along the Ohio and Muskingum Rivers, provided a way station for travelers coming downriver looking for land to call their own. Nearly all of the early pioneers were of an English background, but the lure of the frontier had a multicultural appeal. During the 1780s and the Indian Wars of the 1790s, two significant men of German descent engaged in military and diplomatic work. Maj. Johann Zeigler was stationed at Fort Harmar near Marietta. He worked with Col. Josiah Harmar and Gen. Arthur St. Clair in campaigns to halt Native American confederation in Ohio. Later, he would become the first mayor of Cincinnati. John Heckewelder, son of German missionaries, was an interpreter of Indian languages and noted for his knowledge of Indian customs. He worked with Rufus Putnam to draw up a treaty with the Indians. His journals about the Ohio Valley were published in the German States in 1797 making Germans aware of new opportunities for land, employment, and freedom.

Marietta struggled to survive in the Ohio frontier. Indian wars, clearing of land for crops, isolation, epidemics, and lack of new settlers hindered its prosperity. Only through determination, fortitude, and hard work did the settlement reach the turn of the 19th century. In 1834, leaders of the community formed the Emigrant Association of Washington County in order to attract new settlers. Agents of this group distributed flyers in port cities, such as Baltimore, urging people to consider settlement in the Ohio Valley. Between 1830 and 1860, hundreds of Germans flocked to southeastern Ohio. Flatboats, canoes, and sternwheelers brought the Germans, as well as the Irish, downriver by way of Wheeling, Virginia.

In the first wave of German settlers who came to Washington County in 1833, almost all were from the village of Durkheim in the Rhine Palatinate. The most well-known story is about Jacob and Charles Frederick Peters. In 1832, the brothers were supporters of a political rights gathering at

Homburg. When the movement failed, they looked to America. The brothers with their families and others arrived in Baltimore and traveled overland to Wheeling, Virginia. Charles Peters went ahead of the group to their destination of Cincinnati and found it suffering with cholera. Upon his return, a new plan was laid for the brothers to find a place to settle. After six days of travel, they arrived at Marietta where they found a German speaker at the Brophy Inn in Marietta. A Mrs. Brophy was born in France near the border of the German states and fluent in German. She convinced the brothers that Washington County had much affordable land. Eventually, Charles Peters settled in Salem Township, and Jacob Peters settled in Fearing Township before he later moved to Watertown Township. In 1834, John P. Peters, Conrad Bohl, Conrad Bissantz, Bernard Wagner, Christian Best, and many others came to the countryside, where they spread to other townships and Marietta. This first wave of immigrants set in motion the great migration of Germans to Marietta and Washington County.

In the next decades, Germans were the predominant immigrant group to the area and made a significant impact on the population of Marietta and the county. They had fled Europe for political freedom, for the availability of arable land, and to be free of military conscription that had plagued the German states during political upheavals. However, when the call for volunteers went out for service in the Civil War in 1860, about 200 native Germans and many first-generation Germans in the county participated and were honored for their service. Col. Jesse Hildebrand was one of the oldest men to volunteer. Upon his death, the *Marietta Register* reported on April 24, 1863, "We have lost one who honored his city, his country, his regiment, and his family, by the purity and exaltation of his patriotism, and by the heroism of his conduct on the battlefield of Shiloh." Germans answered the call to serve their country of choice and that did not go unnoticed by the descendants of those first New England pioneers.

Commercial activity at the turn of the 20th century showed the businesses of Germans well established in Marietta and other areas of the county. German speakers from the lands of the many German states, France, and Switzerland found Marietta ripe with business opportunity. Men and women operated some of the largest stores, industries, hotels, and many of the corner grocery stores that dotted the neighborhoods. Their participation in all areas of elected government, civil service, and leadership roles in commerce enabled this immigrant group to become a contributing force in the growth of Marietta.

One

Early German Immigrants

It was on Ohio Street that families came ashore to start a new life in Marietta. With Bibles, musical instruments, and the language of their homeland, many set out for the countryside in Washington County to farm. German merchants and craftsmen prospered in shops along the newly developing Front Street. Yet the Germans intended to retain their heritage in this new land. Socially, the newcomers were a close-knit community where they kept their traditions and language to themselves while fully embracing the ideals of America. Perhaps for this reason, activities at mid-century reflected two groups in Marietta. This can be seen clearly in the two Fourth of July celebrations of 1859. The Germans celebrated the holiday with song and beer while the rest of the citizens held a day of speeches and fellowship.

But it was the value of hard work, frugality, and common sense business practices that brought Germans the respect of the well-established townspeople. Setting up a business, building a home, and securing household necessities were a tall order for anyone coming to the Ohio country in the mid-1800s. In time, the community came to an acceptance of the two cultures. In the local German newspaper, the *Marietta Zeitung*, non-German businesses appealed to the German community with advertisements written in German. By the time of the 1888 Centennial Celebration of Marietta, all citizens participated in activities to honor the first pioneers of 1788.

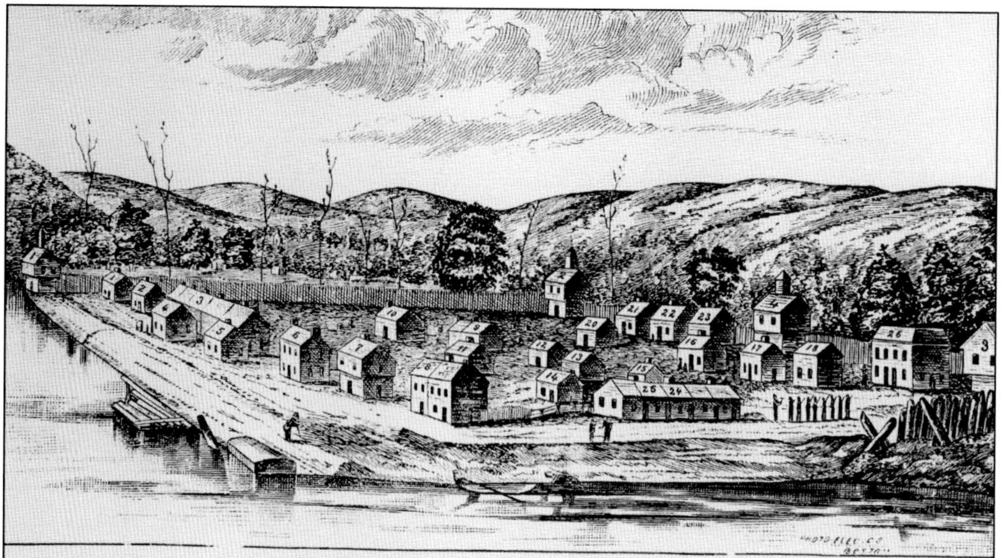

MARIETTA IN 1791.

Frontiersman and scout Peter Nyghswonger, son of a German mother and a Swiss father, had roamed these lands for several years, sometimes with Lewis Wetzel, a famed German Indian fighter. During the Indian Wars of the 1790s, Nyghswonger and family lived in Cabin No. 4 at Picketed Point. Nyghswonger could be named as the first German settler. (Courtesy of Marietta College.)

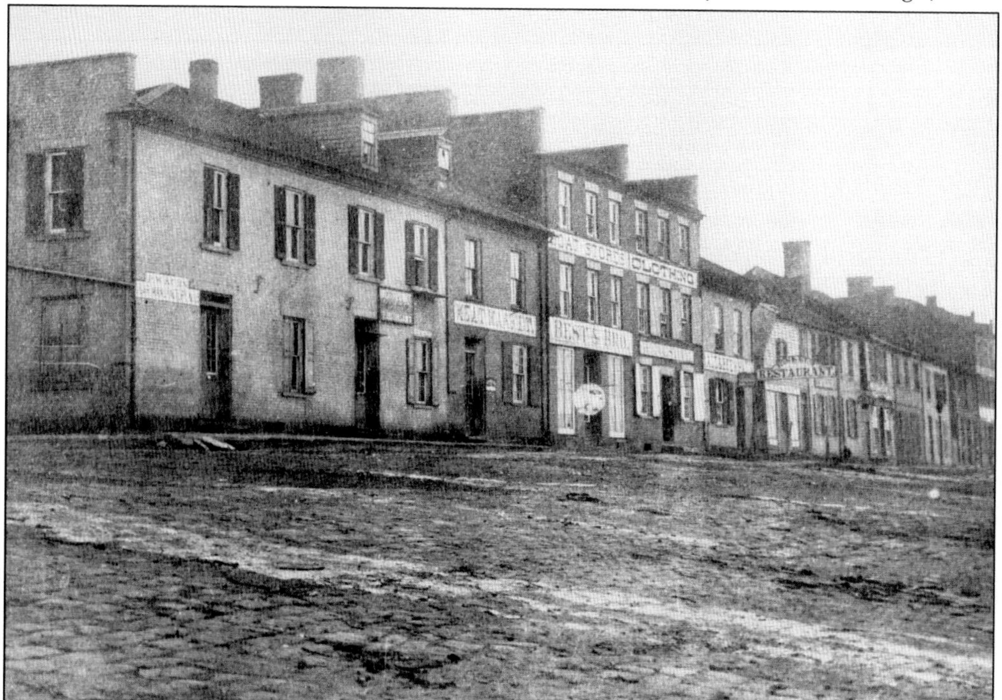

Most early German immigrants would travel the Ohio River to arrive in Marietta. As they stepped on to Ohio Street, a grocery, a meat market, and a clothing store were available to meet basic needs. Germans P.W. Kuhn, a cigar manufacturer, and the Best & Brother, groceries and boat supplies welcomed them in their native language. (Courtesy of Washington County Public Library.)

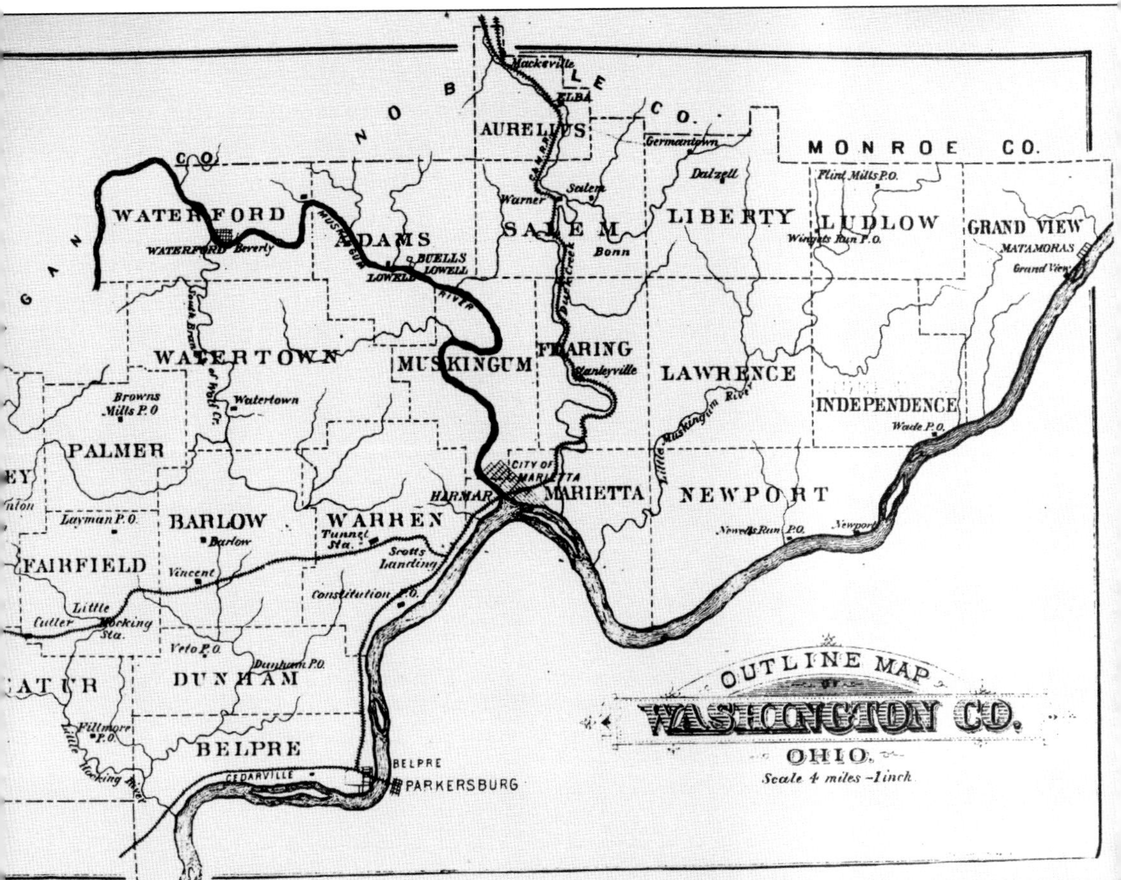

Washington County has 23 townships. The cities of Matamoras, Newport, Marietta, and Belpre, located along the Ohio River, were stopping places for German settlers during the early to mid-1800s. By the latter half of the century, Germans often came to the county by roads from Cincinnati and Zanesville where they had briefly settled. Most Germans were concentrated in the townships north and east of Marietta. Fearing and Adams Townships were heavily populated with German immigrants who formed early churches and farming communities. Of the cities, Marietta had the greatest influx of Germans. Townships west of Marietta had a strong Scot-Irish population. (Courtesy of Marietta College.)

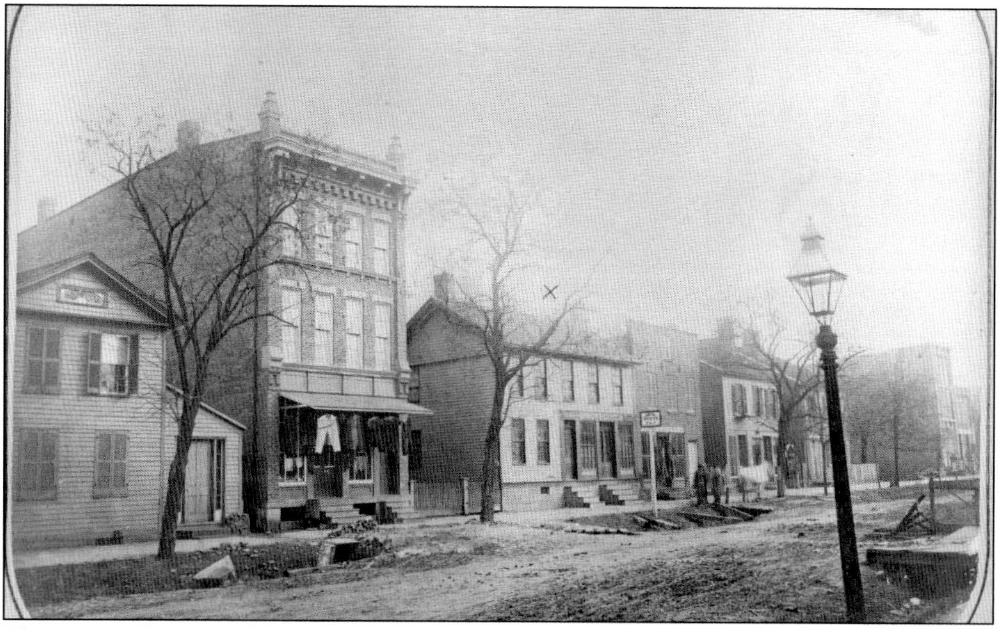

The corner of Front and Butler Streets was quiet in the 1860s. The tall building later became the office for the *Marietta Zeitung*, the local German newspaper. The Union House, a hotel, operated by Frederick and Elizabeth Gross, would later be the site of the St. Cloud Hotel. The next building was that of saddle- and harness-maker Jacob Ebinger. (Courtesy of Washington County Historical Society.)

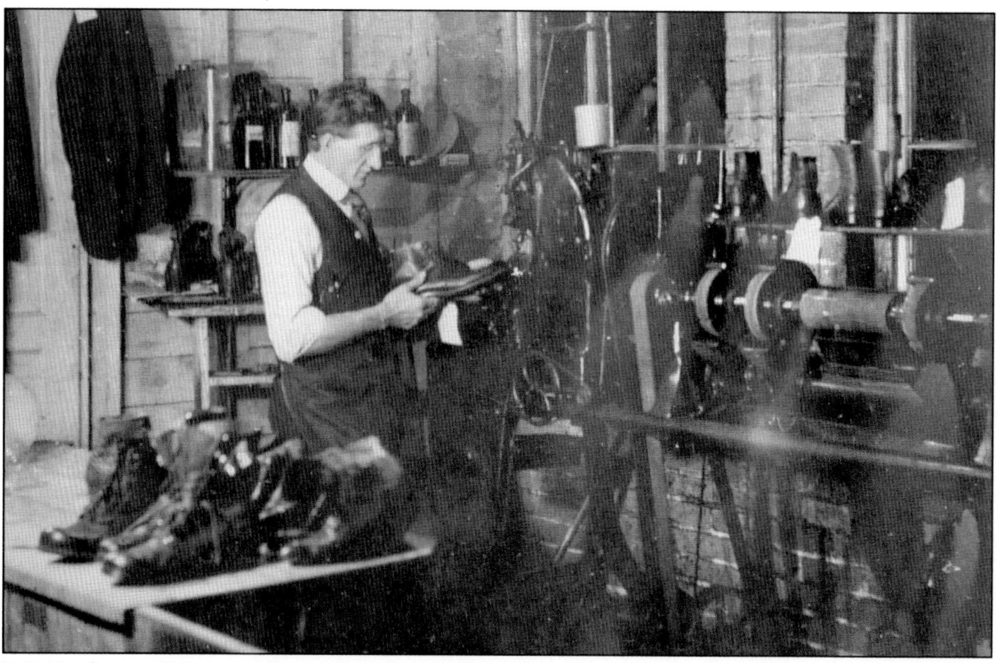

P.C. Fischer, well-known shoemaker, served the city for many years. He and his brother opened a shoe shop as early as 1873 at 104 Front Street. By 1893, P.C. Fischer moved to 246 Front Street where he spent the remainder of his career. In 1905, he went into partnership, and the store was named Fischer and Volkwein. (Courtesy of Washington County Historical Society.)

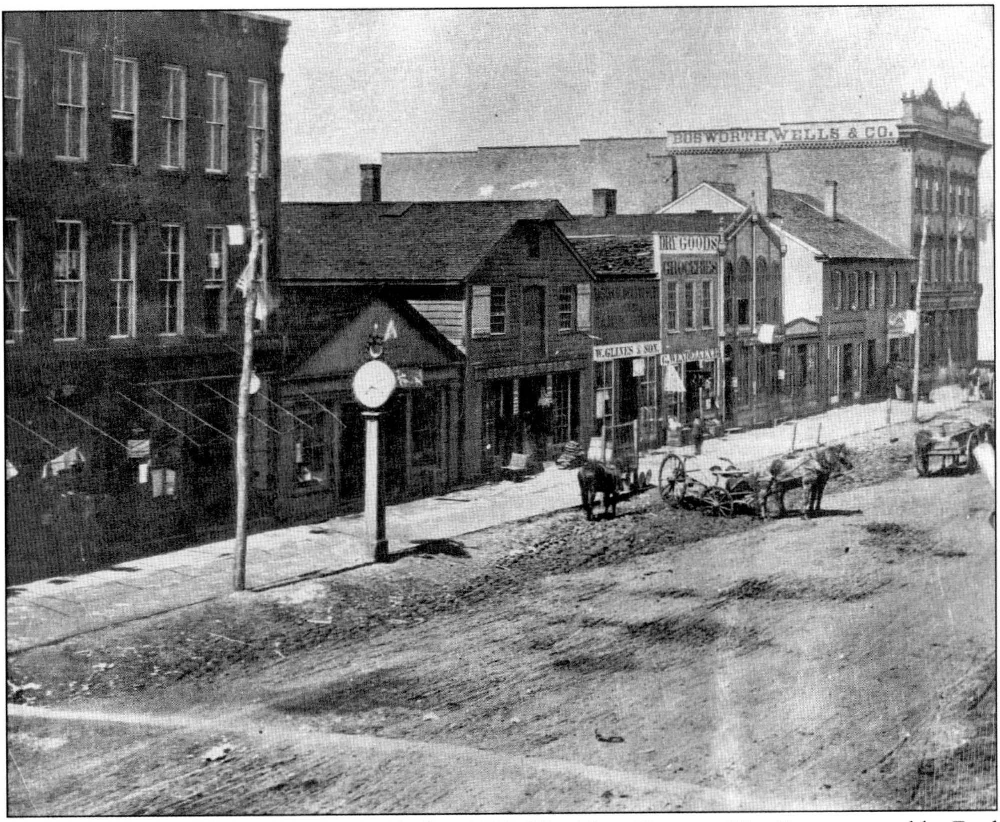

Almost all of these businesses opened after 1858. The New German Hat Store, owned by Fred Weiss; Gerd Wendelken's, grocery and dry goods; and Joseph Wildt's Grocery were on the west side of Front Street. Across the street were the shops of Peter Kunz, John Holst, August Grabe, and Valentine Klueber. (Courtesy of Washington County Historical Society.)

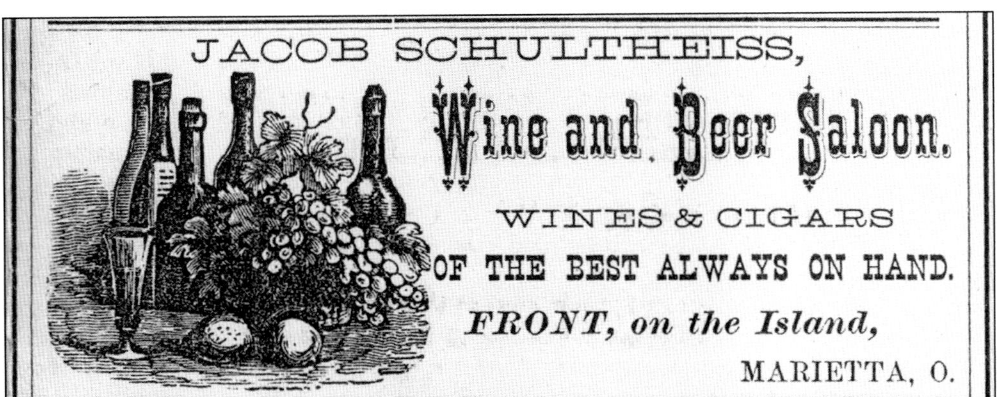

Jacob Schultheiss operated a wine and beer saloon on the second block of Front Street in the area known as the island. When this elaborate advertisement was listed in the 1873–1874 city directory, the second block of Front Street was lowland surrounded by a canal and stream. A significant number of native German businesses were located there. (Courtesy of Washington County Public Library.)

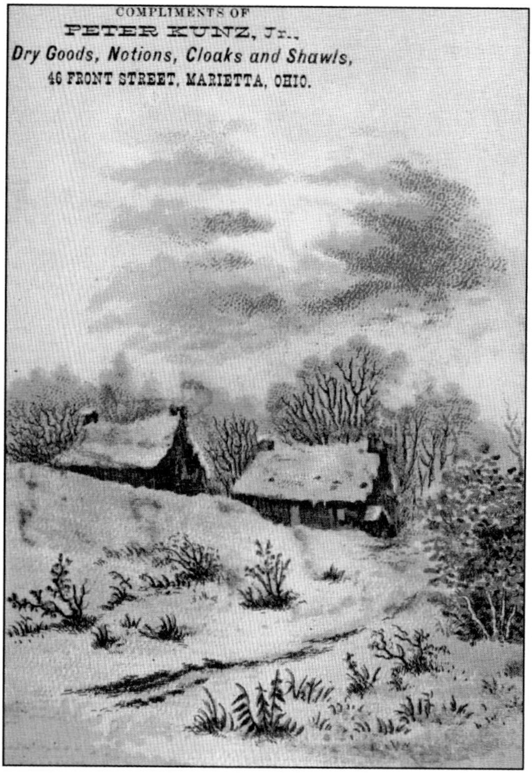

The popular Kunz Store had a full line of fancy and domestic dry goods for ladies and gents including cloaks, furs, and dress goods of domestic and foreign variety. It first opened as a general store in 1861 with Peter Kunz Sr., an early German immigrant, as proprietor. His son Peter Jr. specialized in dry goods in his father's two-story brick building at 162 Front Street until 1913. (Courtesy of Steven Weber.)

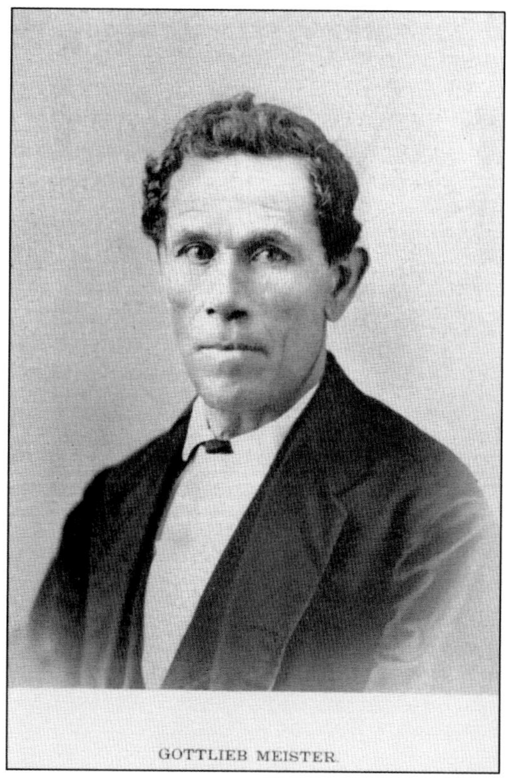

Gottlieb Meister directed all of his energies to building one of the most successful leather manufacturing companies in the Ohio Valley. Meister moved to Marietta, where he worked for Ebinger and Killinger in the tannery business. Beginning in 1860, his tannery at Pike and Greene Streets specialized in products from shoe leather to superior harness making. (Courtesy of Washington County Public Library.)

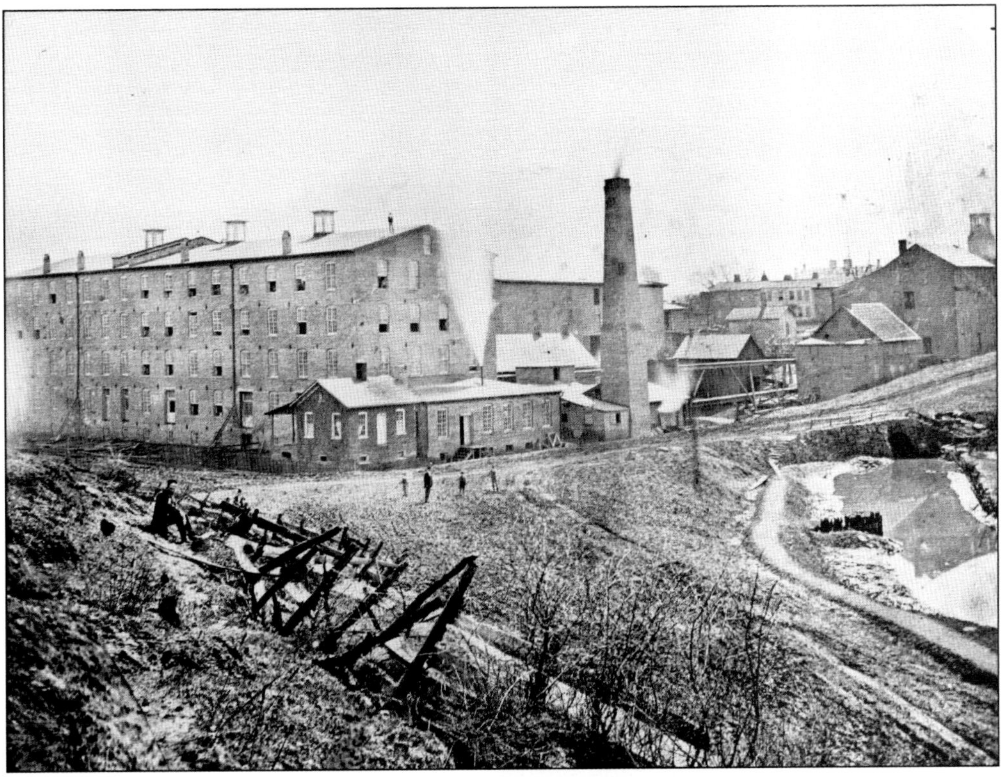

Located at Seventh and Putnam Streets, the Marietta Chair Company, one of Marietta's oldest and leading industries, manufactured wooden chairs, stands, bedsteads, and other furniture. The business started in 1856 and lasted into the 1900s. Because of their fine craftsmanship and work ethics, many employees were of German descent. In fact, the company was nicknamed the "Dutch College." (Courtesy of Marietta College.)

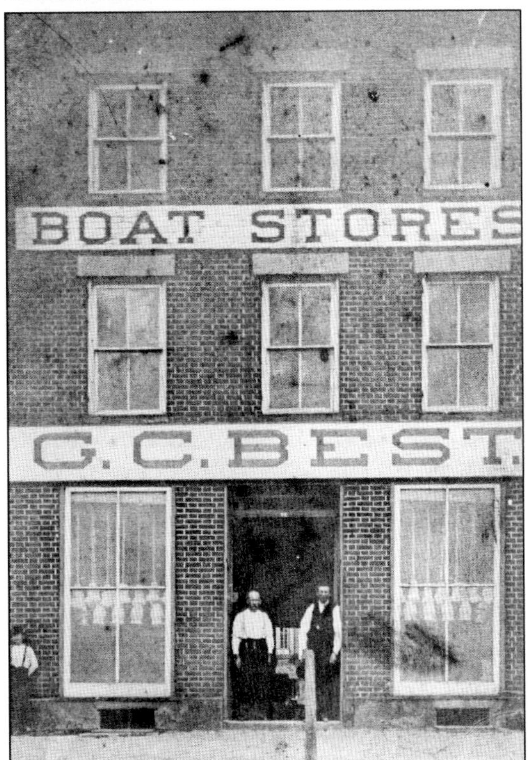

An early German immigrant to downtown Marietta was G. Christopher Best from Bavaria. Upon immigration, he lived in Salem Township and eventually operated a retail grocery on Ohio Street. The store was part of the fading but vital business district at the Ohio River edge. In 1874, the business was Best & Brother. (Courtesy of Marietta College.)

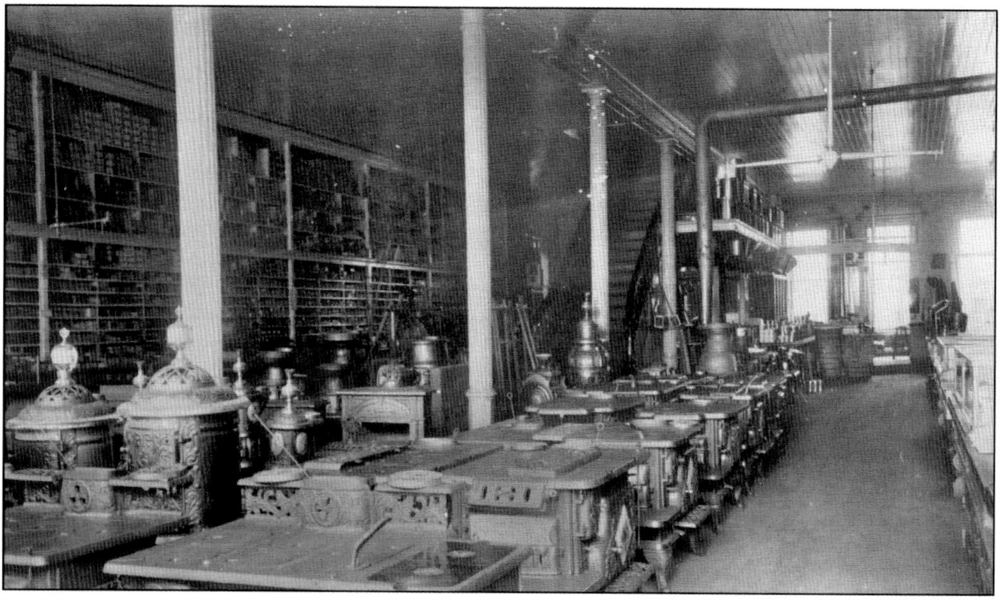

Seyler Hardware was established as a business in 1864 by brothers Jacob and Adam in a store on the island of the second block of Front Street. Twenty years later, it moved to a large building at 158–160 Front Street. The photograph shows the interior of the store with a variety of stoves for home heating. (Courtesy of Washington County Historical Society.)

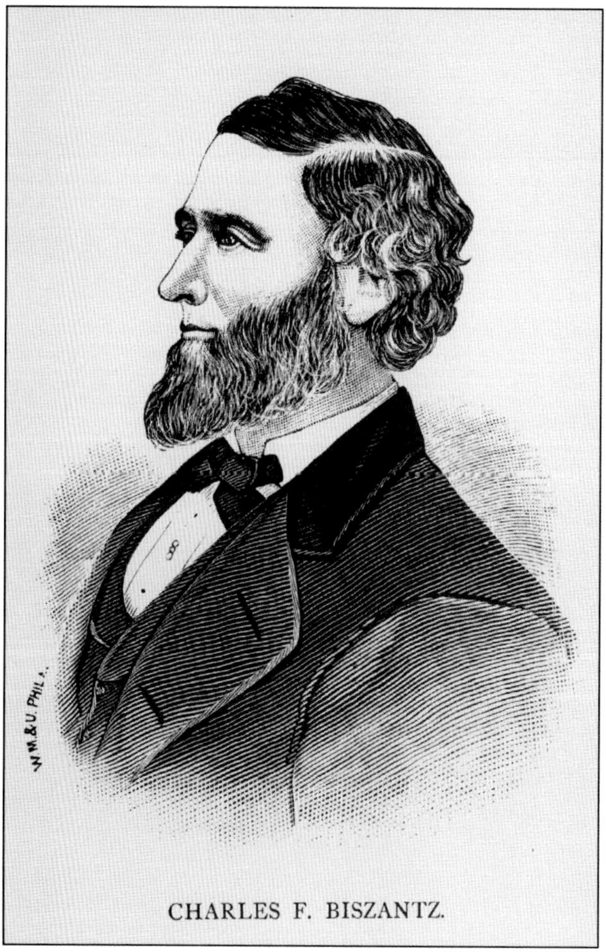

CHARLES F. BISZANTZ.

Businessman Charles Biszantz, a native of Bad Dürkheim, opened a dry goods store on Front Street in 1854. He then tried his hand in the restaurant business with his wife, Philippina. Biszantz later became the hotel proprietor of the Biszantz House. At this time, he also had interests in the oil business, the Harmar Mill, and a ferryboat. (Courtesy of Washington County Public Library.)

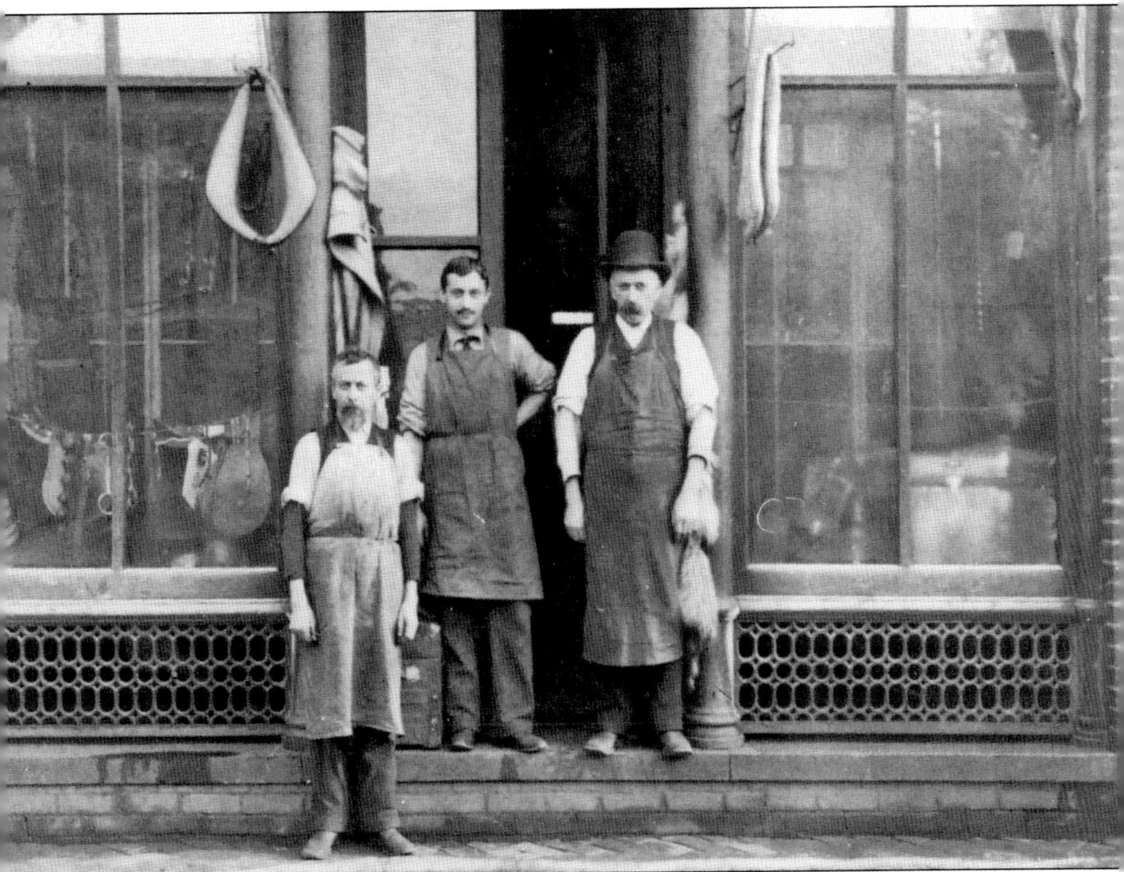

The Schafer Leather Store is the oldest family-owned business in Marietta and has been operated by five generations of the family. Louis and Adam Schafer, native Germans, opened A & L Saddlery at 140 Front Street in 1867. The photograph shows, from left to right, Adam, young Louis P., and Louis Schafer. After the 1884 flood destroyed the building, they erected a new brick structure. Adam left the business, and it was renamed Louis Schafer. Louis's son Louis P. Schafer took over the business in 1925. With the invention of modern machinery threatening the business, third-generation owner Robert Louis added tarps, awnings, luggage, trunks, and handbags. His son Robert Louis Jr. purchased 142 Front Street in 1975 and added western clothing and boots. Fifth-generation Robert H. Schafer has continued to adapt the business to the times since his ownership in 1994. (Courtesy of Marilyn Schafer.)

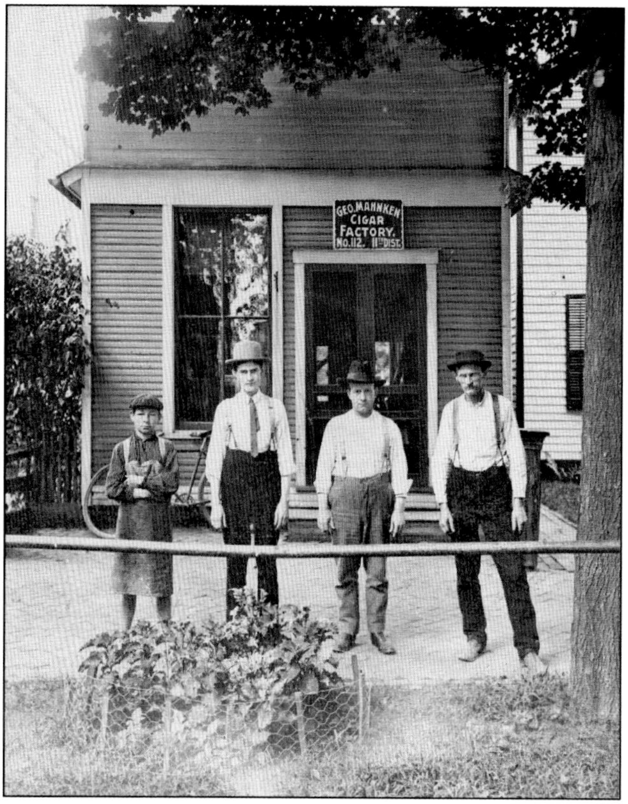

Germans were cigar makers, and Marietta consistently kept four or five manufactories in town in the years around the turn of the 20th century. Tobacco grown in the townships was shipped overland and down the Ohio River to Marietta. The Mahnken Cigar Factory, operated by George Mahnken, was later located at 123 Front Street. (Courtesy of Marietta College.)

August Weber opened a two-story market at Third and Scammel Streets in the 1870s. The store sold fine groceries, produce, hay, grains, feed, and live chickens. As business grew, a third story and section at the rear of the building were added. The nine children of August Weber were expected to work in the store and never marry. (Courtesy of Tony Weber.)

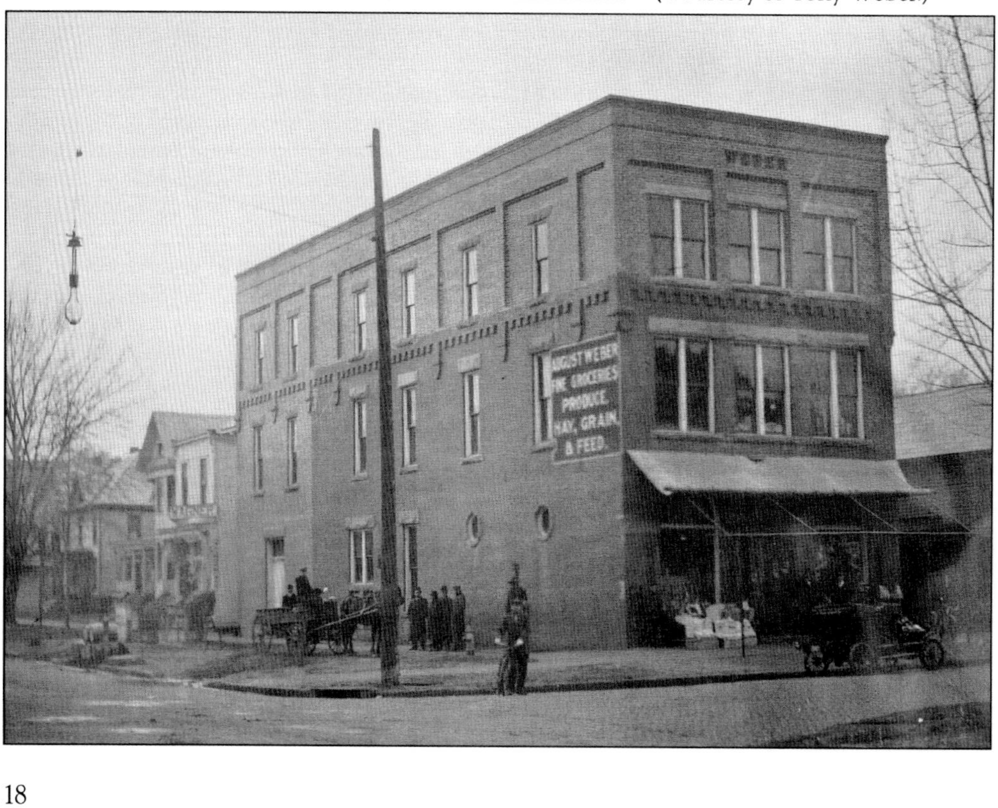

Starting in the 1860s, Jacob Mueller, and later his son Louis, published the *Marietta Zeitung*, a German-language newspaper with a regional circulation. Jacob and Louis, both accomplished violinists, were leaders in local music events, particularly with the Marietta Orchestra. He was considered a "48er." This referred to the year that many people from the German states made an exodus from the homeland. (Courtesy of Sue Trotter.)

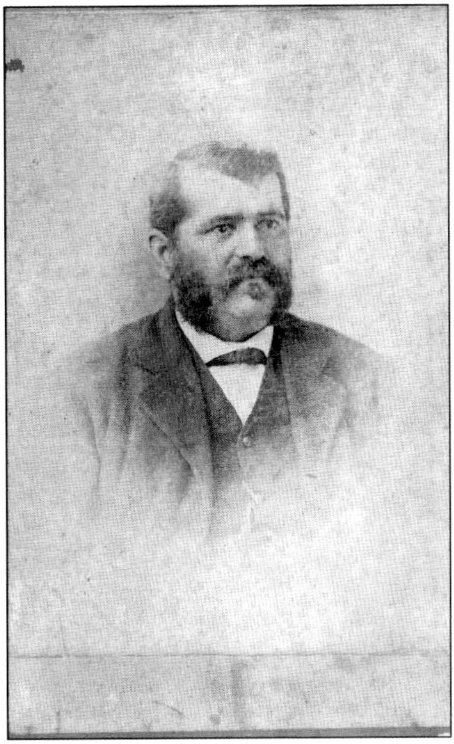

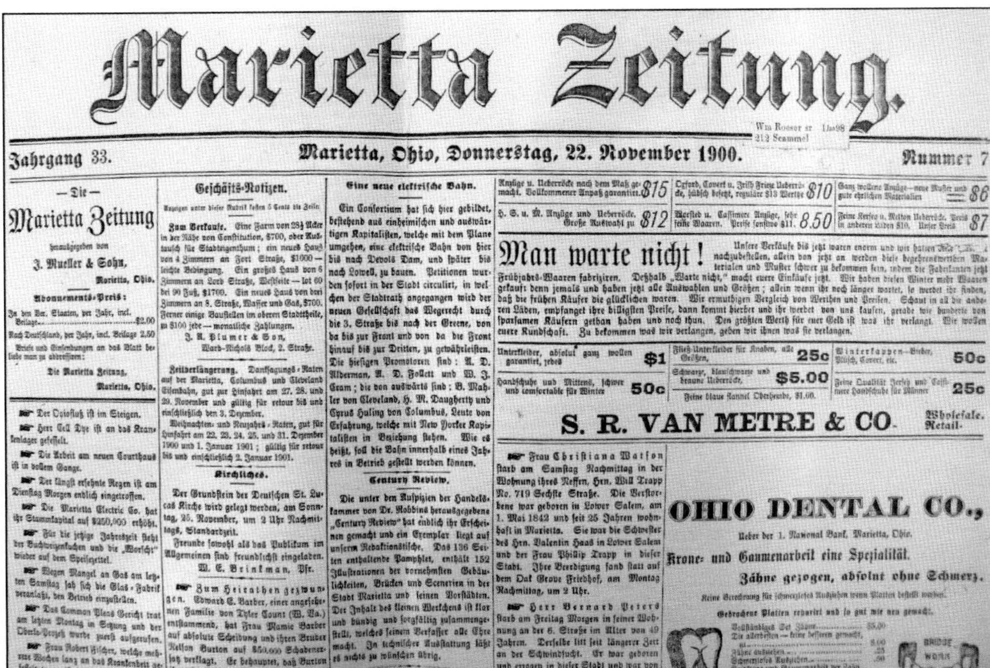

Marietta Zeitung.

Jahrgang 33. Marietta, Ohio, Donnerstag, 22. November 1900. Nummer 7

— Die — Marietta Zeitung herausgegeben von J. Mueller & Sohn, Marietta, Ohio.

Geschäfts-Notizen.

Eine neue elektrische Bahn.

Man warte nicht!

S. R. VAN METRE & CO. Wholesale. Retail.

OHIO DENTAL CO.,

Krone- und Gaumenarbeit eine Spezialität.

Zähne gezogen, absolut ohne Schmerz.

Early Germans came to Marietta knowing little English, and German-language newspapers found a ready audience. *Der Marietta Demokrat* was published from 1856 to 1865. *Der Beobachter* lasted only a year in 1861. The *Marietta Zeitung* found success starting in 1868 with a county-wide circulation until the publication ended in 1904. (Courtesy of Ernest Thode.)

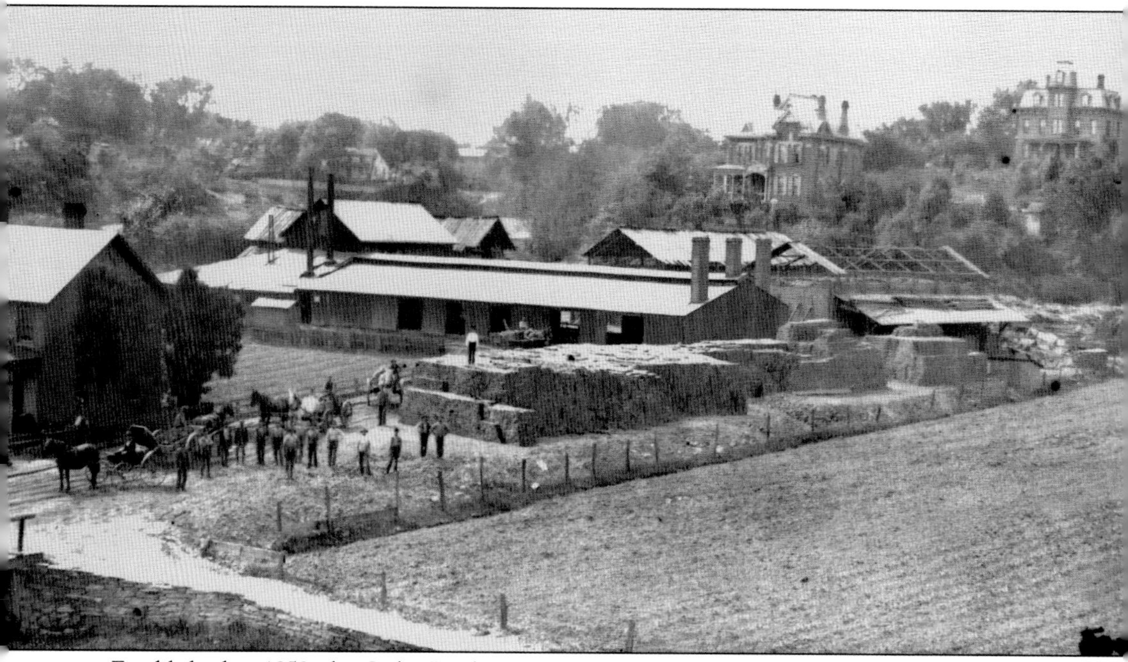

Established in 1858, the Cisler Brick Company was located near the intersection of Putnam and Seventh Streets. In 1900, the Thomas Cisler and Son facility was capable of producing about 25,000 building and paving bricks per day. The premises of the plant covered about 25 acres. The shale material for the bricks was found locally, often from the property of the Cisler family. The Cisler home overlooking the brickyard also served as the office for the business. Many of Marietta's brick streets were paved with Cisler brick. The last project of the company was to build a new high school on Cisler land that overlooked the brickyard. The family traced its roots from the pioneer German immigrants Heinrich and Anna Zeissler, who arrived about 1836. They soon changed their name to Cisler. Thomas, their son, was responsible for the business and building the house. The business closed in the late 1920s. (Courtesy of Laurie Ada.)

Two

German Business Boom

By early 1870, the German community in Marietta had significantly impacted the business district. At the same time, Washington County experienced the development of oil production that brought companies, businessmen, and workers into the area. Marietta Germans took advantage of this. The 1871–1873 Wiggins and Weaver Ohio River Directory stated, "A large portion of the citizens of Marietta are Germans, and are noted for their industry, and as reliable business men, and to them the city is indebted for the fact that it is now fairly awakened from its Rip-Van-Winkle sleep and is rapidly progressing in all elements of material wealth and prosperity."

The Gay Nineties brought inventions, modern conveniences, entertainment, and dollars into the pockets of many people. Germans participated in city services and were leaders in local business. In the last 20 years of the century, many native German businesses were being passed to the next generation who were more integrated in the community and engaged in all aspects of the city. By the end of the 19th century, Germans were fully incorporated in commerce, but they still found solace in the greater German family, particularly German-language churches for sharing tradition and socializing.

Like many communities across the nation at the advent of World War I, the allegiance of Germans was questioned. However, the doubts subsided near the end of the war. The headline of an article in the *Sunday Morning Observer* on November 24, 1918, was "Our German Sons That Came In 48." The endearing headline particularly honored Jacob Mueller as a citizen with proven loyalty. Due to political strife in the German states in 1848, he came to America. The paper stated that the "men of '48" have been a valued contribution to this county. They fought for the Union, they voted for liberal ideas, and have always been opposed to Kaiserism." It is important to note that Germans across the nation suffered criticism during the war years and took measures to quiet their German culture and traditions in order to prove allegiance.

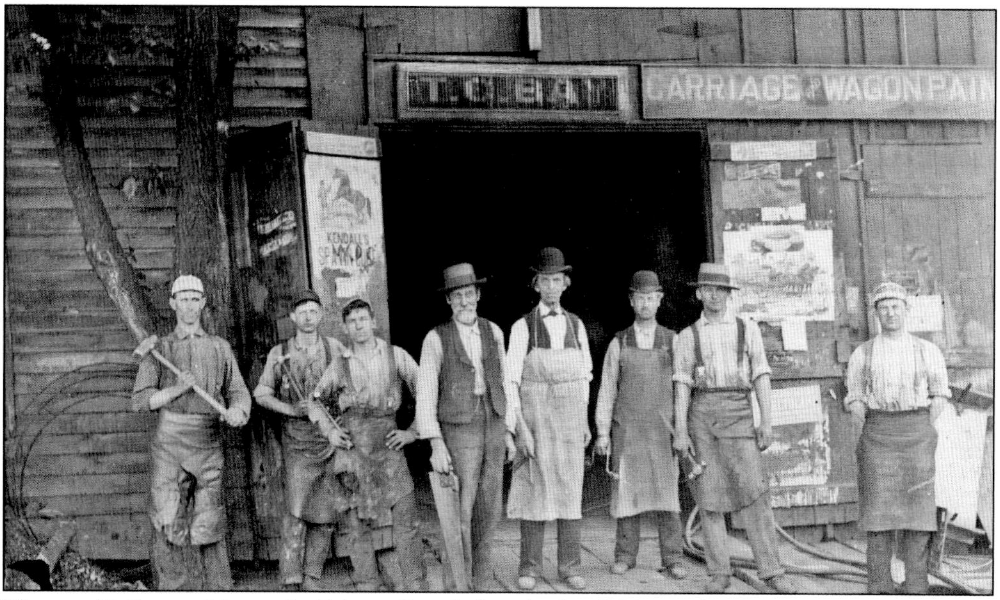

Thomas C. Bay and his wife, Sabina Greishaber, both of Wurtemburg, were early immigrants to Salem Township. Their son Thomas C. Bay Jr. moved to Marietta about 1861 and operated a wagon and carriage shop. By 1885, the Bay Wagon Works was located at 217 Second Street. Around 1905, Bay built the large three-story brick building next door with the address of 217 ½ Second Street. The top of the building indicated it was named the Bay Block. Initially, Bay shared the building with the Huber Machinery Company. Over the next couple of decades, the building was home to the Eagle's Club, the Improved Order of Red Men, the Day Brothers Barber Shop and Bowling Alley, Rempe Beer Distributor, and Weihl Autos. Today, the address is 219 Second Street. (Both, courtesy of Marietta College.)

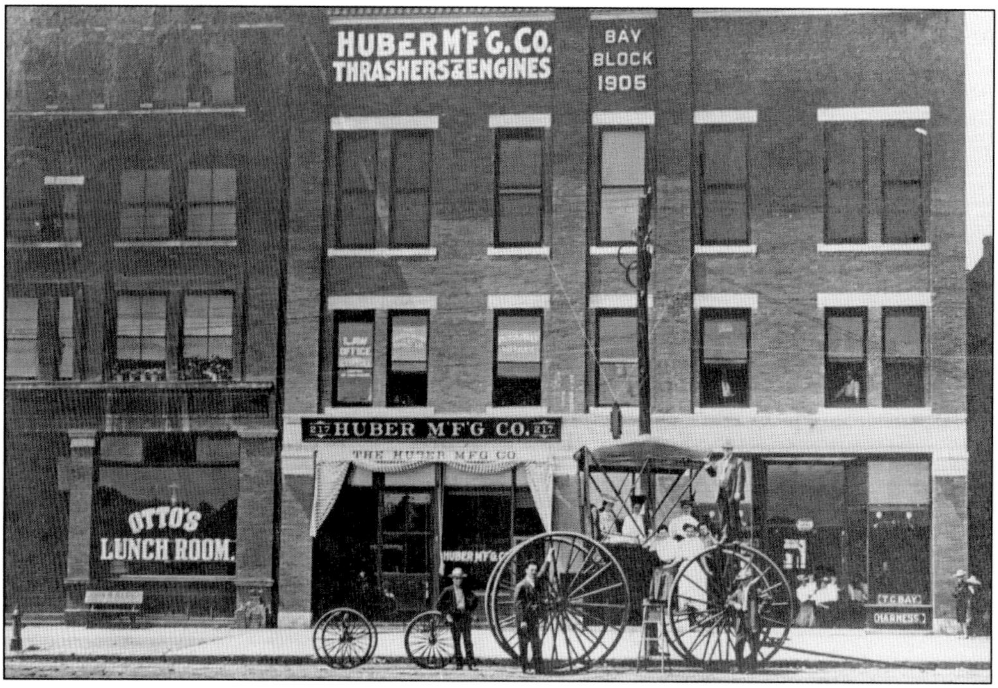

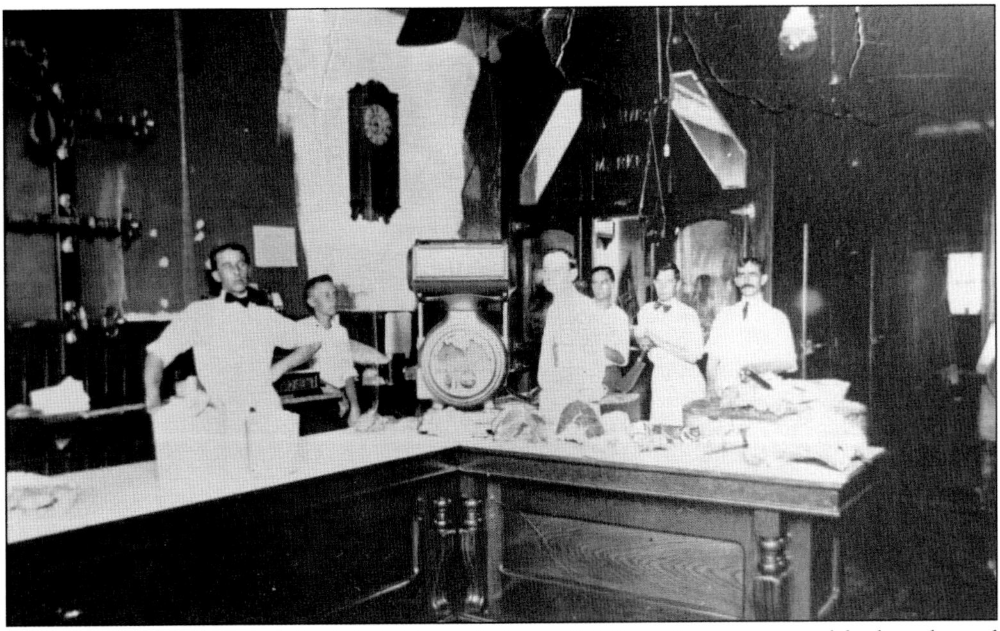

From 1883 until the late 1940s, Jahn's Meat Market at 284 Front Street prepared fresh and cured meats. They would bring livestock from pasture to the "backyard" of the store for butchering. Herman Jahn, a native German, married Catharine Reiter and had eight children. Four sons learned the trade and worked in the family business. (Courtesy of Washington County Historical Society.)

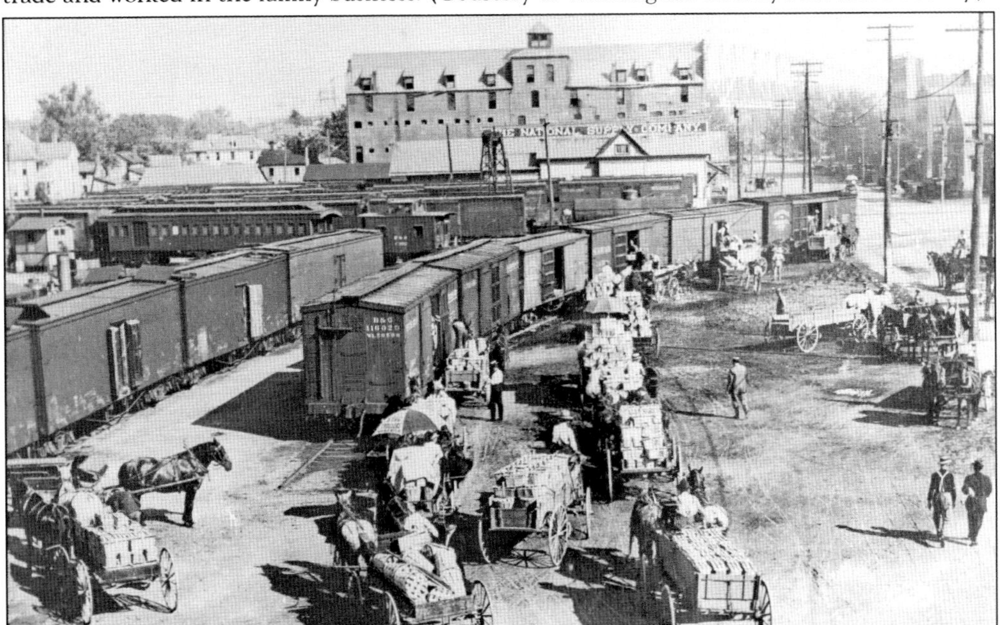

Farmers from the townships brought produce to the railroad depot on Second Street. Southeastern Ohio was well known for tomatoes and other crops that were shipped by rail. The National Supply Company in the background of this photograph opened in 1895 under the management of John Kaiser, and the company supplied necessary items for the surrounding oil fields. (Courtesy of Marietta College.)

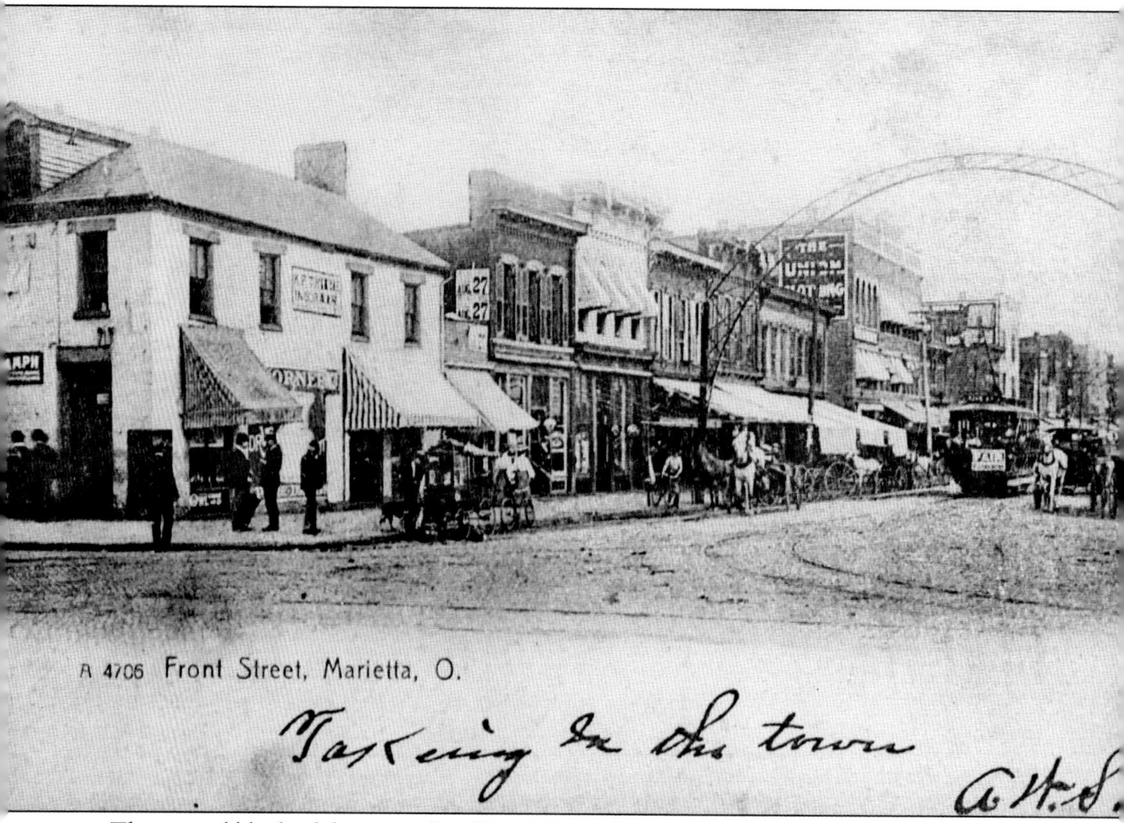

The second block of the east side of Front Street housed so many German businesses that it was often referred to as Dutch Row. In 1898, at least 27 German businesses were along the street, some of which were on the second stories. Popular businesses were Kestermeier Shoes, Blume Insurance, Schramm Brothers Florists, Wehrs Grocery, and Roeser Cigars. (Courtesy of Marietta College.)

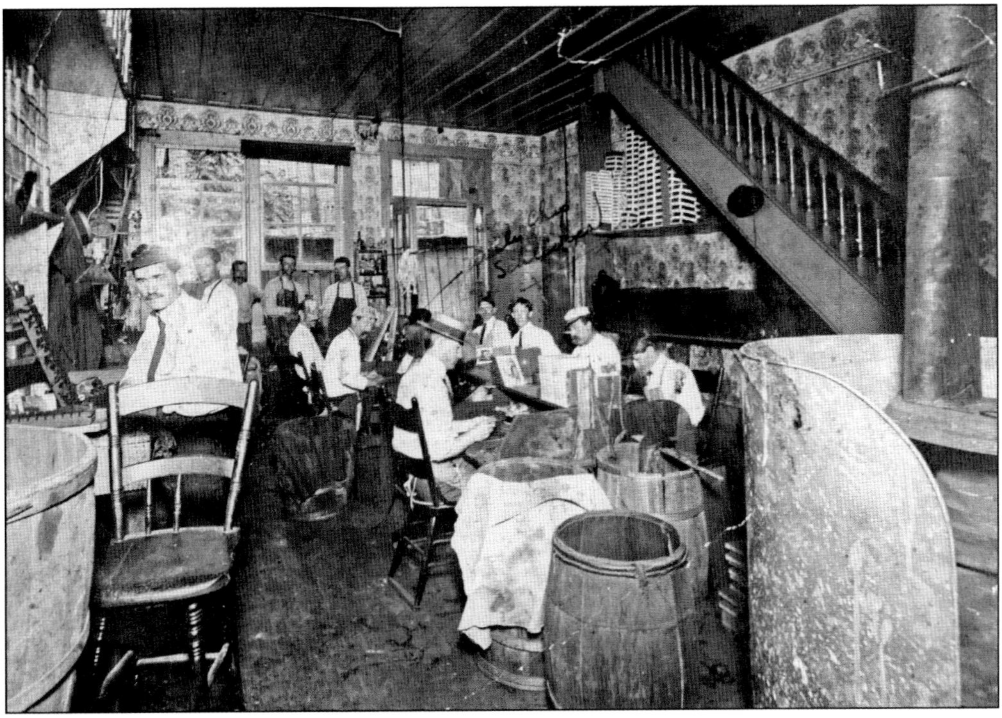

In the 1890s, the Schlicher Stogie Shop was one of the leading cigar businesses. The popular brands sold were Safe Deposit as a 10¢ cigar while the Havanna View, and the Silver Lining were a 5¢ grade. In 1902, the shop's prime location at 110 Front Street afforded many customers. Nearby to the Ohio River landing, tobacco could be taken off boats and hung to dry in the shop. The shop employed many workers to handle the tobacco. Peter Schlicher emigrated from Bavaria in 1854 and married his wife, Margaret, a year later. Their son Peter Jr. took over as the cigar manufacturer until his death in 1914. (Above, courtesy of Marietta College; right, courtesy of Steven Weber.)

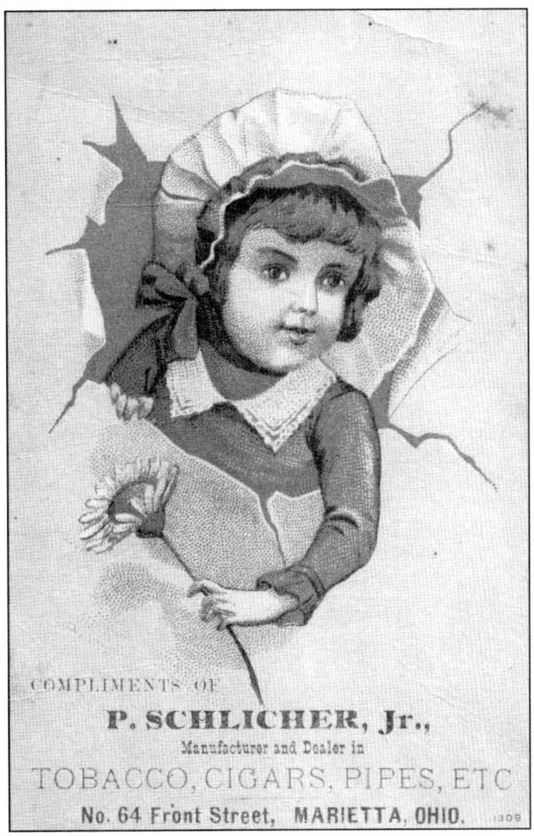

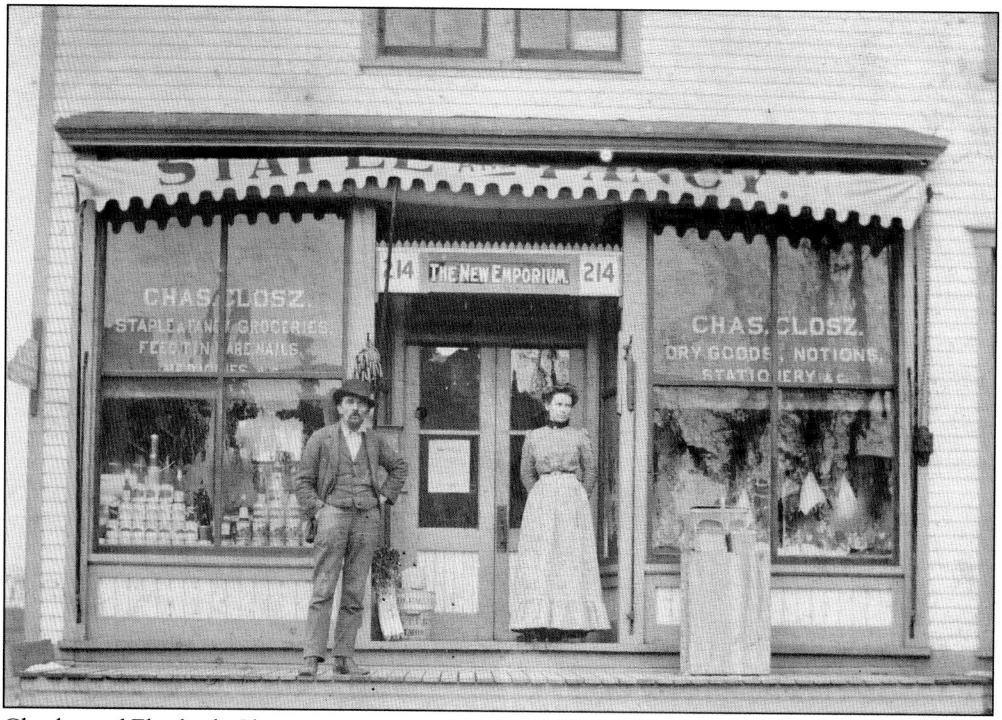

Charles and Elizabeth Closz ran a grocery store and lived on the second floor at 214 South Sixth Street at the turn of the 20th century. Young Charles came to America in 1856 from Bavaria with his family who settled in Fleming for a time. When the children grew up and their father died, Elizabeth changed the spelling of Closz to Close. Many Germans did this to fit into society. (Courtesy of author's collection.)

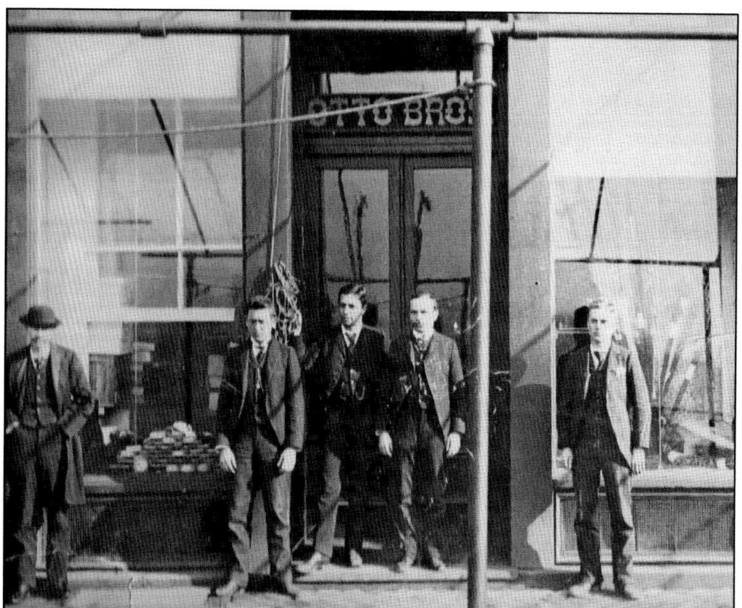

A very young John Wesley Otto convinced his older brother to take a risk and open their own dry goods business in 1886. To get started, they used "loaned" merchandise from a closing business and borrowed $500 from the German National Bank to open a shop. John Wesley (left) and Charles Otto stand in the doorway of 286 Front Street alongside brother Harry Otto (far right). (Courtesy of Gretchen Otto.)

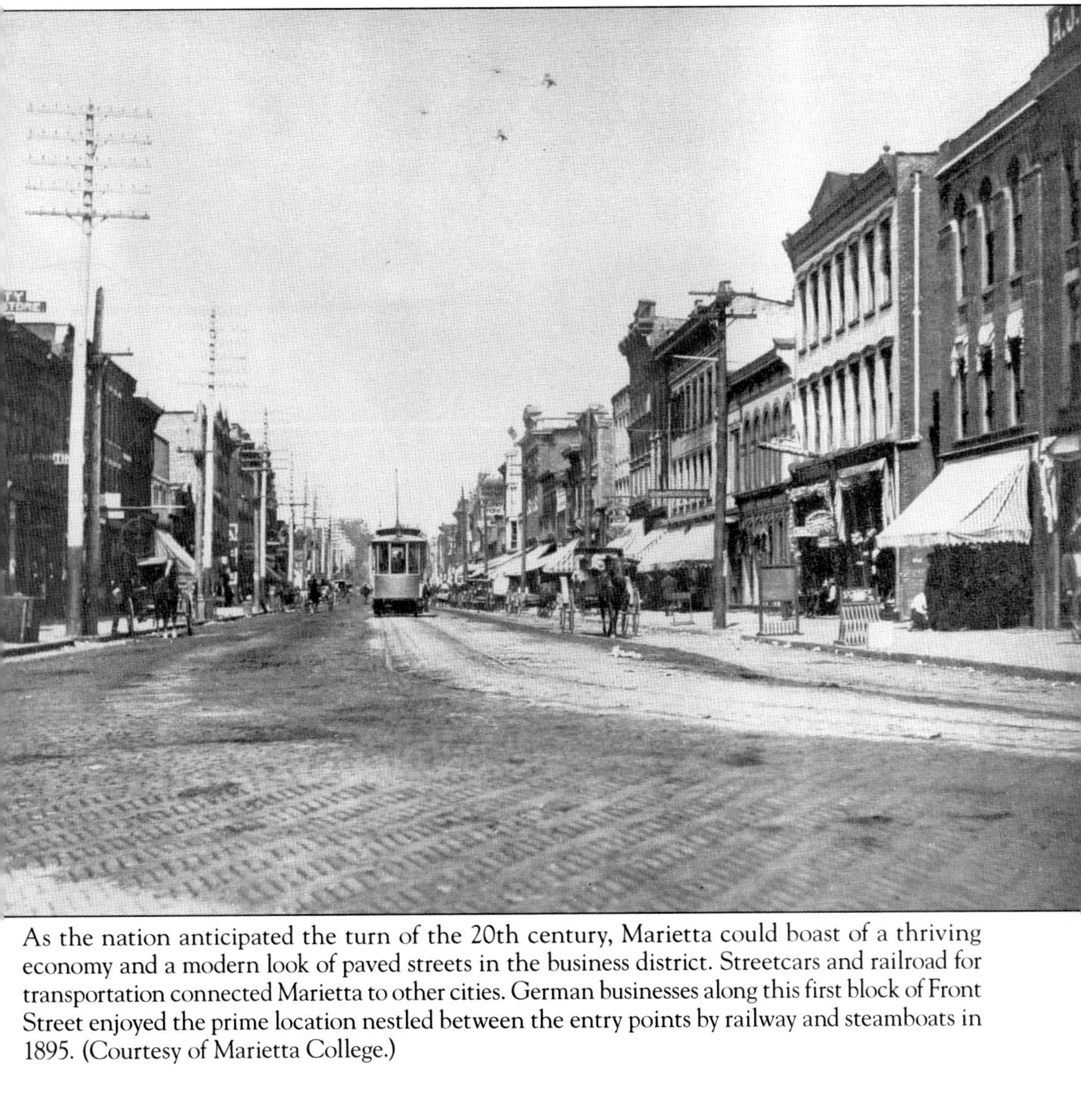

As the nation anticipated the turn of the 20th century, Marietta could boast of a thriving economy and a modern look of paved streets in the business district. Streetcars and railroad for transportation connected Marietta to other cities. German businesses along this first block of Front Street enjoyed the prime location nestled between the entry points by railway and steamboats in 1895. (Courtesy of Marietta College.)

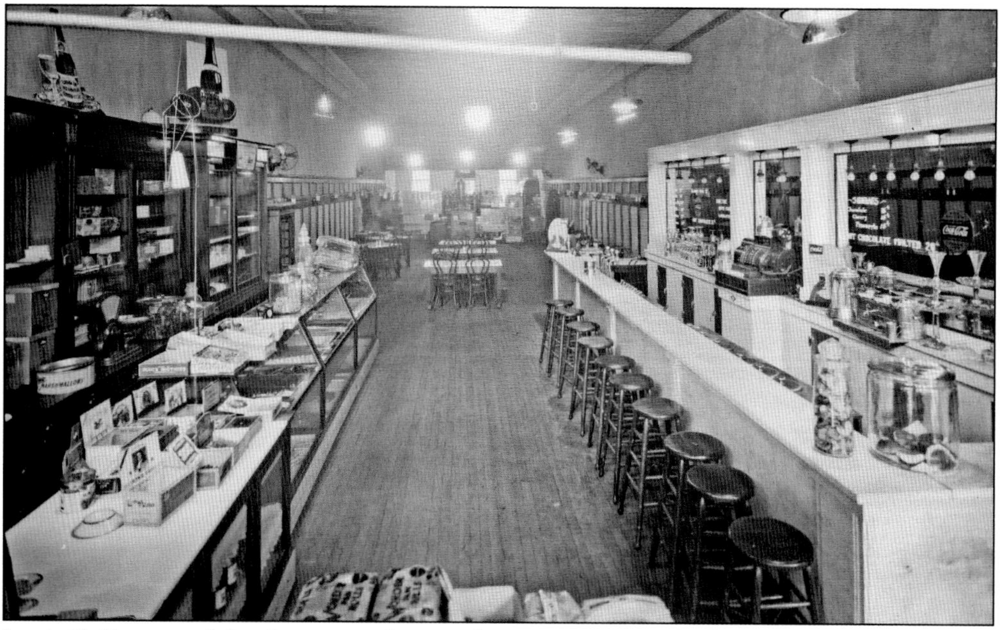

Louis C. Braun and family operated a popular restaurant at 138 Front Street. The business specialized in bake goods and ice cream with a catering service. It was in operation from about 1888 to about 1930. Braun's was touted as having modern appliances with an oven that had cost nearly $1,000. (Above, courtesy of Marietta College; below, courtesy of Washington County Public Library.)

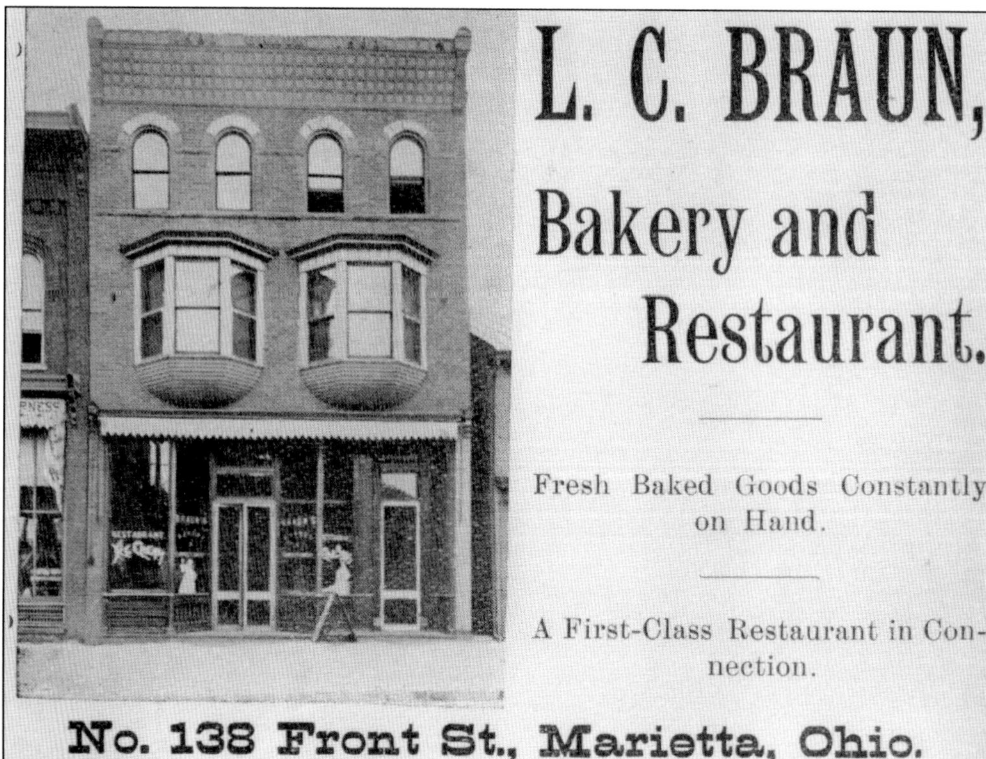

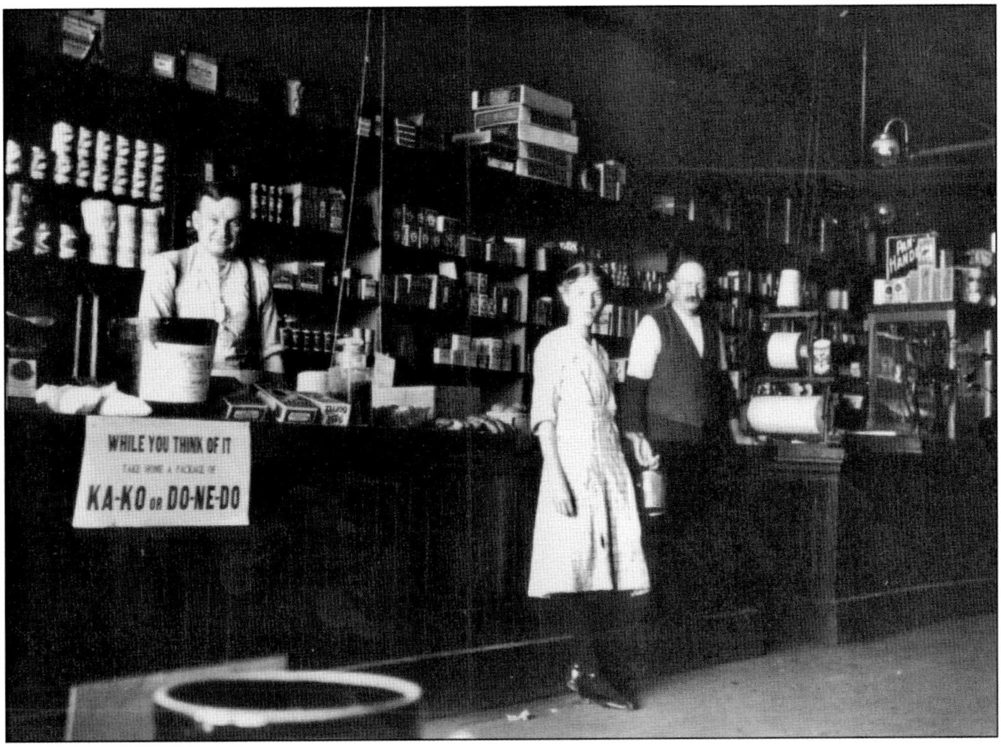

Henry and George Beltz started a general store in Harmar in 1890. The brothers operated the general merchandise shop for nearly 37 years mostly at the 329 Gilman Avenue address. Both of the brothers married native German women and lived as neighbors on Warren Street. (Courtesy of Washington County Historical Society.)

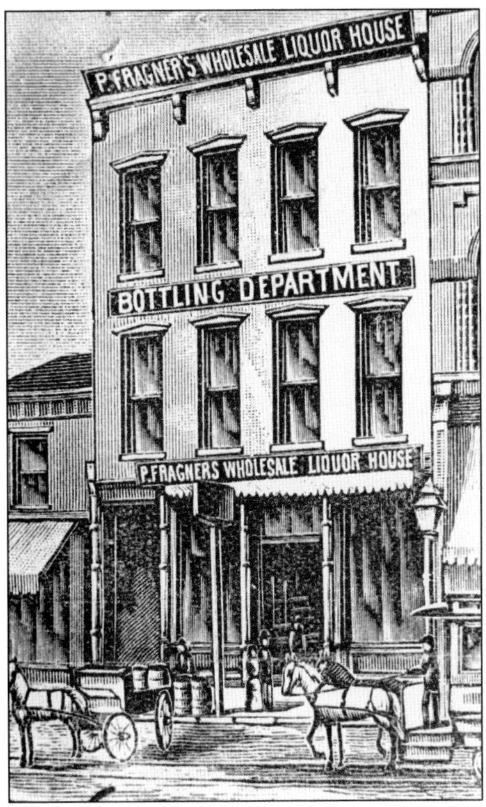

Peretz Fragner, of Austria, dealt in wholesale liquors and wine at 130 Front Street for about 10 years. He opened the store in Marietta about 1898. The family left Marietta about the time that the Rose Law passed, which did not allow the sale of alcohol. (Courtesy of Washington County Historical Society.)

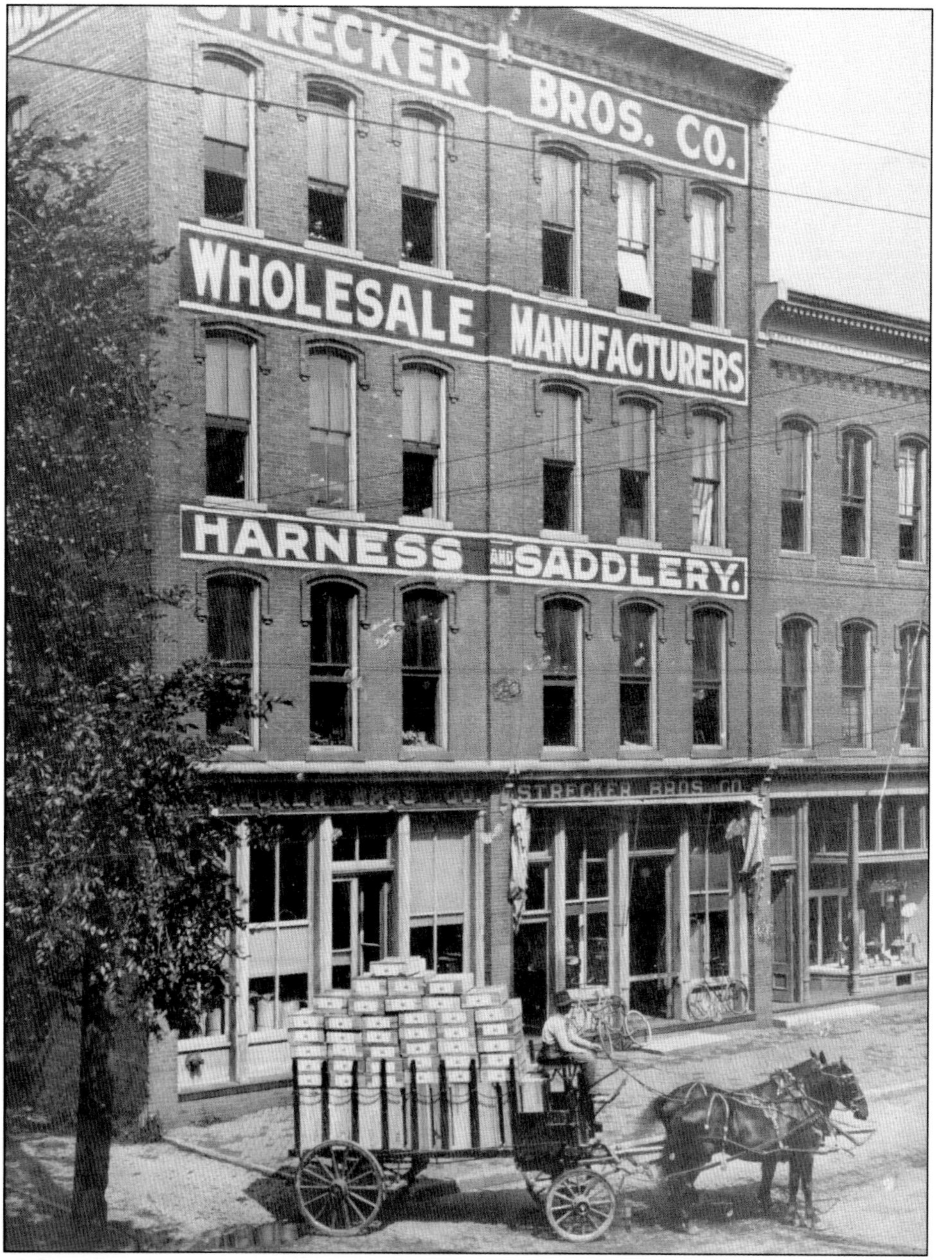

In 1881, Strecker Brothers Company, located at 117–119 Putnam Street, started a leather business that included hides, sheepskins, tallow, and furs that could be shipped outside the city. The business grew into manufacturing horse collars, saddles, and patent leather goods. Charles and Benjamin Strecker personally marketed the business within 100 miles of Marietta. By 1922, Strecker Brothers expanded its trade to cover the entire nation and won international accounts with the British, the French, and the Imperial Russian Army during World War I. In the community, Benjamin F. Strecker was instrumental in initiating a plan to build a local hospital. Marietta Memorial Hospital opened in 1929 on a portion of the Strecker farm owned by Carrie Strecker. Hayward Strecker, a cousin, was known for generosity and leadership. Following his death, his wife, Nancy, donated funds in his memory to establish a cancer center in Marietta. (Courtesy of Marietta College.)

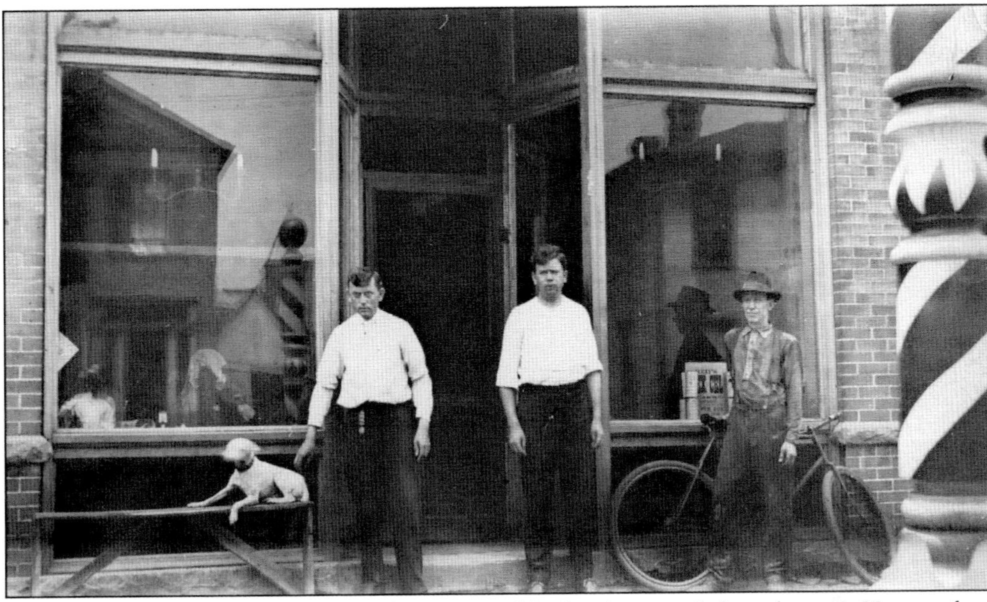

Four generations of the Neader families operated barbershops and shoe shops in Harmar for a total of 108 years. In this photograph, brothers George and Albert Neader stood ready for the long business day at 122 Maple Street. They worked from 6:00 in the morning to 8:00 at night during the week and longer on weekends. (Courtesy of Theresa R. Thomas.)

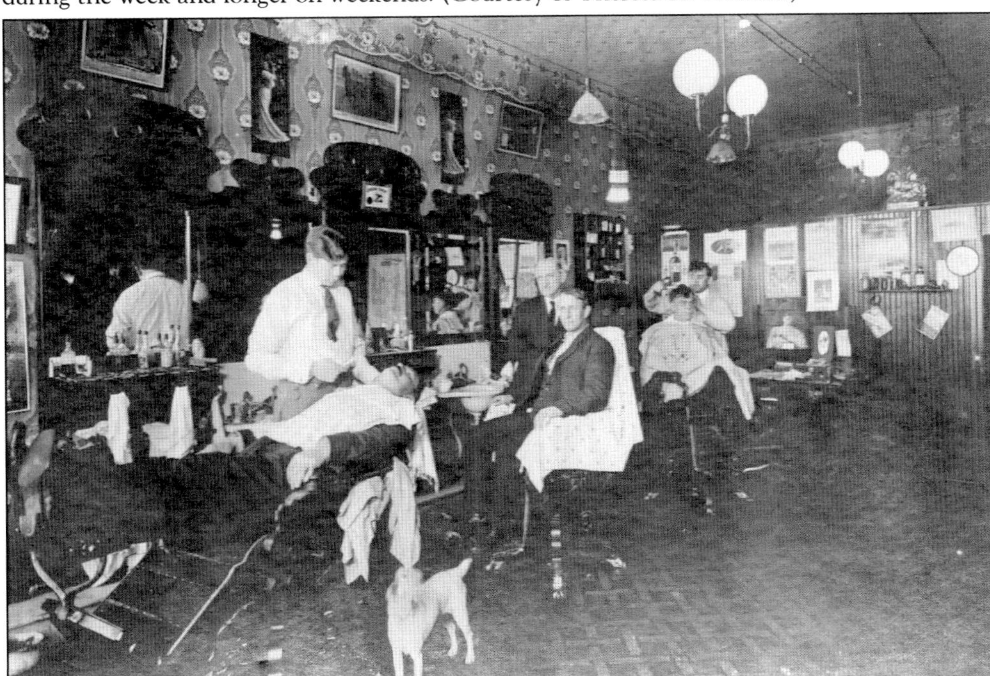

The entire Neader family helped with the barbershop. Wife Bertha and children sewed, washed, and ironed barber shirts and towels and cleaned the shop, including the spittoons. Albert Neader was the first barber in Marietta to have electric clippers. Women in the 1920s went to the shop for the bob hairstyle. A barbershop quartet entertained before advent of radio. (Courtesy of Theresa R. Thomas.)

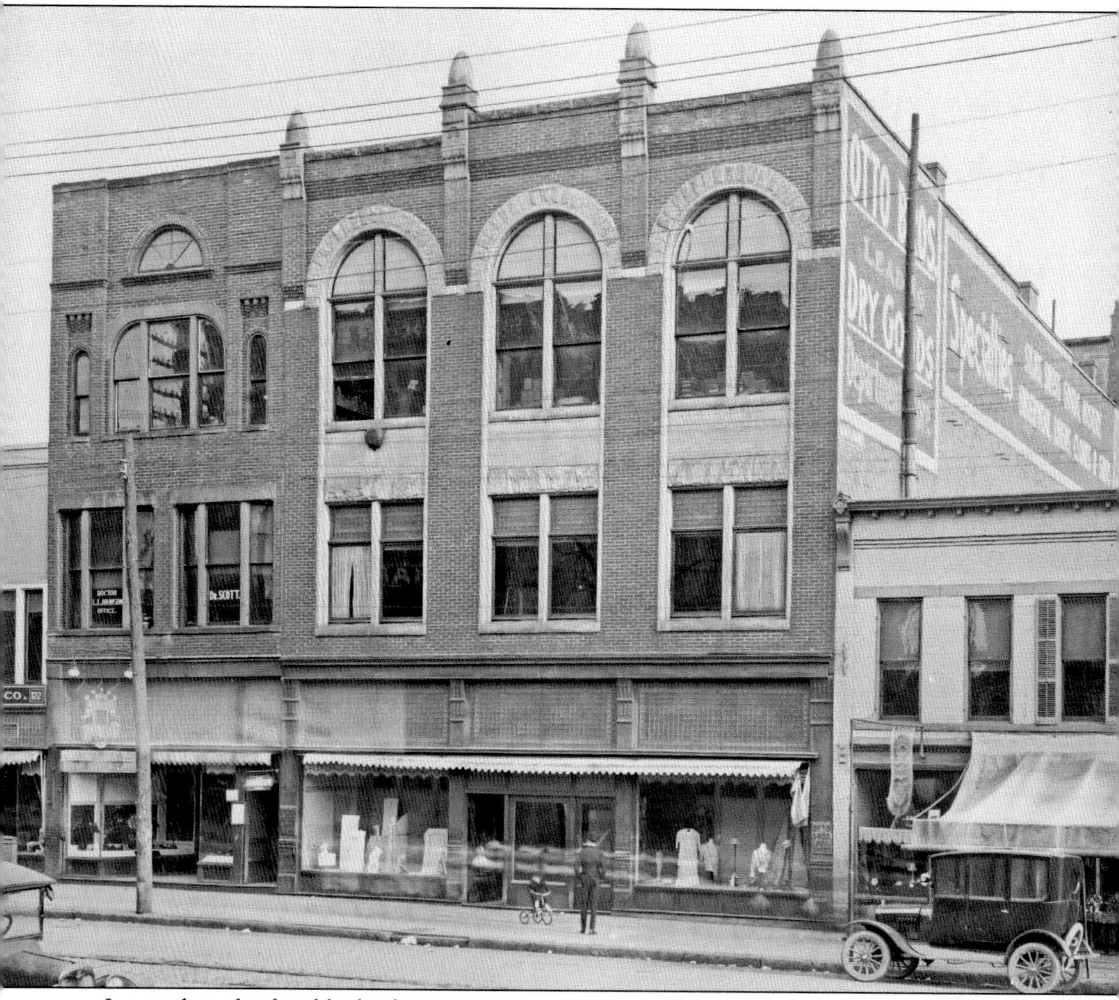

Located on the first block of Putnam Street, Otto Brothers department store was the largest dry goods store in southeast Ohio during the first half of the 20th century. Deciding to enlarge because of their successful Front Street store, John Wesley and Charles Otto erected a large three-story store with a later addition at 110–112 Putnam Street. Some people thought this was a great risk since, at the time, this street was not considered part of the main shopping area. Otto Brothers department store sold a full line of dry goods and notions. Ready-made wear clothing was purchased and displayed, making Otto Brothers one of the first to offer factory-made clothing in the area. Interestingly, clerks assisted customers, but did not have cash registers. The cash would be sent through an array of tubes to the office where staff would make change and receipts. (Courtesy of Marietta College.)

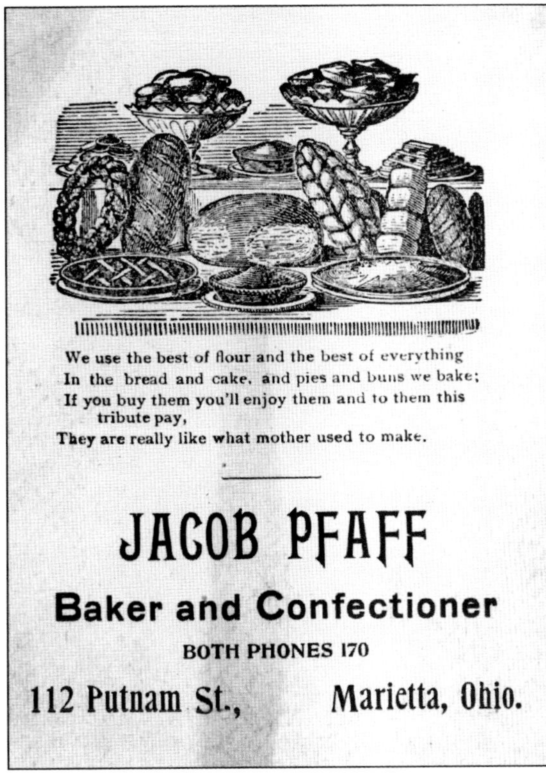

Pfaff Bakery, located at 112 Putnam Street, operated the business from the 1880s to the 1950s. The shop contained a confectionery, a lunch counter, and a bakery. The bakery carried breads, cakes, crackers, fine candies, fruits, oysters, and ice cream. They also offered delivery of fine cakes and other fancy supplies for special occasions, such as weddings and parties. (Courtesy of Washington County Historical Society.)

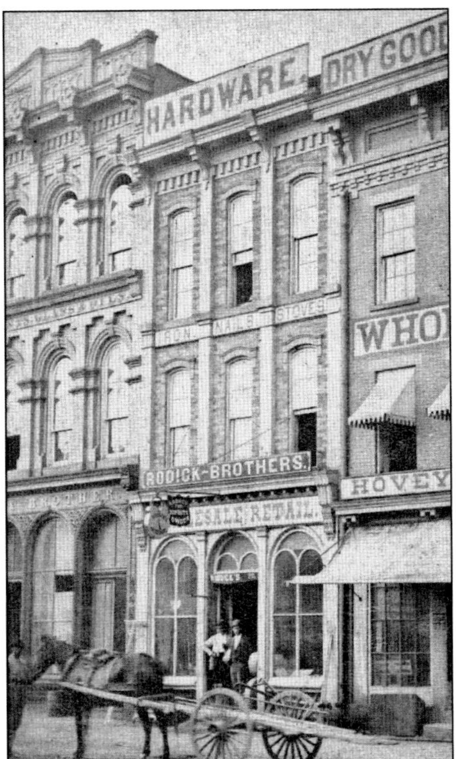

Brothers Henry and Bernard Rodick, from Oldenburg, came to Marietta with their parents in 1850. As teens, Henry worked at the A.T. Nye Company, and Bernard worked at the Woodbridge Store. In 1867, the brothers became partners in Smith and Rodick Hardware. After the death of Smith in 1871, Rodick Brothers became a major hardware store in Marietta. (Courtesy of Marietta College.)

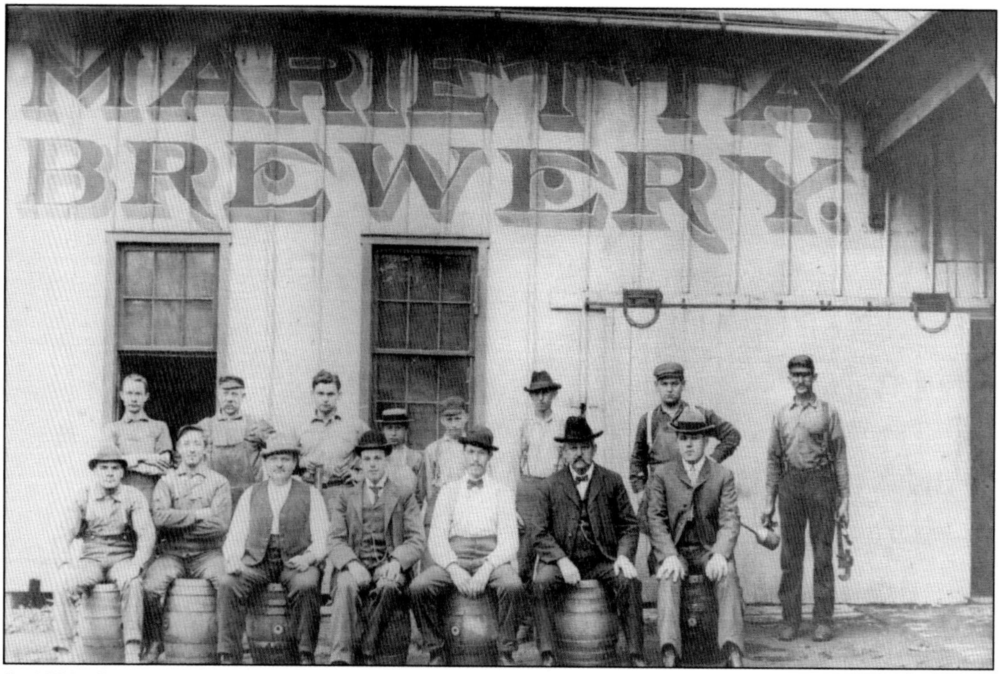

In 1898, German immigrants Jacob Epple, William Feller, and August V. Kuehn (men with ties in front row, from left to right) started the longest-lasting beer-making establishment in the area. In 1903, Kuehn and Epple renamed it the Marietta Brewing Company and continued operation until a local temperance law in 1908 curbed production, but National Prohibition in 1919 completely halted the production of beer. (Courtesy of Washington County Historical Society.)

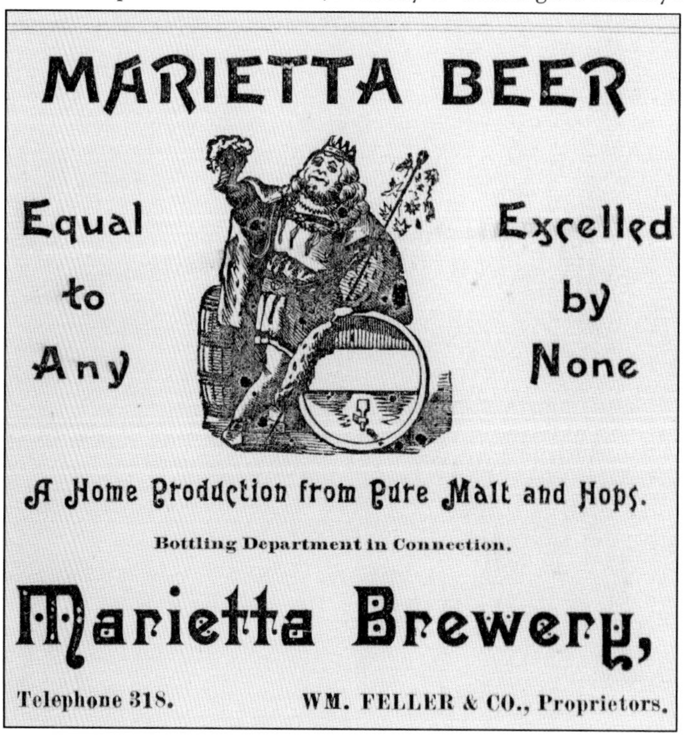

The Marietta Brewery placed this large and artistic advertisement in the city directory of 1902–1903. Feller, shown as president, later left the business, and new partners Kuehn and Epple renamed the company the Marietta Brewing Company. (Courtesy of Washington County Public Library.)

In 1868, Swiss-born and German-speaking Jacob Wittlig was on his way to Cincinnati for a job when his boat made a stop in Marietta. Peddinghaus, jeweler and optician shop needed a trained jeweler, so he stayed. In 1877, he opened his own shop at 208 Front Street. In 1899, a third story was added, and an adjacent building and a common stone front joined the two. (Courtesy of Marietta College.)

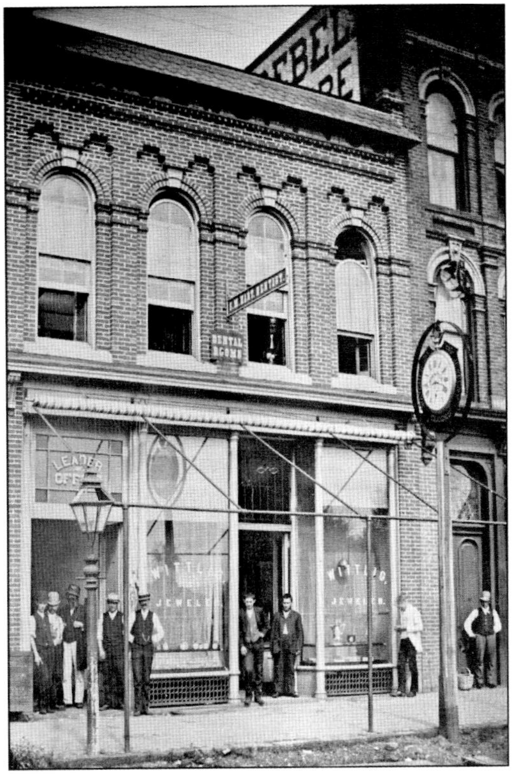

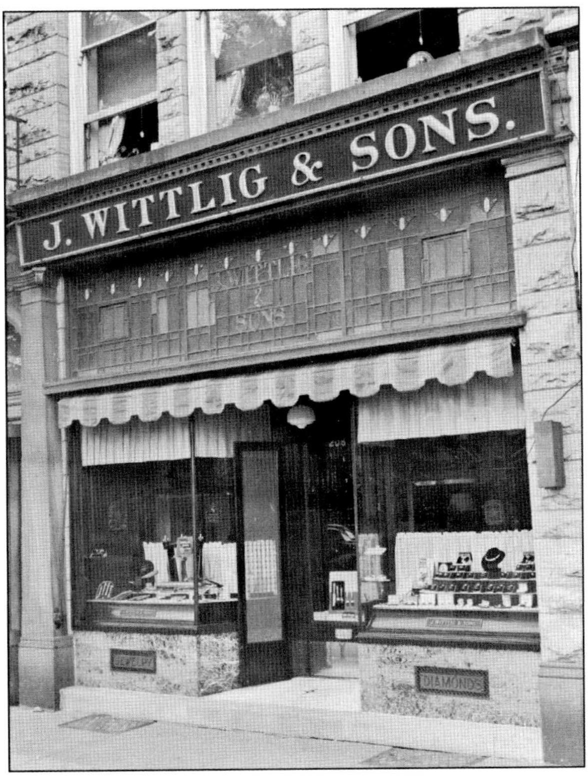

The sons of Jacob Wittlig joined him in the jewelry store and continued the shop after their father died. Grandson Alfred Wittlig operated the firm until he retired in 1977. The store also sold gold and silver watches, silverware and silver-plated ware, clocks, and opera glasses. The Wittlig safe is still in the store. (Courtesy of Marietta College.)

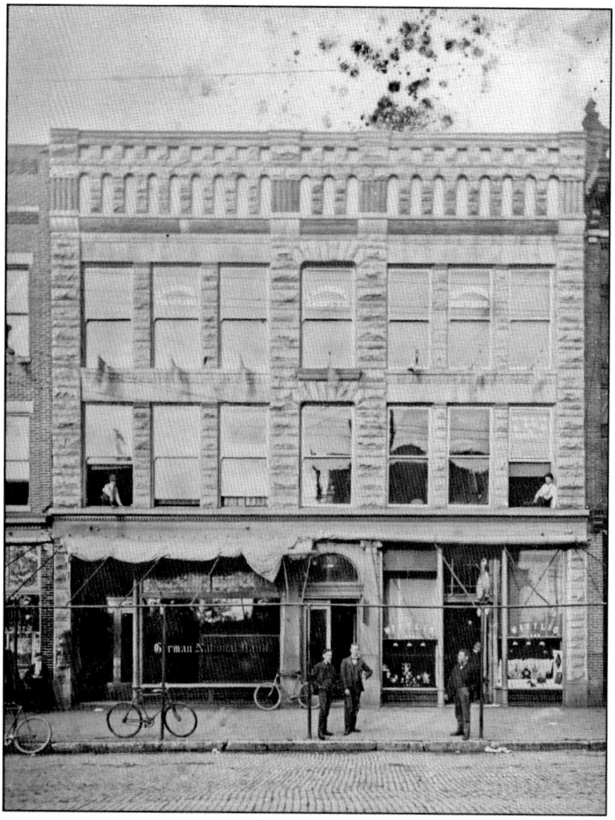

At the turn of the 20th century, the German National Bank and J. Wittlig Jeweler shared the front facade of this building. Actually, Wittlig constructed the German National Bank building separately and added a third floor to both, with a center doorway leading to upper-floor business. (Courtesy of Marietta College.)

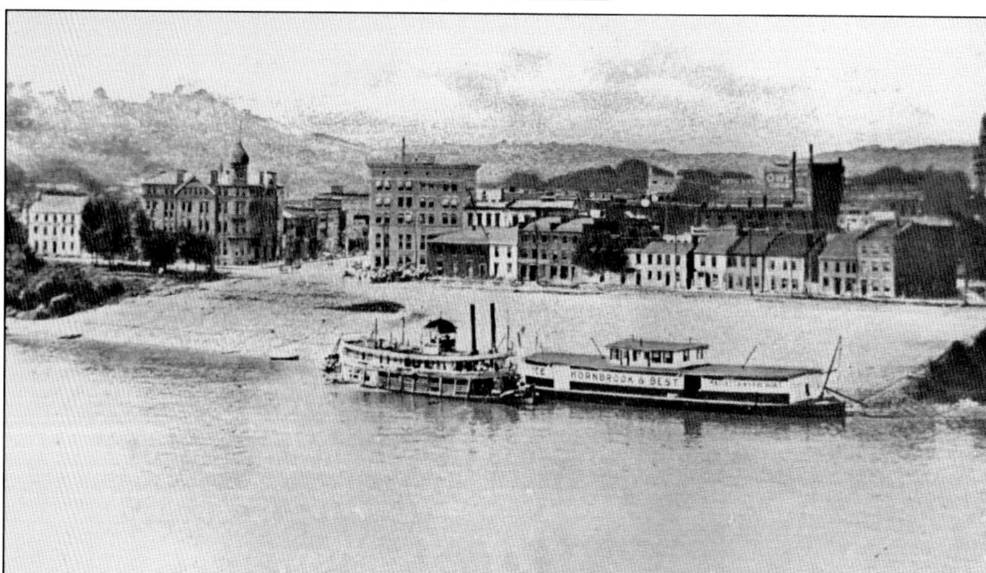

The Ohio River was a highway for immigrants, cargo, and mail that came to Marietta and Washington County. The Hornbrook & Best–owned wharf boat, moored near the bank of the river, allowed for sternwheelers to easily load and unload cargo. Partnerships between non-German and German businessmen, such as Henry Best, were more likely to occur with first-generation Germans. (Courtesy of Washington County Public Library.)

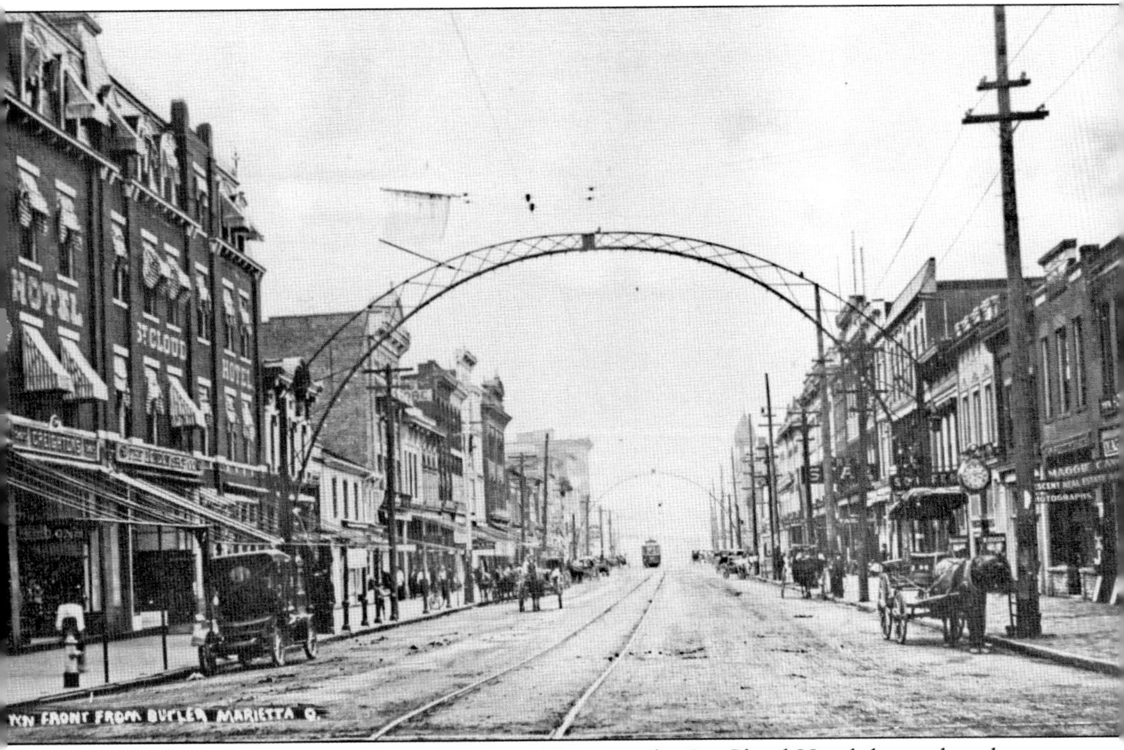

The leading hotel in the 1890s in southeastern Ohio was the St. Cloud Hotel, located at the corner of Front and Butler Streets. The proprietor was Elizabeth Cisler Gross. After her husband died in 1866, leaving her with three children and a debt, Gross continued to run the St. Cloud Hotel, which was a framed building. Being in a great location at Front and Butler Streets, she built an all-brick, four-story hotel. New and modern in every respect, the hotel welcomed guests into its broad entryway on attractive tiled floors to steam-heated, spacious rooms. The hotel could accommodate over 100 people and had some apartments for guests with a lengthy stay. The dining hall had a seating capacity for at least 100 people, complete with signature dinnerware. The left side of the first floor was a breezeway that allowed for horse and carriage entry. (Courtesy of Marietta College.)

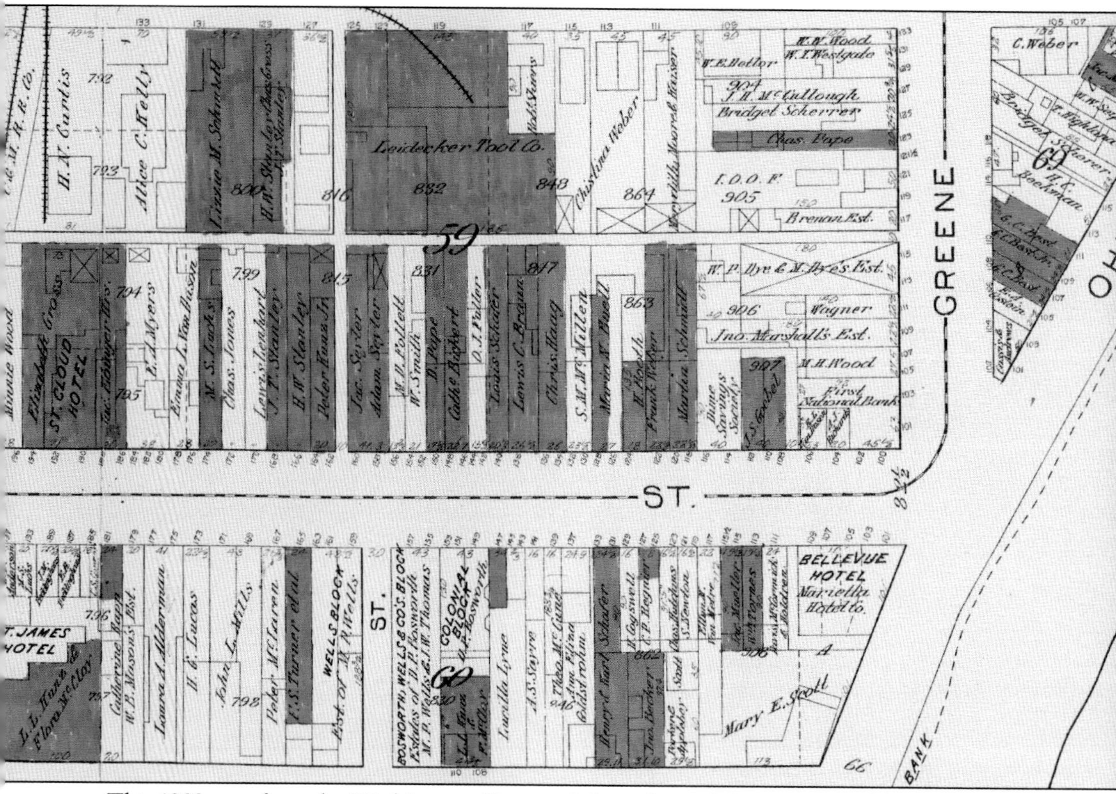

This 1902 map from the Washington County Atlas indicated the owners and location of businesses on the first block of Front Street. The businesses marked in gray were owned or operated by native and first- and second-generation Germans. At 192 Front Street, Elizabeth Cisler Gross owned the St. Cloud Hotel. Next door at 186 Front Street, Jacob Ebinger had a long-established leather shop. His son Henry became part owner of the Turner-Ebinger Store across the street. The Stanley family at 164–168 Front Street partnered with Grass. The name Stanley and Grass is still on the building. The Schafer building, located at 140 Front Street, is still owned by the family, and they bought 142 Front Street for expansion. This block also housed the Marietta Zeitung offices at 115 Front Street. The triangular block at Greene and Ohio Streets had the Best businesses that had survived nearly a half-century. (Courtesy of Washington County Public Library collection.)

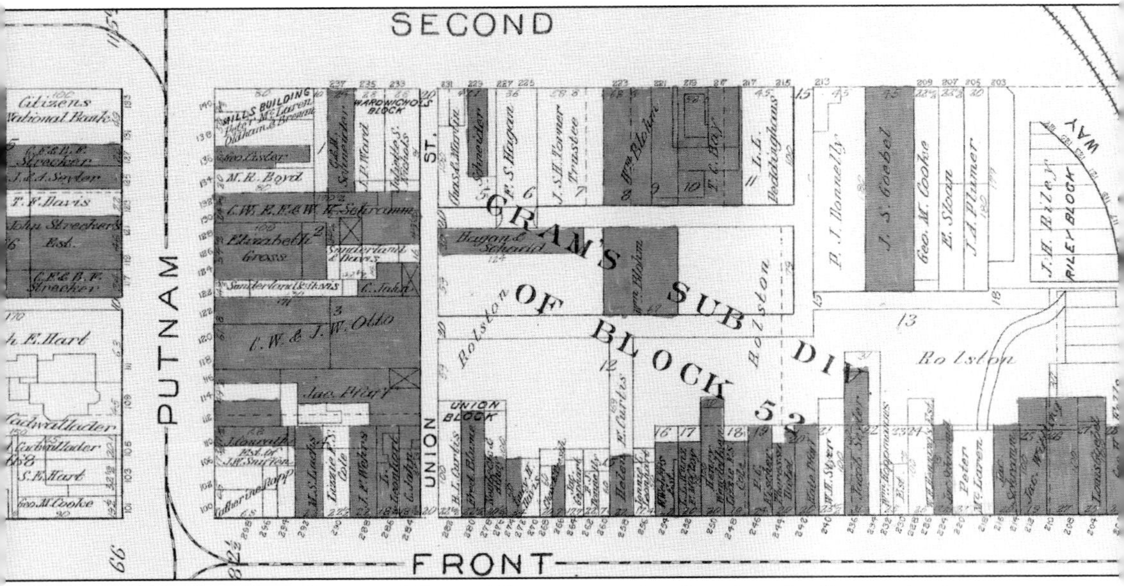

The second blocks of Front Street and Second Street were prime locations for German businesses, as shown on this 1902 map. Many Germans had businesses on Front Street for over 50 years, thus the block was nicknamed Dutch Row. In the beginning, the area may have not been favorable to commerce due to the fact that it was located on a low island. A creek nearly parallel to Butler Street emptied into the Muskingum River on the western side of Front Street. The creek joined with a waterway behind the businesses on Front Street that flowed out to the Muskingum River along Union Street. Thus, the businesses between Union and Butler Streets were on an island with bridges over the streams. In the 1890s, to prevent continual flooding, Front and Butler Streets were filled in with dirt, and the waterways were diverted. Today, patrons really walk into the second floor of old buildings. (Courtesy of Washington County Public Library collection.)

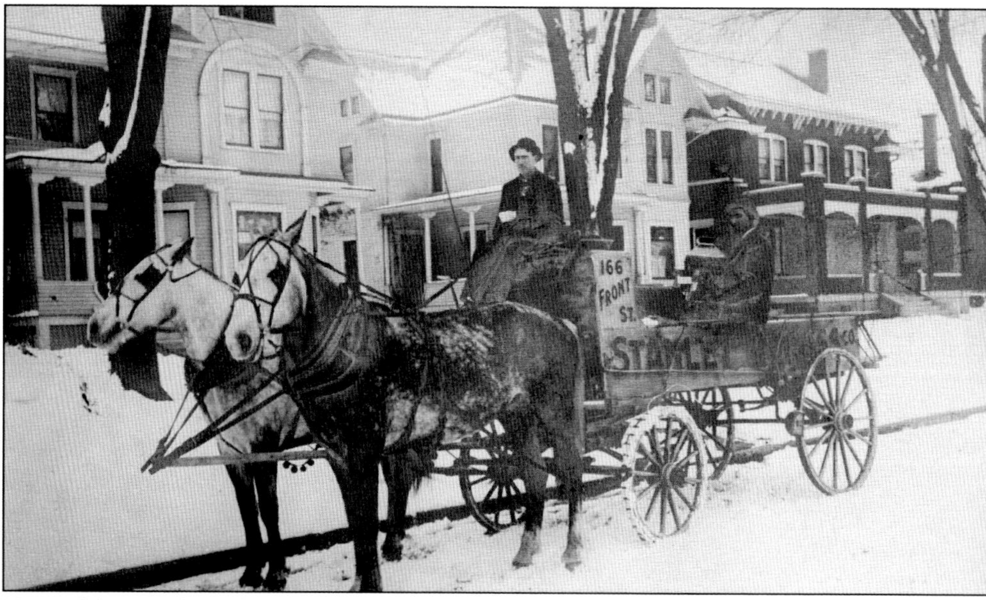

Home delivery of merchandise and food was part of business for many shops. This photograph shows delivery from Stanley & Grass who sold furniture, rugs, and wallpaper. Wehrs Grocers and Frank Weber's Meat Market were among those who had their own horse and wagons to transport goods. Schramm's Bakery drove the bread wagon to various neighborhoods. The Stanley & Grass Company opened in 1883 at 166–168 Front Street. Starting with a modest store, they later expanded to this modern, larger store with its signature name in the front glass. The company was noted for their fine domestic and imported furnishings. In the 1920s, advertisements included the rich designs of the Royal Ka Shan and Savalan Royal Wilton Rugs, as well as curtains, specialty wooden bedroom suites, and Turkish davenports. Home furnishings included gas ranges, electric washers, and high-grade solid oak refrigerators. The store sold wholesale and retail furniture, carpets, wallpaper, and window shades. H.W. Stanley and Charles Grass, of German descent, owned the business. (Both, courtesy of Marietta College.)

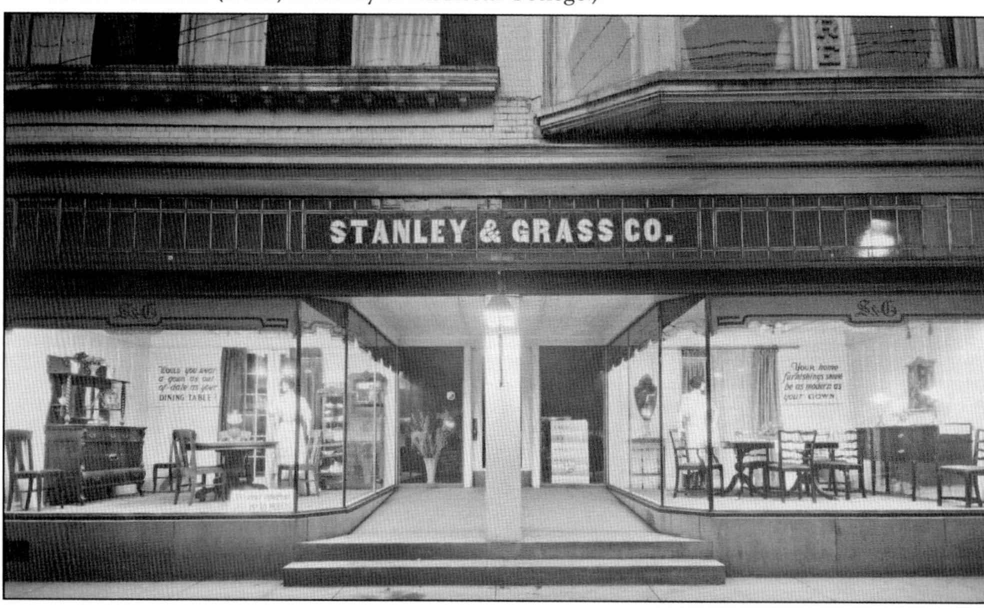

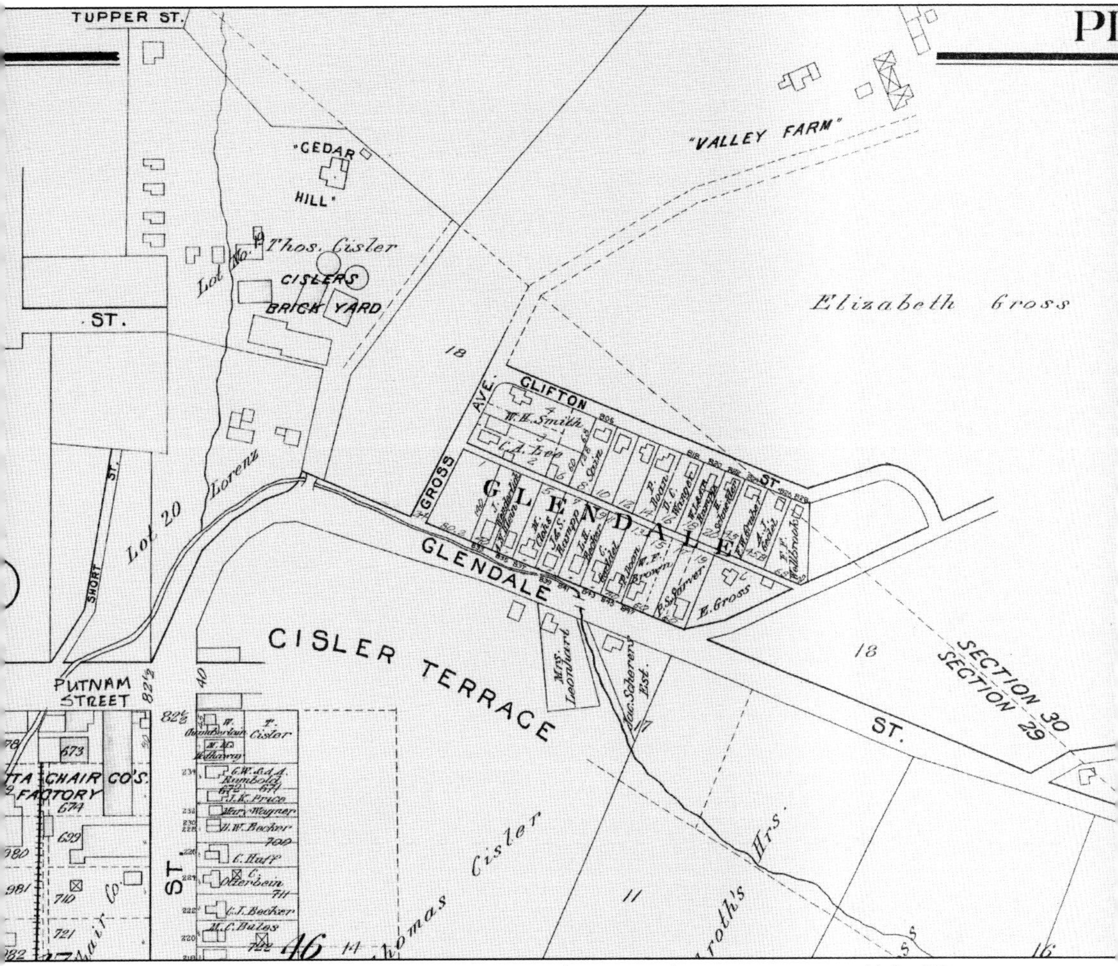

In 1902, this area of town looked very different from what it is today. To orient oneself, find Putnam and Seventh Streets at the lower left-hand corner. Cisler Terrace was the property of Thomas Cisler and would later be the site of the high school built in 1924. The brick store across from the Marietta Chair Factory was the company store for Cisler Brick Company. Note there was not a northbound Seventh Street from the intersection in 1902. Following a very small creek north brings one to the Cisler Brickyard. Cedar Hill is where the Cisler home was built. West of the brickyard there are four small houses that were used by workers. Those houses still stand today, but most of the brick has been covered. Elizabeth Cisler Gross, sister to Thomas Cisler, owned 150 acres and had her farm where Frontier Shopping Center is today. She developed Gross Street, Clifton Street, and Glendale Road. (Courtesy of Washington County Public Library collection.)

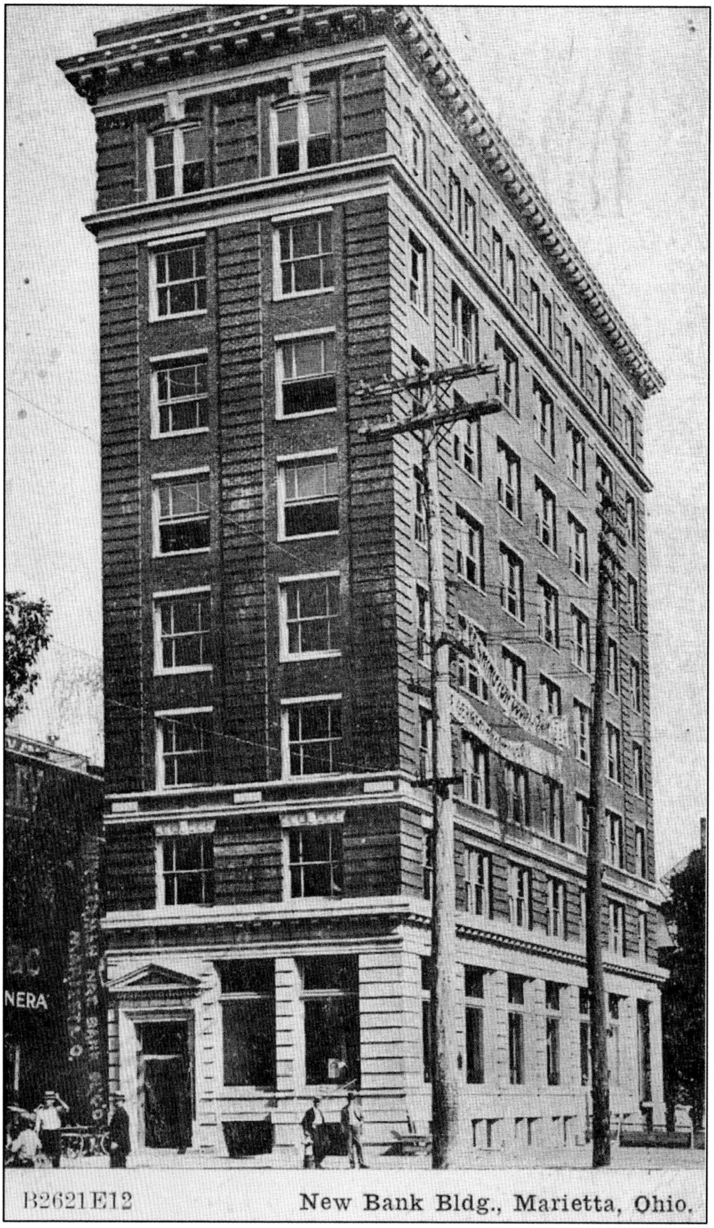

The first German National Bank was located at 212 Front Street. It opened in 1899 as one of the city's four banks. The greater financial community as well of the German community welcomed and supported the bank. William H. Ebinger held the office of president, and J.S.H. Torner was vice president. The German National Bank moved from the original building on Front Street to Marietta's skyscraper at the corner of Second and Putnam Streets. This 1912 postcard shows the first half of the building. Behind it on Second Street was the Hippodrome Theatre, operated by Weber, Frantz, and Schafer. In 1912, it was one of four banks in Marietta. It closed about 1918 during the era of World War I. The German National Bank was not the only German financial institution in town. The German Savings and Loan was first organized in 1870. By 1900, it had 1,200 members. The officers were John Rech, president; John Lenz, vice president; John Bickert, treasurer; and Fred Blume, secretary. (Courtesy of John Miller.)

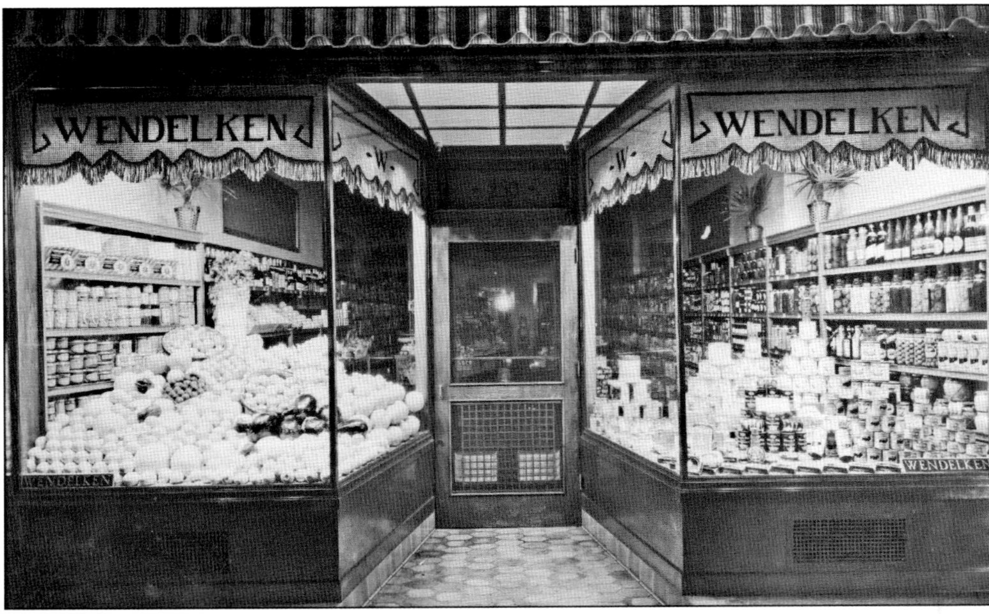

Many people today fondly remember the unique shop of Wendelkens that was located at 250 Front Street. Henry Wendelken came to America as a boy in 1853. His father, Gerd Wendelken, had a grocery and dry goods store on lower Front Street. Henry opened his own business in 1866. Henry died in 1906, but his family still lived upstairs of the business until the 1913 flood reached the ceiling and they lost everything. The grocery passed on to son Sargeant, who had spent his boyhood making deliveries—perhaps this is why Sargeant purchased the city's first delivery truck. The store traditionally sold groceries and dry goods, including the best trades of coffee, teas, confections, canned and bottled goods, fine cigars, and notions. In later years, the company specialized in gourmet and health foods, gift baskets, and party items. It could send specialty baskets worldwide. (Both, courtesy of Marietta College.)

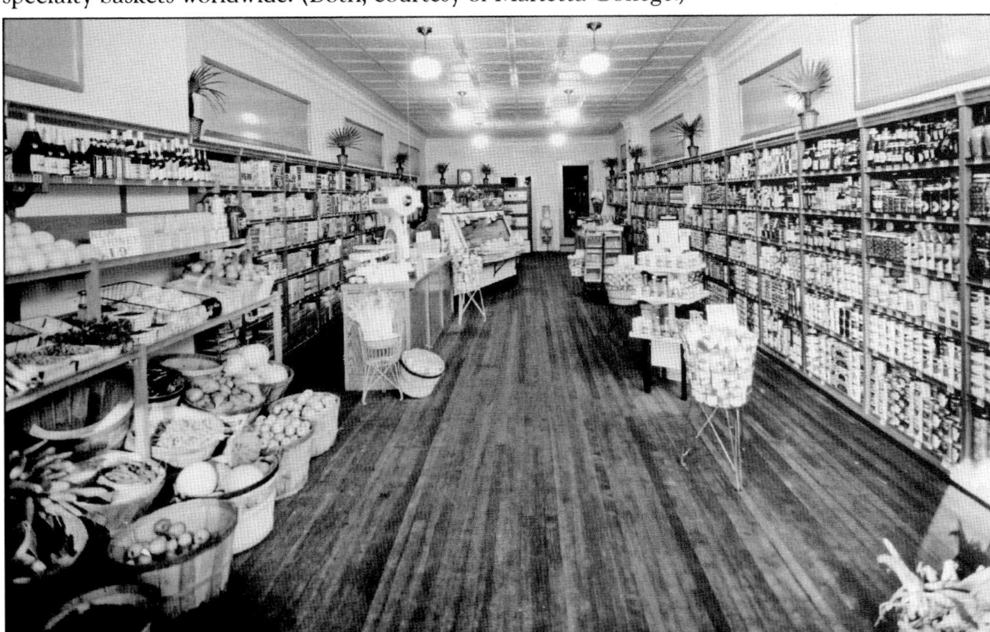

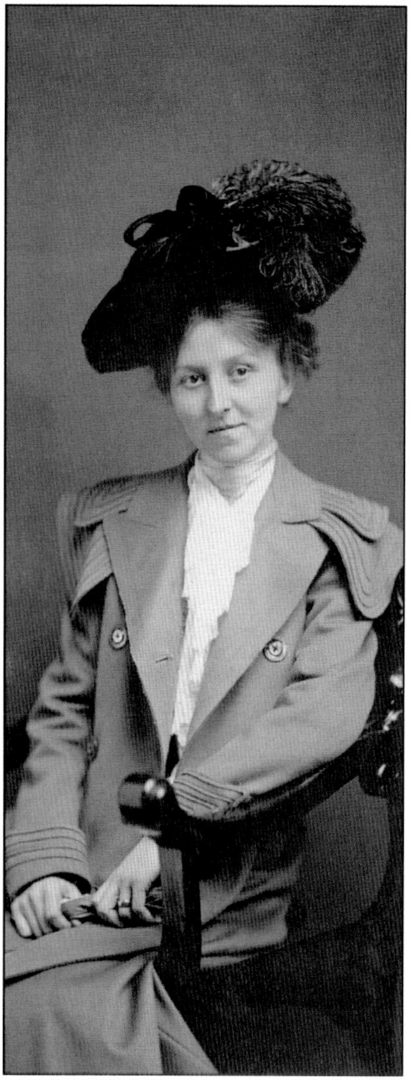

Living the American dream came true for the Best family. G. Christopher Best, upon arrival to Ohio, lived in the county and then opened a business on Ohio Street. As first-generation Germans, two of their children found their livelihoods in the nearby First National Bank. Oldest son, G.C. Best Jr. born in 1852 was a cashier, banker, and then, vice president of the bank from 1910 until his death in 1924. Youngest daughter, Laura, born in 1873, was the private secretary for many years to bank president John Mills. The photograph shows a fashionable Laura comfortable in her role in the bank and community. From immigration to raising a family, G. Christopher Best saw two of his children rise to successful careers in America. (Both, courtesy of Marietta College.)

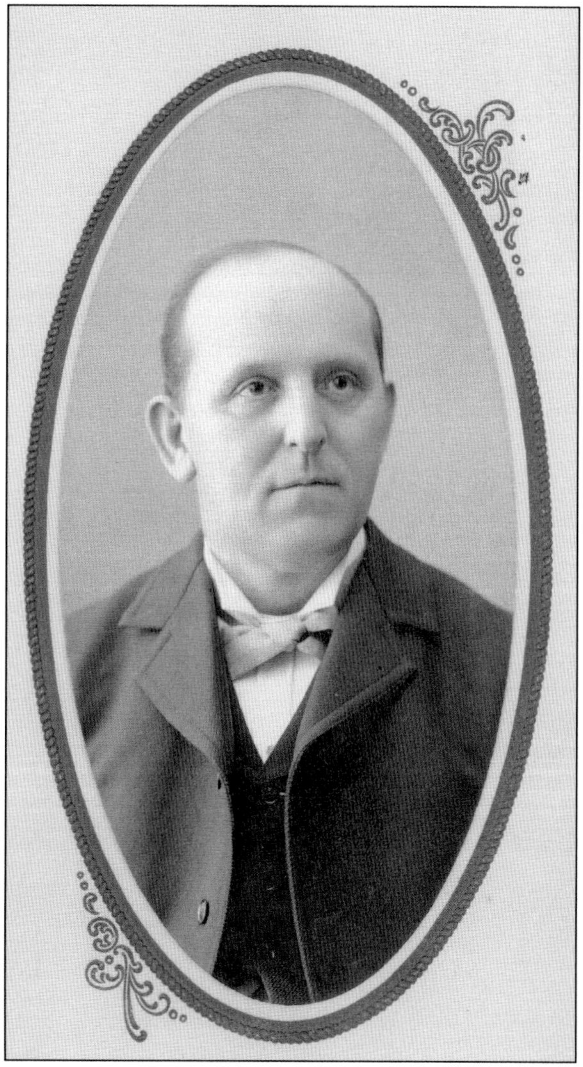

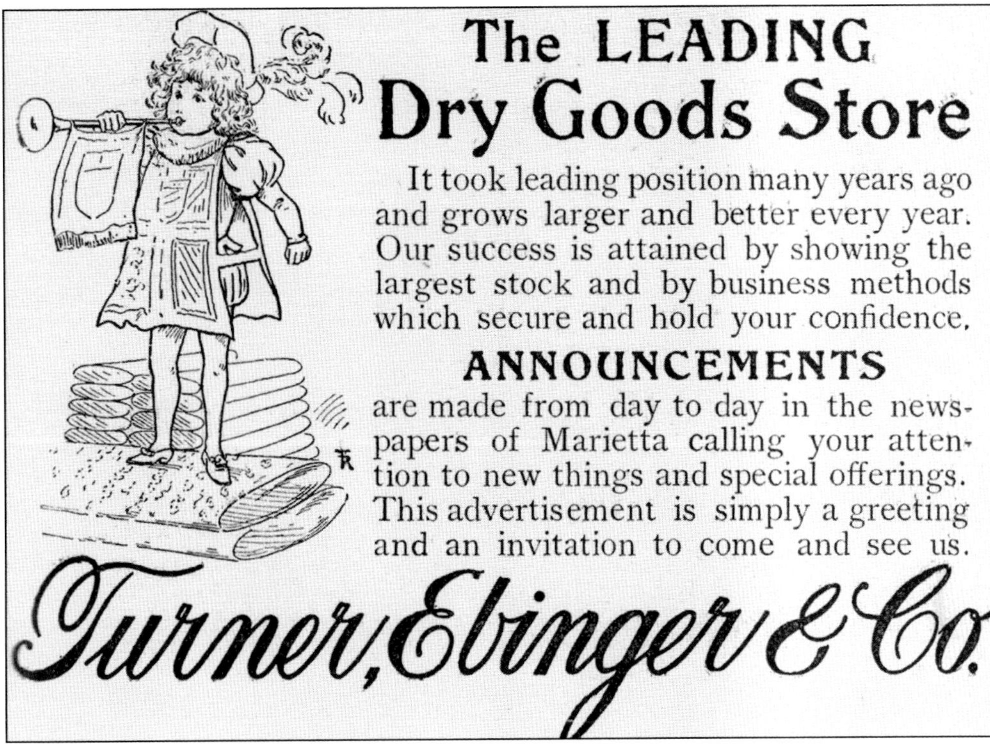

In 1846, S.R. Turner & Sons established a dry goods store on Front Street, and for over 40 years, it was a leader in the trade. A young German, H.J. Ebinger was hired as a clerk at age 14 and became part of the Turner family. By the 1880s, Ebinger became a partner in the firm, and the name changed to Turner & Ebinger. The three floors of the business carried dry goods, fancy goods, carpets, and other general merchandise. The first floor displayed a comprehensive line of dry goods of the newest design as well as furnishings, domestic goods, and notions. A passenger elevator made of cherry wood could access the floors. In 1925, it moved to the commodious accommodations at 206–210 Putnam Street. The three-story building was a part of the "big" stores of the 20th century. After successful years of business, the Turner & Ebinger Company closed its doors about 1946. (Both, courtesy of Washington County Historical Society.)

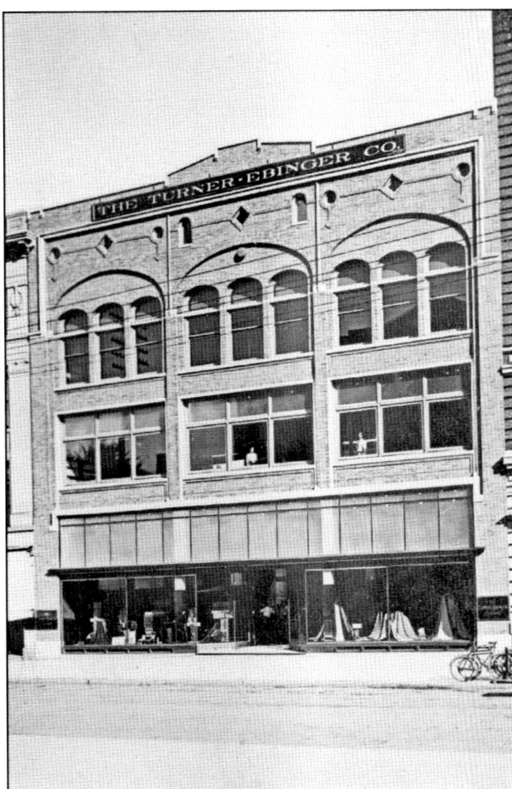

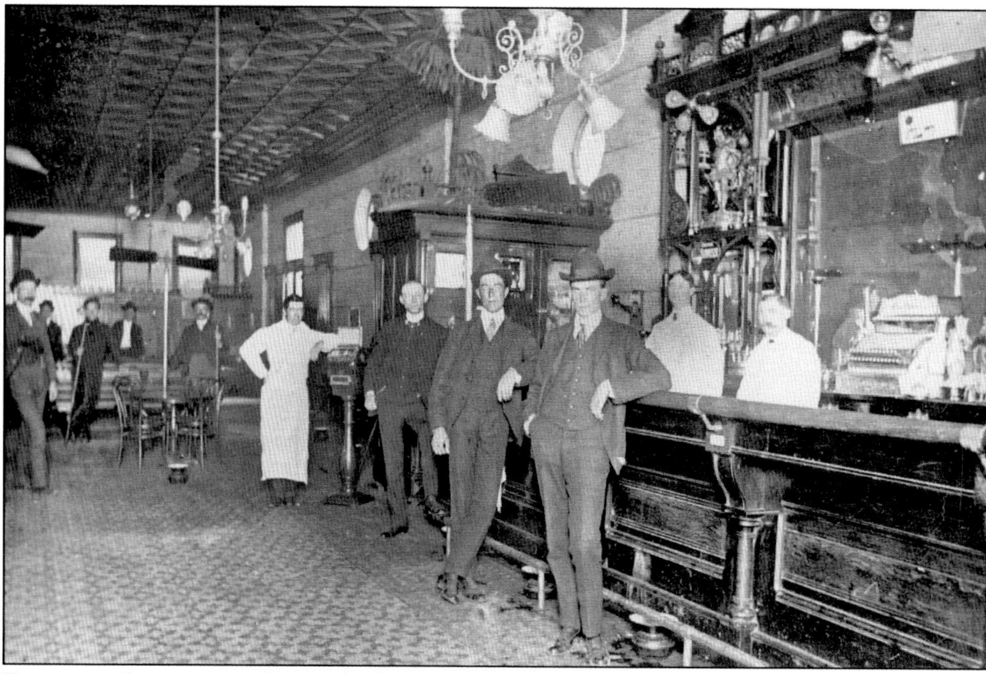

From its earliest times, Marietta had an assortment of drinking establishments. Germans were known for their preference for beer. Sample rooms could often be found in the back rooms of businesses. Saloons, such as Baum's at 237 Second Street, were places where men would gather to socialize, drink an alcoholic beverage, and play billiards. (Courtesy of Marietta College.)

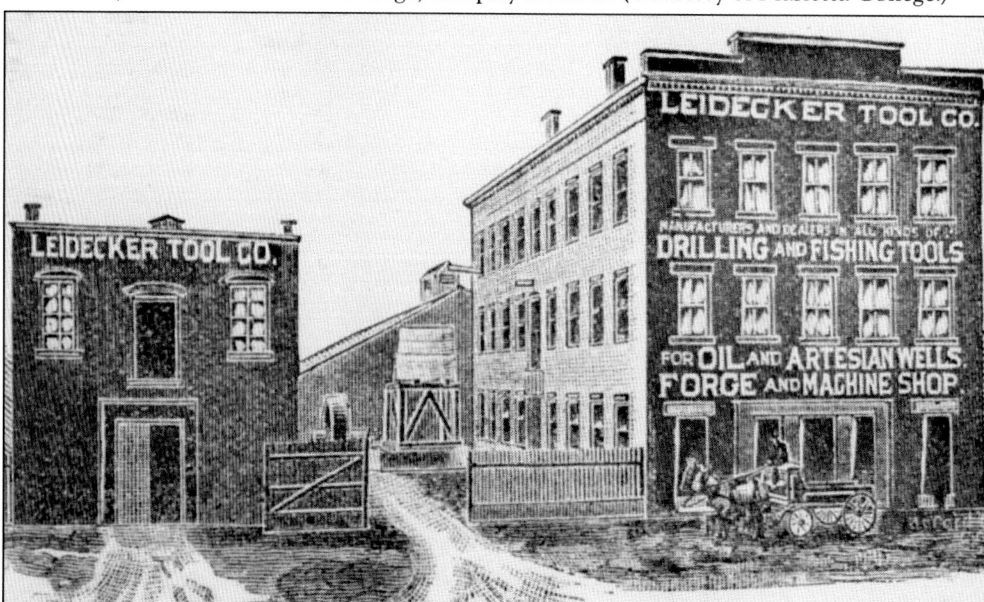

The Leidecker Tool Company opened in 1891 during the oil boom. In 1915, Foster Leidecker announced that the company had a long-term contract with the US government for orders of projectiles and shells to be used in war. The Leidecker plant at 119–127 Second Street in Marietta was one of the nation's largest and oldest drilling and fishing manufacturers in the oil industry. (Courtesy of Marietta College.)

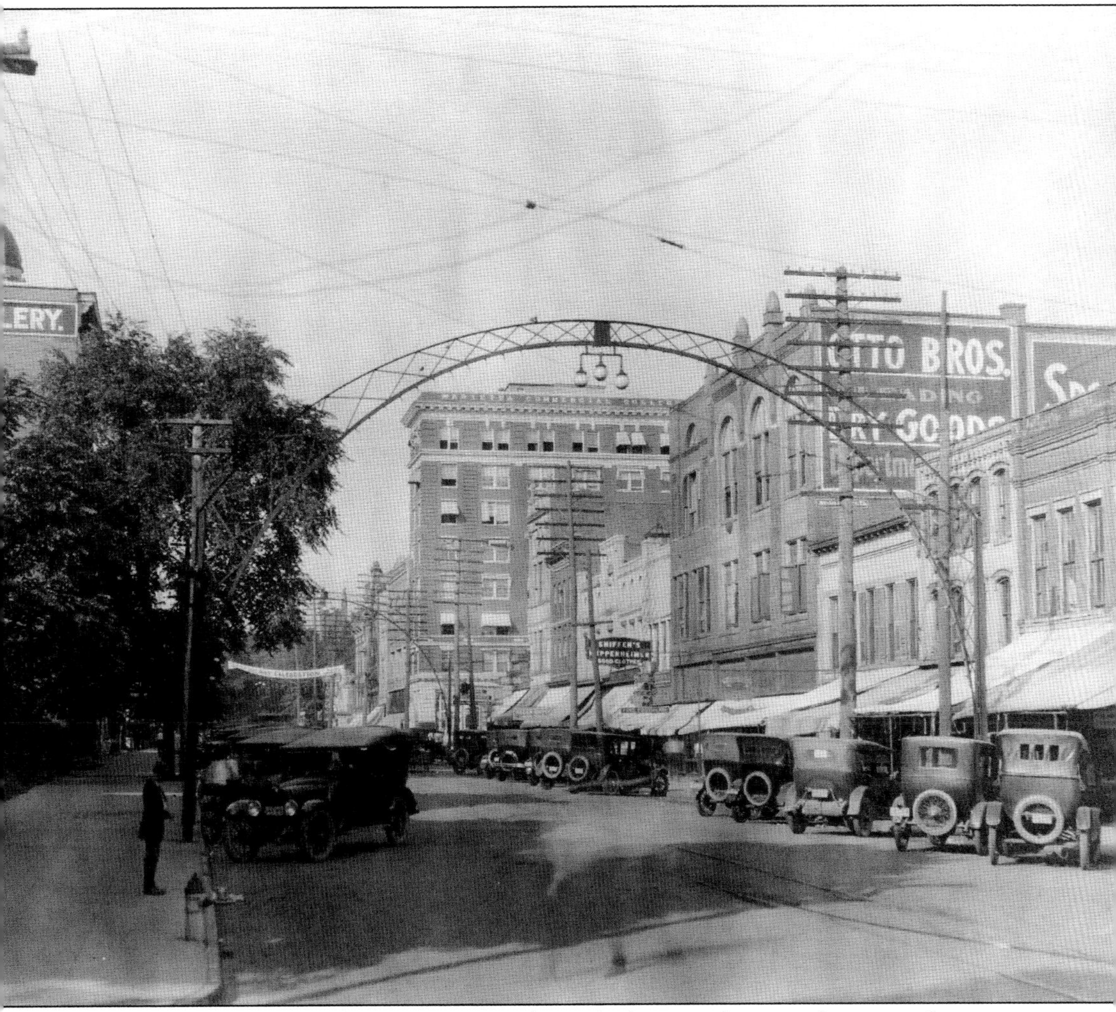

Marietta's Putnam Street was thriving in 1923. This street became the main downtown business district in the 20th century. At the turn of the century, some merchants feared moving from the Front Street shopping area that had served the town for decades. The Otto Brothers took the lead and became the largest and most-modern dry goods store in southeastern Ohio. Unlike Front Street shops, Otto Brothers and Strecker Brothers were very large multistoried structures. Strecker Brothers (saddlery ad on top floor) was nationally known for leather goods. In the background, the new German National Bank built the skyscraper, Marietta's tallest building. These anchor stores shared the street with other smaller German-descent businesses, such as the Pape Cigar Company, Schramm and Pffaff Bakeries, Karl Schafer Insurance, and Kropp & Son Hardware Store. (Courtesy of Marietta College.)

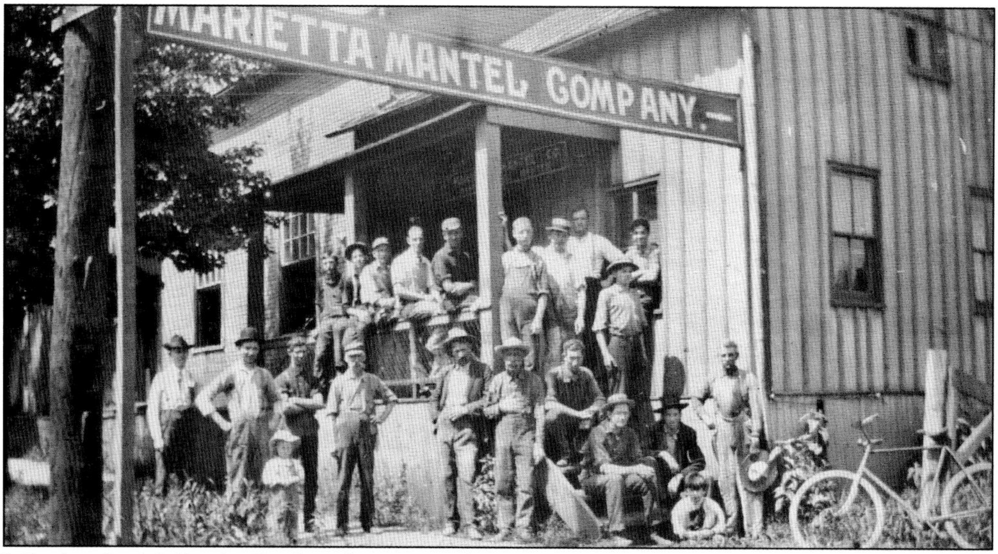

J. Frederick and Charles Brickwede were employed at a young age as woodworkers at the Stevens Organ and Piano Company. By 1903, they started the Marietta Mantel Company near the corner of Gilman and Wood Streets. Since cabinetry for mantels was found in nearly every home at the time, the business flourished. This single business lasted for over 21 years. (Courtesy of Kurt Ludwig.)

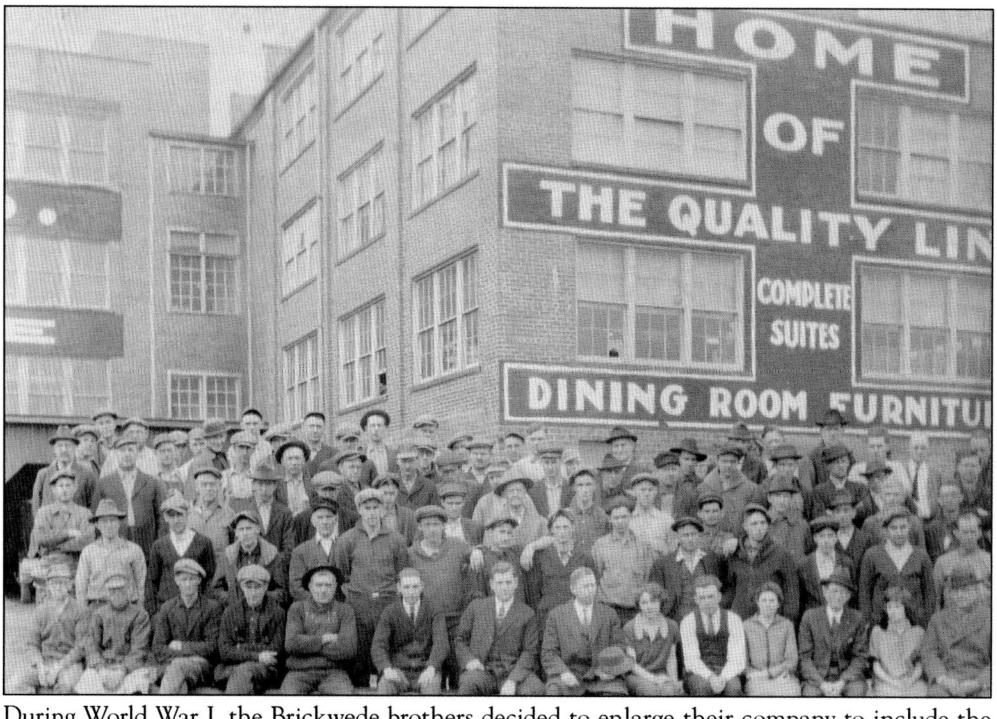

During World War I, the Brickwede brothers decided to enlarge their company to include the manufacturing of dining suites that included tables, chairs, china cabinets, and buffets. With the support of additional investors, they built a large, modern furniture factory in the Westview business area. In 1923, the name of the firm was changed to Brickwede Brothers Company, and the fine-quality furniture became known nationally. (Courtesy of Marietta College.)

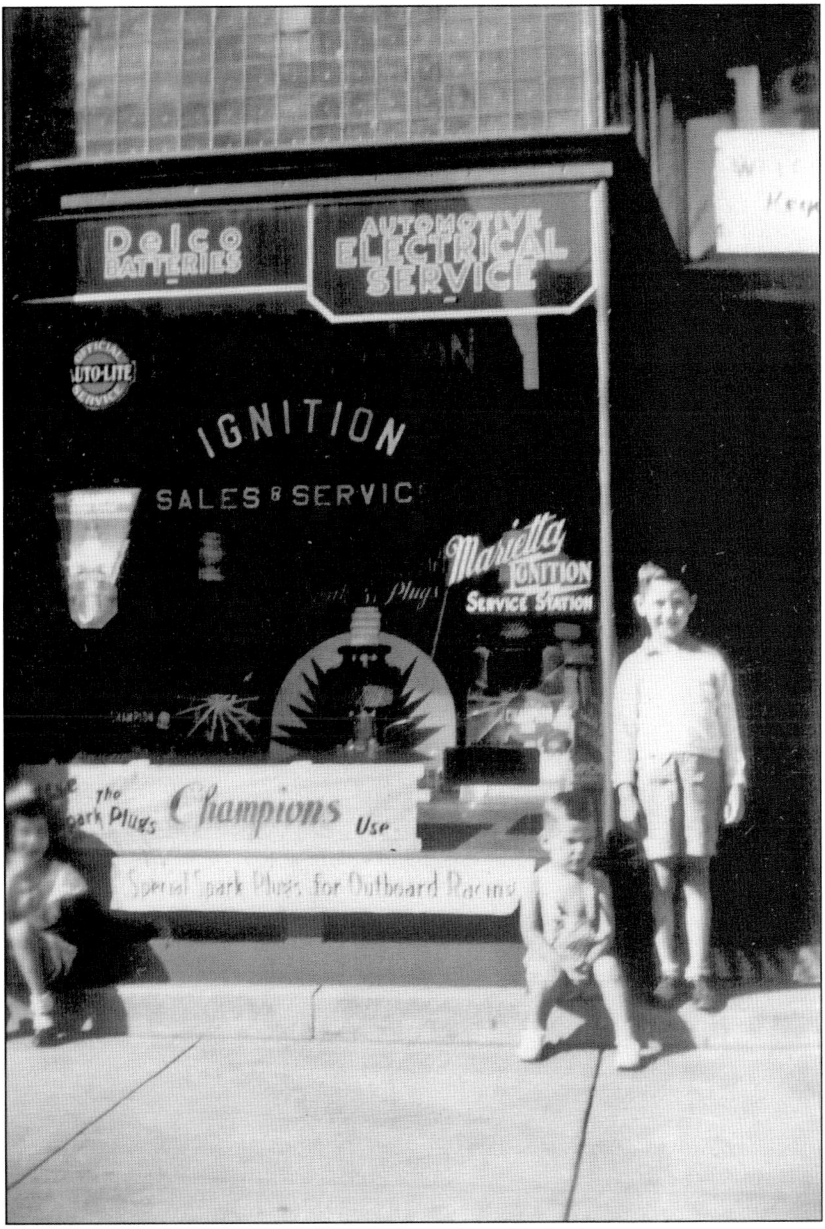

William F. Wesel arrived in Marietta about 1920 and established a service station at 130 Greene Street. By 1925, he moved the Marietta Ignition Service Station, the first business of its kind in Marietta, to 181 Front Street with a specialty in electrical parts for automobiles. The photograph shows the Marietta Ignition Service Station in 1935. William and Genevieve Wesel and family lived upstairs at this address. Pictured in this 1935 photograph are, from left to right, Catherine and her brothers C. William and young Joseph. All of the children, including the youngest, Mary Agnes, would later operate and enlarge the Marietta Ignition Company. Following the death of her husband in 1945, Genevieve became chairman of the board. Later, eldest son, Joseph, became president, with his siblings and relatives holding other key positions. The business grew to house one of the largest inventories of automotive parts in southeastern Ohio with three warehouses in the region. (Courtesy of Joseph and Luada Wesel.)

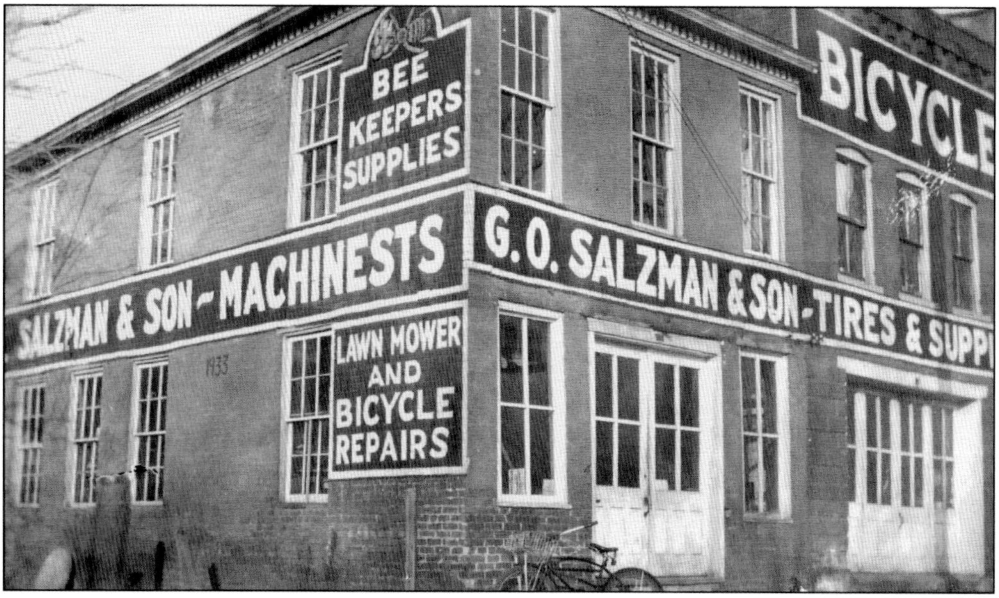

In 1898, the first bicycle made in Marietta was the work of George O. Salzman at his bicycle shop at 225 Ohio Street. Though still awkward in appearance, the bicycle was an improvement over the high-wheeled structure of the past. Bicycles were a significant form of transportation. (Courtesy of Washington County Historical Society.)

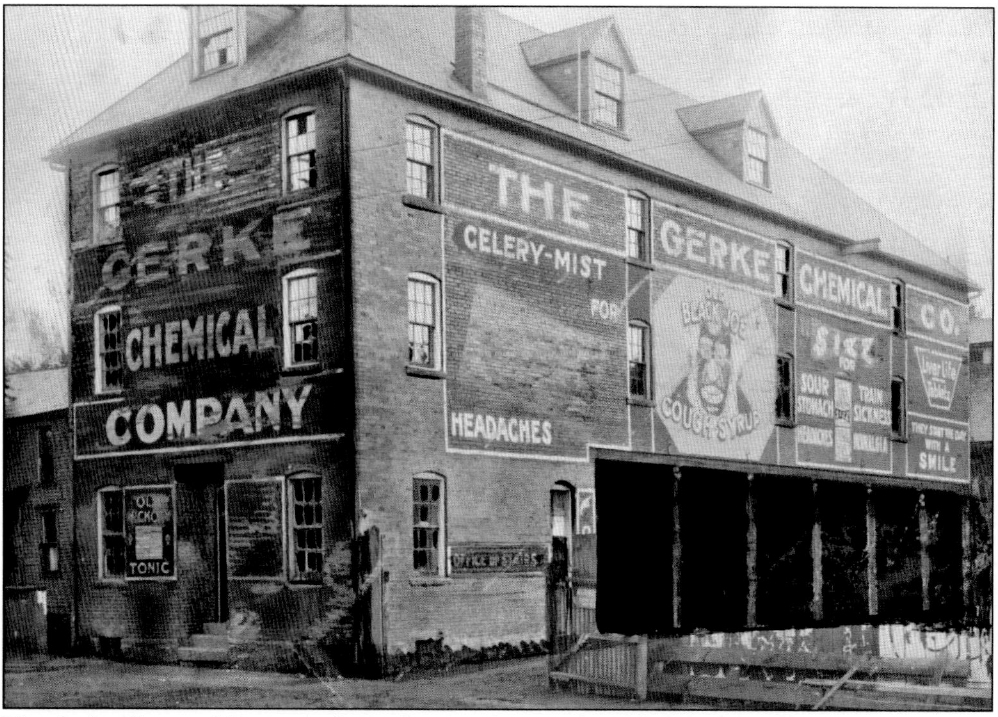

The Gerke Chemical Company, located on Market Street in Harmar, manufactured medical and household preparations. The patent medicine company was famous for Celery-Mist, which was used for headaches. The chemical composition was made from aspirin and ground celery seeds, placed in wrappers with a twist. It was then snorted for fast relief. (Courtesy of Marietta College.)

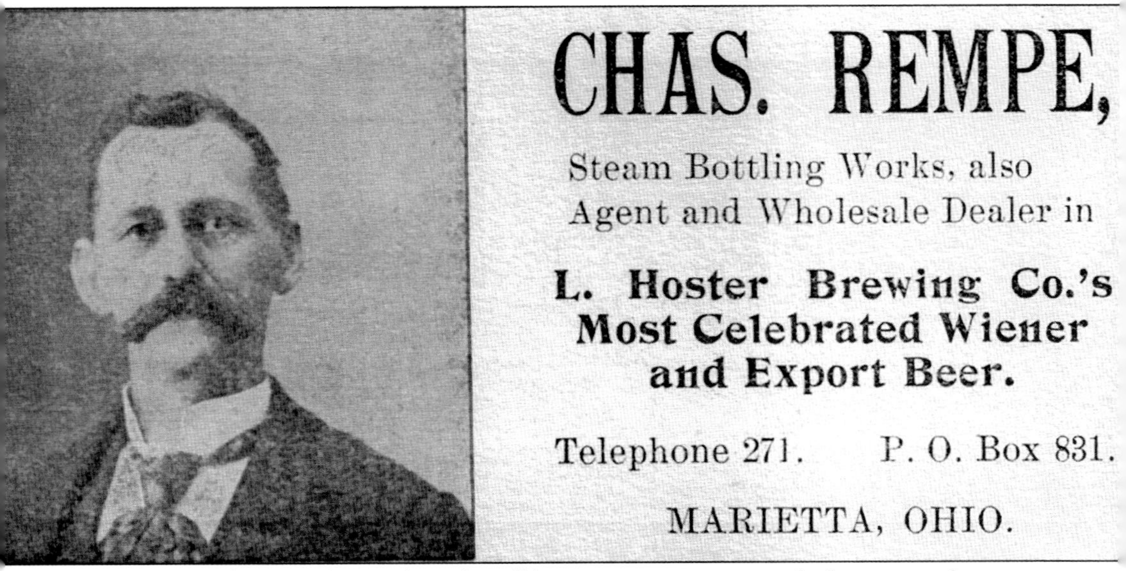

Germans owned and operated a number of small breweries or were agents for larger out-of-town companies. Charles Rempe & Son was a firm that represented the L. Hoster Brewing Company in Columbus, Ohio. It was a wholesale business that started in 1895. The facility at the corner of Butler and Fourth Streets had a bottling plant that could produce about 300 dozens of bottled beer per day. German B.E. Stoehr was noted as the first person to produce lager beer in the area. His property at 703 Fifth Street was known to have a beer garden. By 1900, he was a wholesale dealer for the Christian Moerlein Brewing Company in Cincinnati. Phil Bachman had a bottling works at 112 South Second Street. Bachman received product from the Cincinnati Beer Company in refrigerated cars, and then he would bottle it to sell. The Marietta Distillery at 217–219 Greene Street handled wholesale liquors and exported the keg beer of George Wiedimann of Kentucky. (Courtesy of Washington County Public Library.)

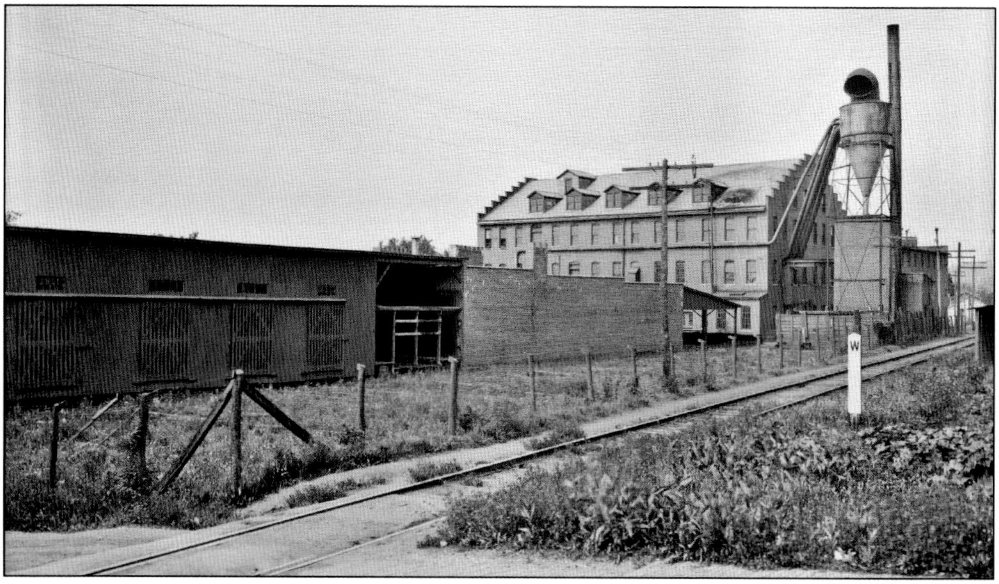

J.H. Becker first started his planing mill on Wooster Street above Second Street. Later, he added buildings on Sacra Via and Front Streets that covered about an acre of land. The company turned out rough and planed lumber as well as sashes, doors, and blinds. Business demand required that Becker build this plant on Greene Street for lumberyards and additional buildings. (Courtesy of Marietta College.)

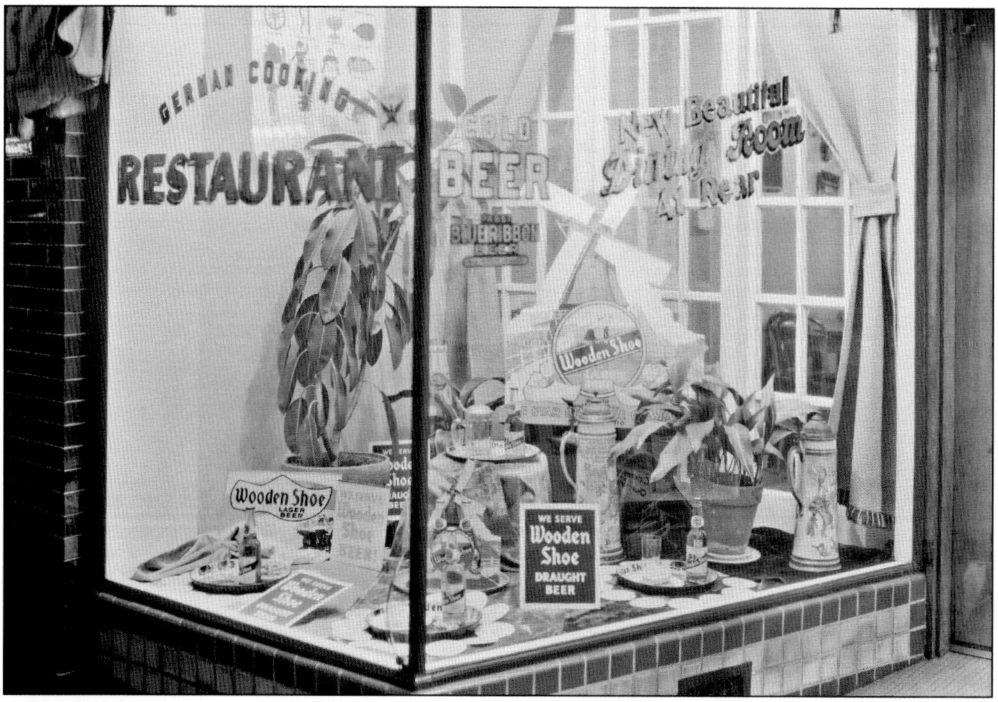

Benjamin G. Conrath and his wife, Grace Klintworth, operated the Conrath Café. The photograph indicates the couple's heritage by advertising German cooking and Wooden Shoe draft beer. He was associated with the restaurant business for a number of years. The café's address was 216 Putnam Street, which was later the location of the Mecca Café. (Courtesy of Marietta College.)

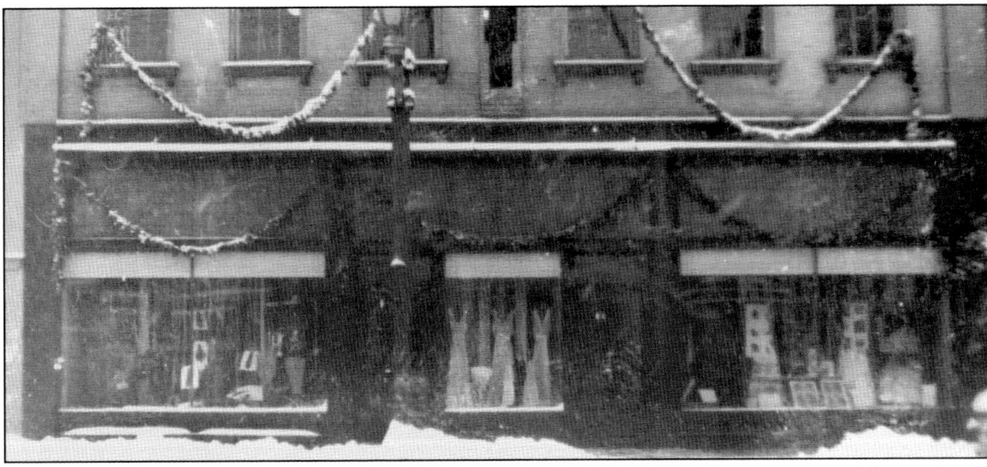

L.C. Gruber and Sons opened at 153–155 Front Street in 1903. The three-story building sold dry goods, notions, men's and ladies' wear, carpets, linens, and hardware. In the back of the store was a grocery with fresh produce supplied by local growers. Farmers could trade eggs and produce for home necessities. Gruber's store was the largest full-service department store in the area. Gruber's survived the 1913 and 1937 floods, but a fire in 1946 ended the business. (Courtesy of Vera Gruber descendants.)

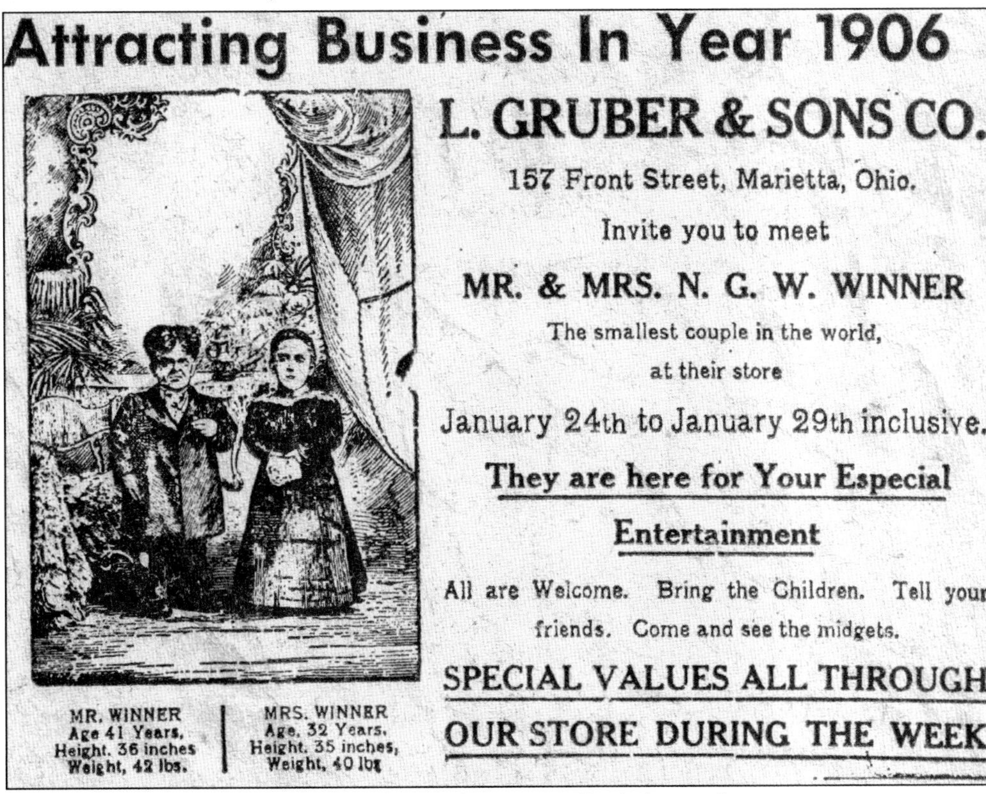

After only three years in business, the Gruber Store afforded a marketing strategy to attract a wide range of customers. Today's mores would question using such an attraction for entertainment. These kinds of events and attention-seeking publicity were not uncommon in the days of vaudeville acts and three-ring circuses. (Courtesy of Vera Gruber descendants.)

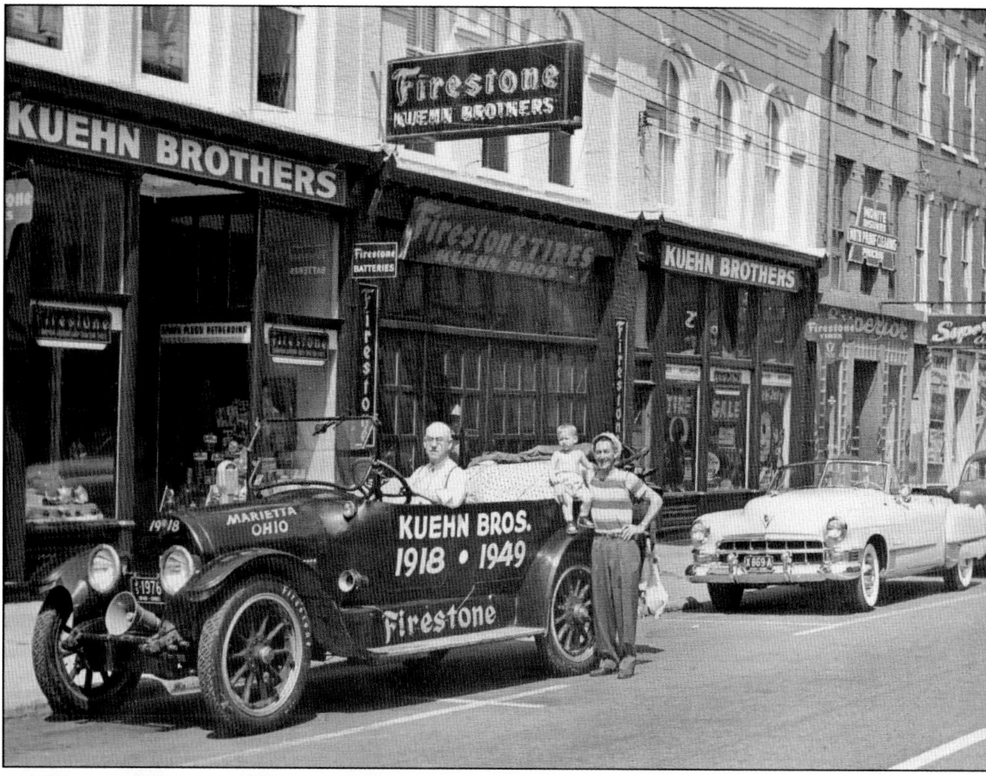

Kuehn Brothers, located at 113 Front Street, was a tire and auto accessory store, which opened in 1918. George and John Kuehn, and later Orland Wolford, were the proprietors. It specialized in Firestone and Barney Oldfield tires and had a service station for fuel. The store was purchased by the Lafayette Hotel for its addition and parking lot, and the business moved to the bus terminal building. (Courtesy of Marietta College.)

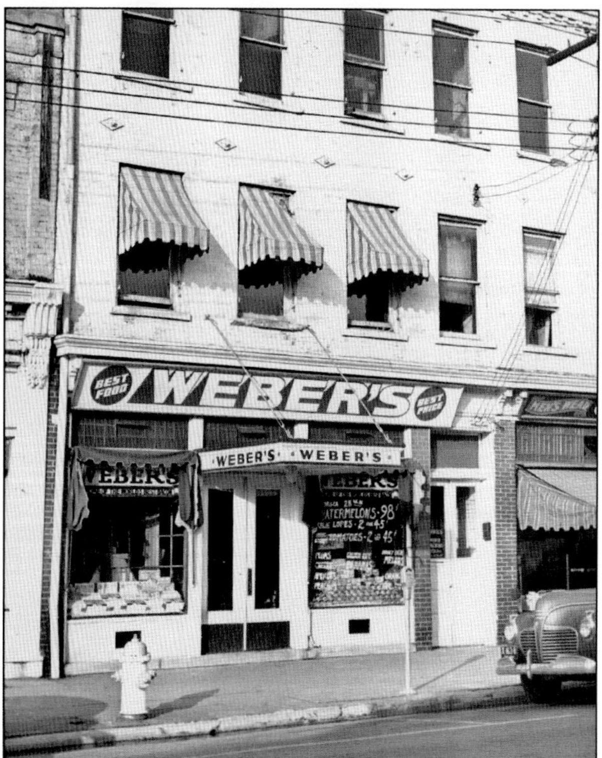

Weber's Meat Market was located at 122 Front Street. In the 1890s, it advertised as a pork packer and offered fresh and salt meats. Frank and his wife, Christina, operated this popular store for about 35 years. In 1928, William Weber took over the business. (Courtesy of Marietta College.)

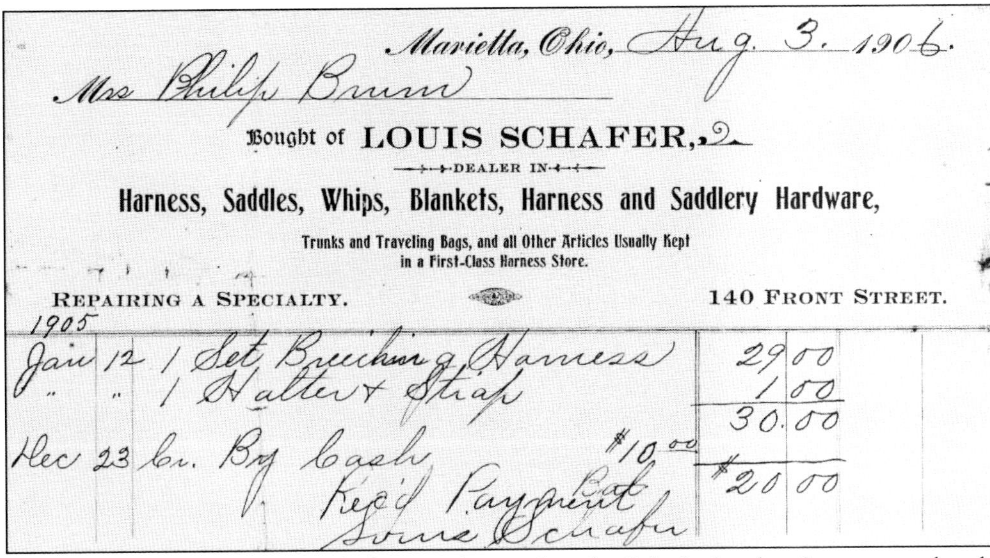

Marietta, Ohio, Aug. 3. 1906.

Mrs Philip Brunn

Bought of LOUIS SCHAFER, 2

DEALER IN

Harness, Saddles, Whips, Blankets, Harness and Saddlery Hardware,

Trunks and Traveling Bags, and all Other Articles Usually Kept in a First-Class Harness Store.

REPAIRING A SPECIALTY. 140 FRONT STREET.

1905			
Jan 12	1 Set Breeching Harness		29 00
" "	1 Halter & Strap		1 00
			30 00
Dec 23	Cr. By Cash	$10.00	
	Rec'd Payment Bal		$20 00
	Louis Schafer		

The 1906 receipt from Louis Schafer Jr. indicates that the Schafer Leather Store not only sold leather goods, but also other items that were kept in a "First-Class Harness Store." The store also did repair work. This repair was for one set of breeching harness and halter. A breeching harness was used for workhorses. (Courtesy of Marilyn Schafer.)

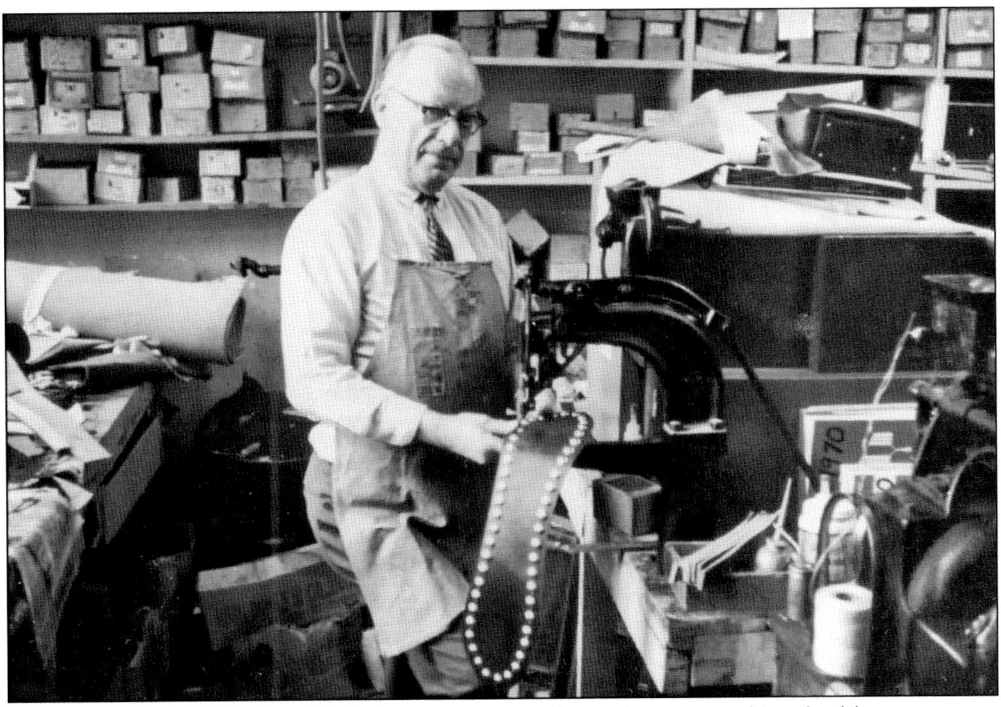

As time passes, a business must adapt to survive. Once, harness making had been a strong demand. Robert L. Schafer Jr. determined that the days of necessity for handmade harnesses had come to an end. He is shown here making the last harness in 1970 for the Schafer Leather Store. (Courtesy of Marilyn Schafer.)

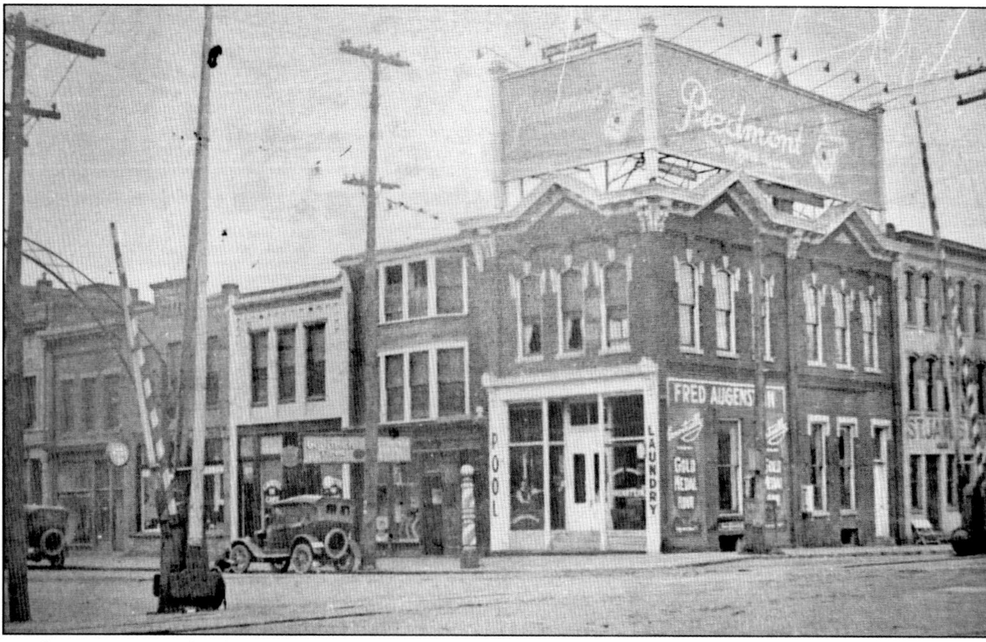

Fred Augenstein's barbershop located at 197 Front Street served the community at this location for over 10 years. In the mid-1930s, he opened the Augenstein Restaurant on Putnam Street. One of his children, Betsy, was well known for her dedication to youth as a teacher and her work with children services. (Courtesy of Washington County Historical Society.)

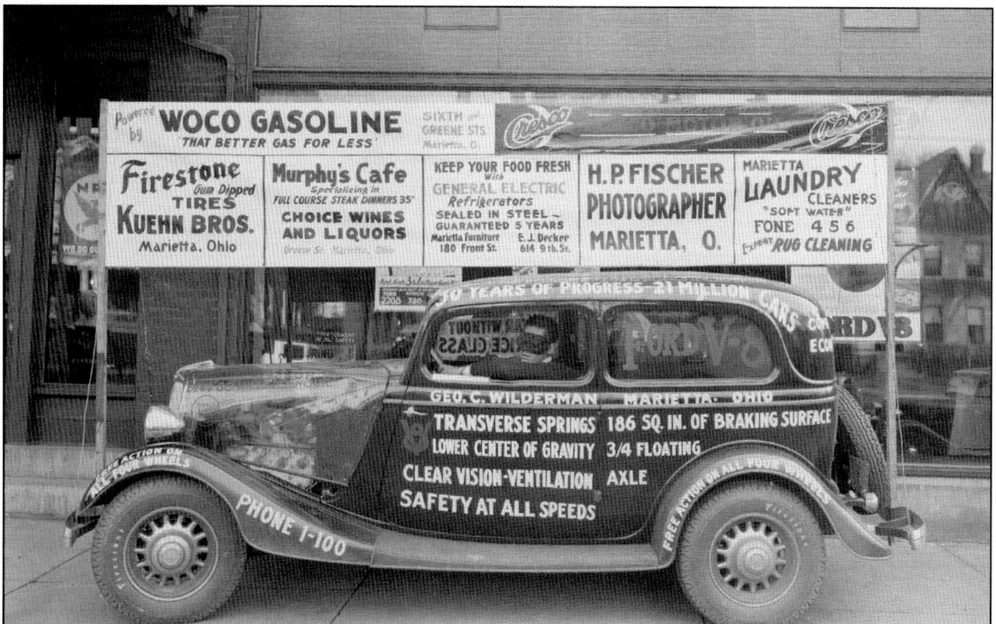

George C. Wilderman started the Ford dealership in 1912 in a small shop in Harmar. He needed to expand, so he built a suitable structure at 317 Second Street. In 1916, the store was fully stocked with a variety of Ford model cars with Ford parts ready for distribution around the county. Wilderman opened branches in Matamoras and Beverly and added Ford trucks and tractors to his line. (Courtesy of Marietta College.)

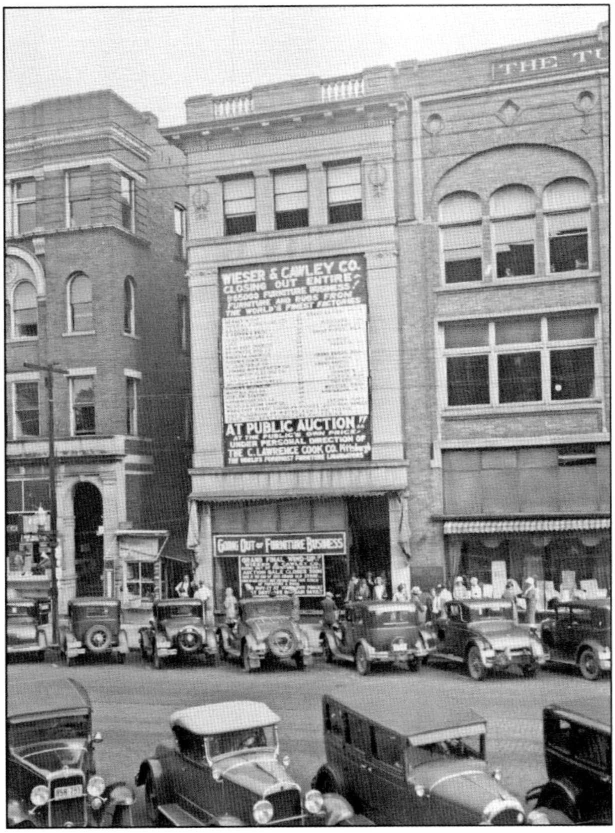

German carpenters, who often made coffins, made undertaking their connected business. In 1886, George Wieser opened a furniture and undertaking business on Front Street and then partnered with Dan Cawley. They built a store across from the courthouse. Furniture was shown on each floor except the second floor that was reserved for the funeral parlor. Later, the business opened at another location. (Courtesy of Marietta College.)

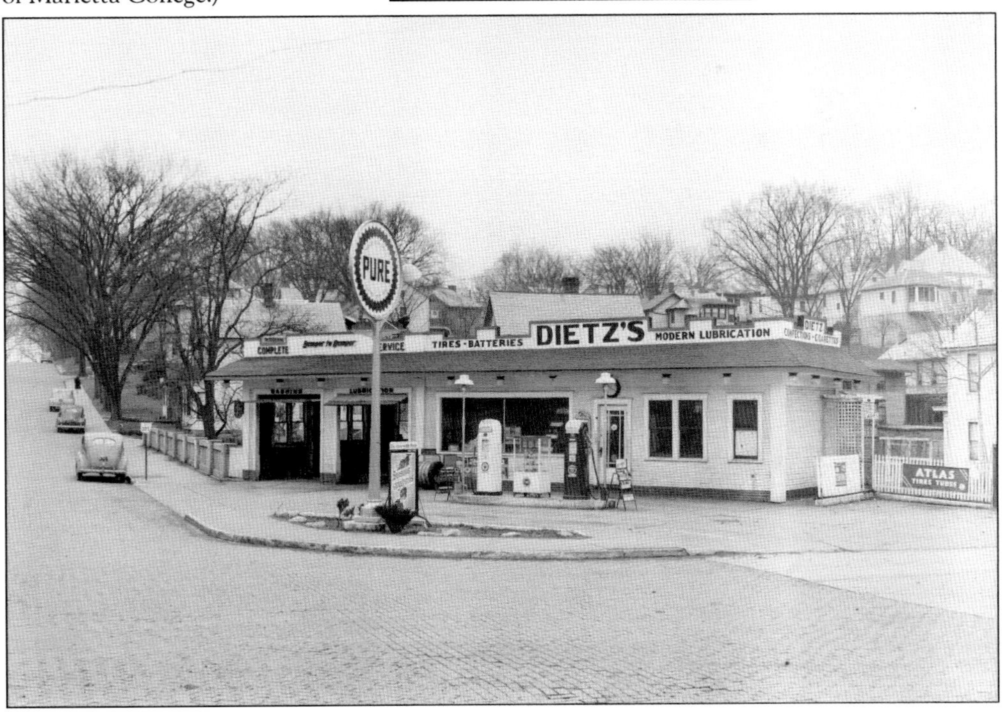

The building on the northwest corner of Seventh and Greene Streets was a service station in the 1930s, owned and operated by Paul C. Dietz. As a young man of 26, he profited at the location at the foot of the high school entrance. Upon leaving this business, Paul Dietz moved to Beverly where he made a significant impact on the community. (Courtesy of Marietta College.)

The family story of Josef Georg and Seraphina Rampp, who arrived in 1856, portrayed the common immigrant family pattern. Father and sons had typical German occupations in German-identified businesses. Josef Rampp was a shoemaker at Roesser's Shoes. Their eldest son, John, was a baker with Pfaff's Confectionery. Benny was a woodworker for the Marietta Chair Factory, and Joseph was a leatherworker at Strecker Brothers. They married Germans. The father had wanted the children to speak English outside the home in order to be "good Americans." One of the grandchildren, Martin Rampp, after 25 years with the Leidecker Company and International Derrick & Equipment Company, founded the Rampp Company at 111 Third Street. This company specialized in water and oil well supplies. (Right, courtesy of Helen Rampp Morris; below, courtesy of Marietta College.)

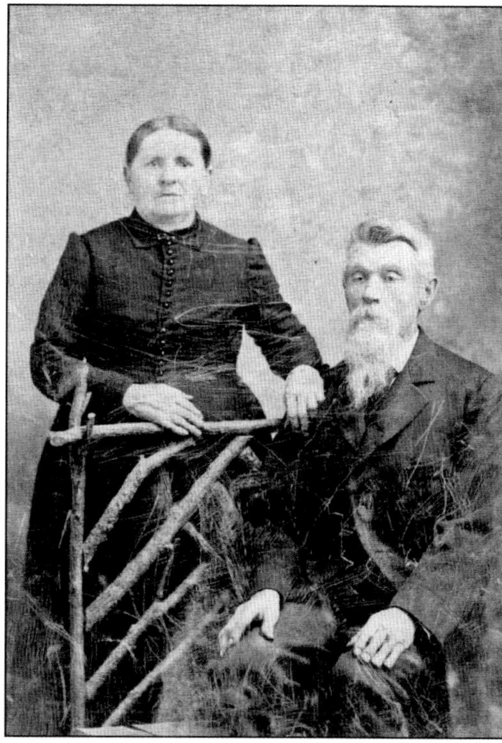

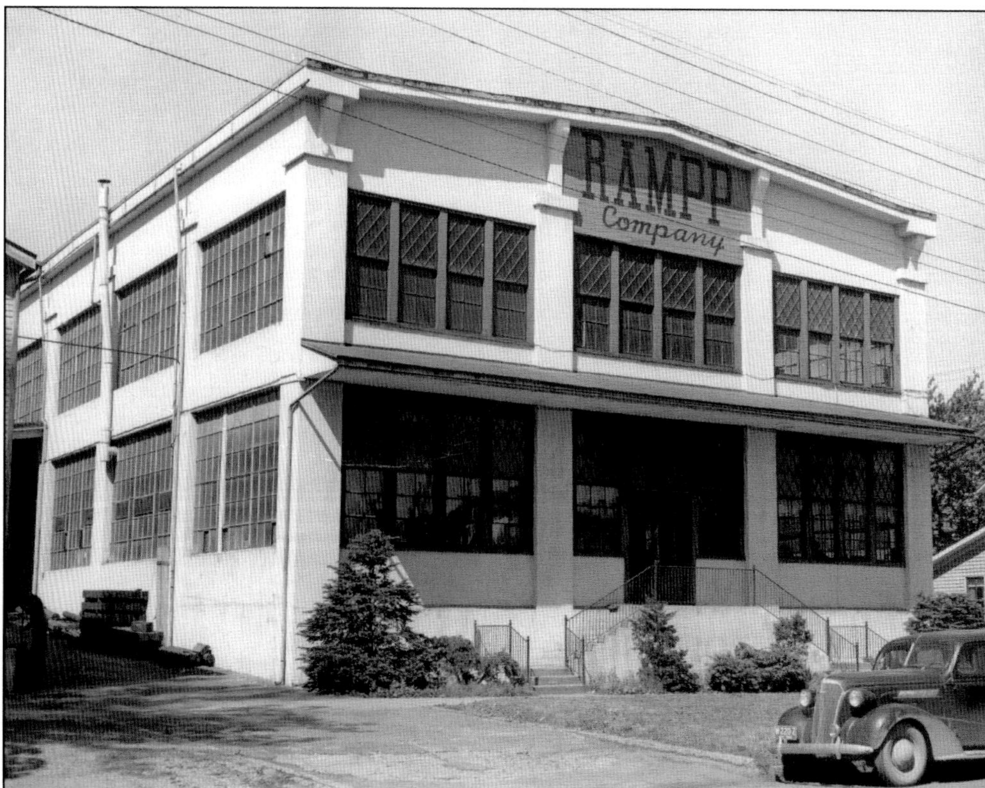

Three

Culture of Community

When the German immigrants first arrived in Marietta, they would take comfort in finding other Germans in which to converse and share traditions. People from all German-speaking lands, such as Switzerland and Austria, were members of the German community. Church services were a binding force in establishing a German community. Meeting for Sunday worship was a top priority, even if at first they attended the English-speaking churches and had one of their own interpret. Understandably, Germans wanted to use their German Bibles and listen to sermons and hymns in German. In the early days, they instructed their children to speak English outside of the home like a good American. However, often, there was a grandmother or parent at home who only knew German, so the language was retained in the cultural community.

Drinking beer and playing music were signature activities of the German culture. The major brewers of Marietta were all German. Though some people of the temperance movement thought Marietta had too many saloons, those were not all owned by Germans. The English gents liked their whiskey. In 1854, the Little German Band floated downriver to Marietta. These German musicians were so well liked, they were convinced to stay. From this event, Germans created the Marietta Band and the Marietta Orchestra.

Germans were civic minded. From the early volunteer fire departments to paid firefighters, the Germans were involved. They knew the risk of their own businesses being lost to fire, like the fate of many during the disaster of the 1859 downtown fire. The offices of mayor, city council, trustees, and clerks were jobs filled by Germans. Fraternities or secret societies were abundant in Marietta. Germans formed their own groups that raised money to care for others. First-, second-, and third-generation Germans were now part of the cultural fabric of Marietta.

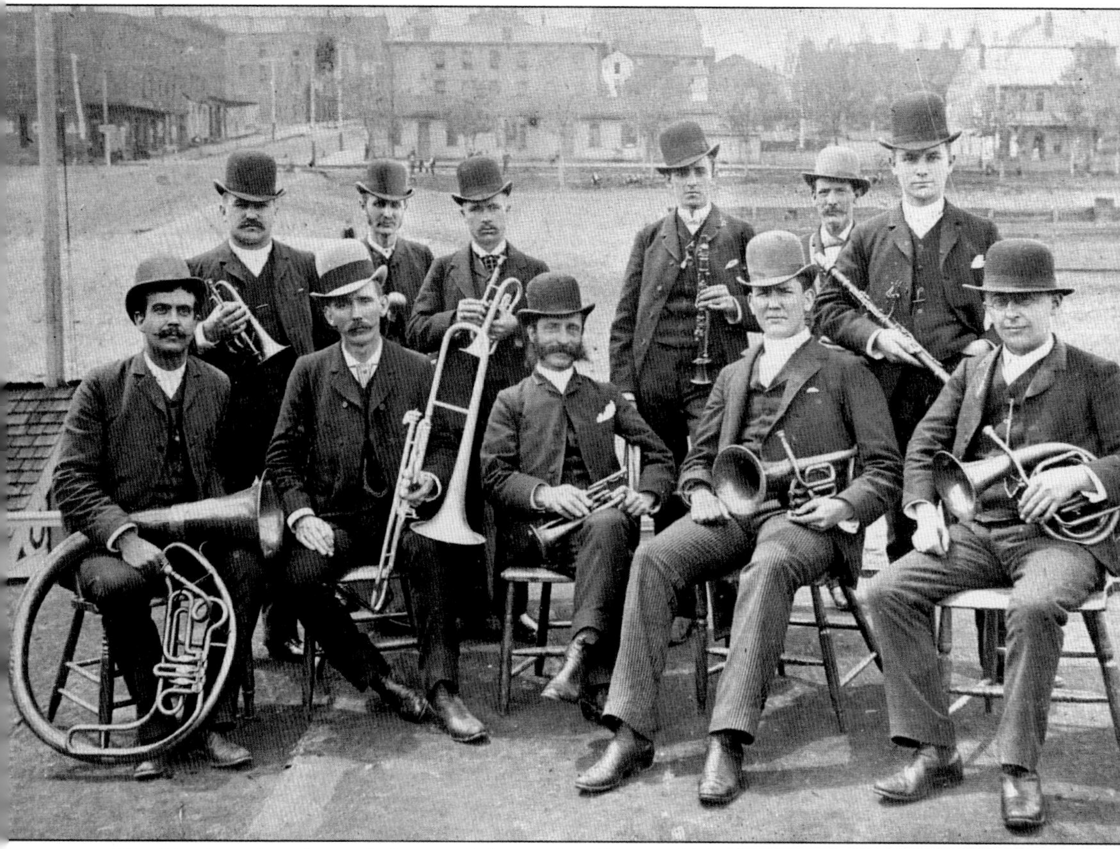

The Marietta Band traveled up and down the Ohio and Muskingum Rivers to perform in towns and would often be seen in parades. The tradition of the local band appealed to musical families with the players often being fathers and sons passing down the love of music. Band concerts were held in the East Muskingum Park to great crowds. Daniel Becker Sr., Carl Becker, Daniel Becker Jr., Jacob Mueller, Jacob Becker, and Louis Mueller were given most credit for the band's organization. The photograph shows the band on the road for a performance at Steubenville in 1888. Most of the players were of German descent. The inspiration to form a band occurred after the 1854 visit of the traveling Little German Band that arrived by steamboat. This band, mostly the Schlicher family, had left Germany in 1852 to tour Europe and America. When meeting the Marietta musicians, most of the family stayed and formed the Marietta Band. (Courtesy of Marietta College.)

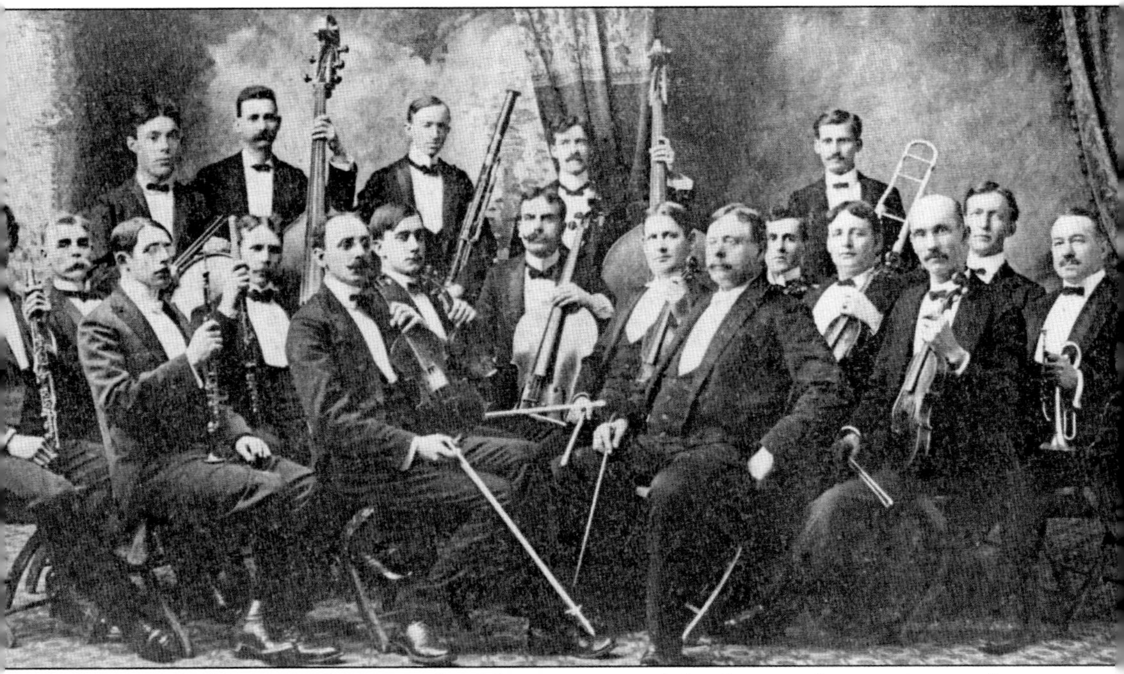

The Marietta Orchestra, made up mostly of Germans, provided culture and entertainment for many years while performing at the Auditorium in the city hall. In 1904, Francis MacMillen, a distinguished American violinist and Marietta native, played with the orchestra. Some of the noted members of German descent were Carl Becker, Fred Wehrs, Henry Theis, Henry Weis, David Gerken, Peter Schlicher Jr., and Henry Wittlig, who was a German speaker from Switzerland. Jacob Mueller, Louis Mueller, and Prof. Franz Schmiedeke, who came from the Pittsburgh Symphony Orchestra, served as directors during the years when the Marietta Orchestra was most active. Most of these men owned thriving businesses in town yet found a great deal of time to devote to practice and performance in the popular Marietta Orchestra. (Courtesy of Marietta College.)

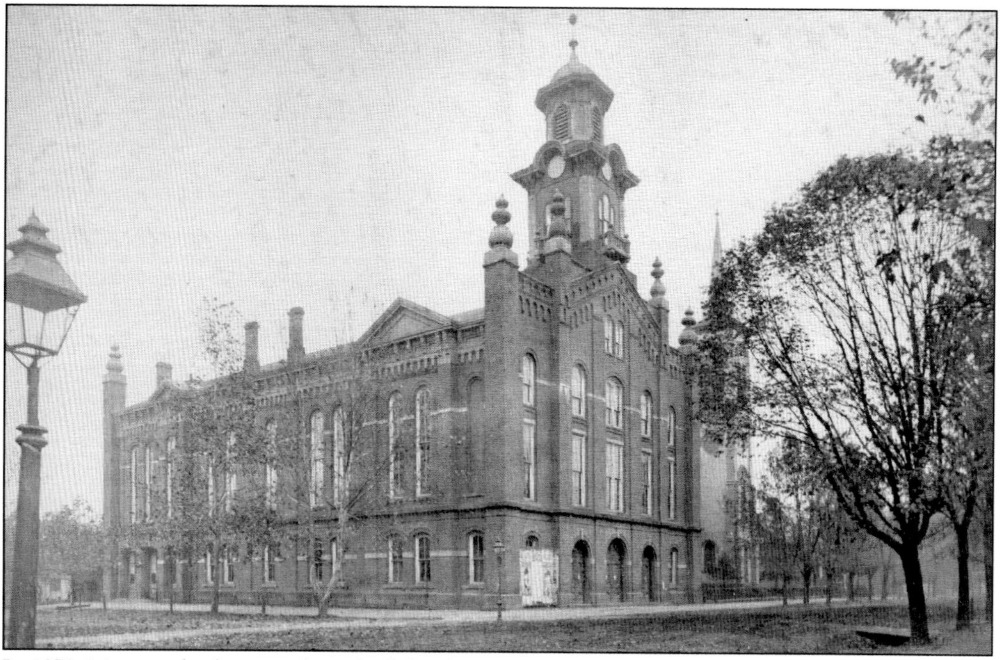

In 1872, Marietta built a grand city hall for the mayor's office, jail, and other city departments. On the second floor was an opera house that was commonly called the Auditorium. It had a seating capacity of 1,500. The large stage allowed for a variety of local productions as well as professional groups from out of town. One of the biggest events of the year was the musical program of 125 trained voices and orchestra performing the *Messiah*. Two of the most noted directors were Jacob Mueller and his son Louis. With the advent of popular films, the auditorium began showing movies. Unfortunately, the entire building burned in 1935. (Above, courtesy of Marietta College; below, courtesy of Washington County Historical Society.)

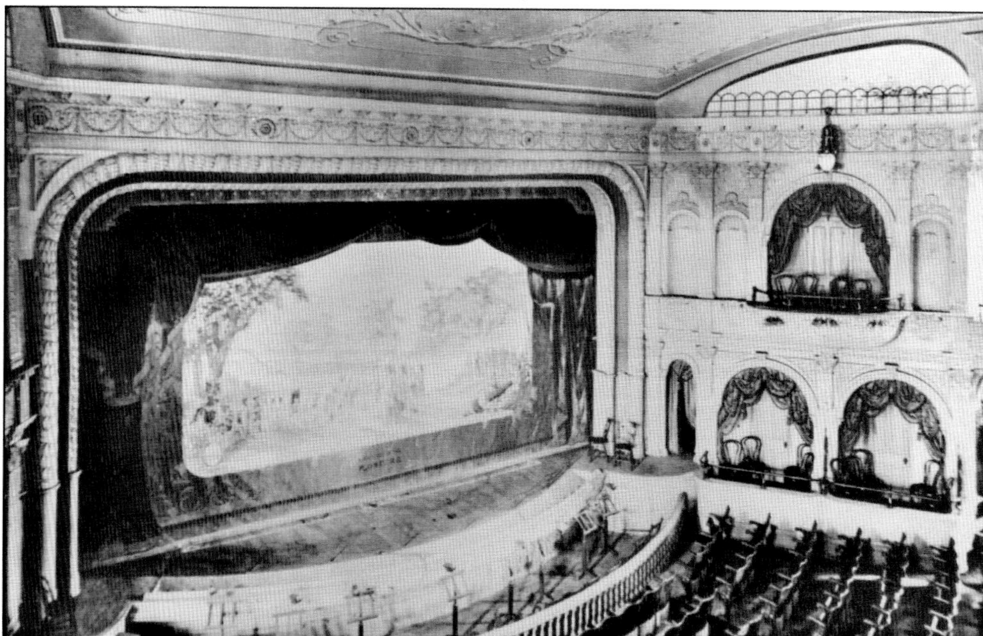

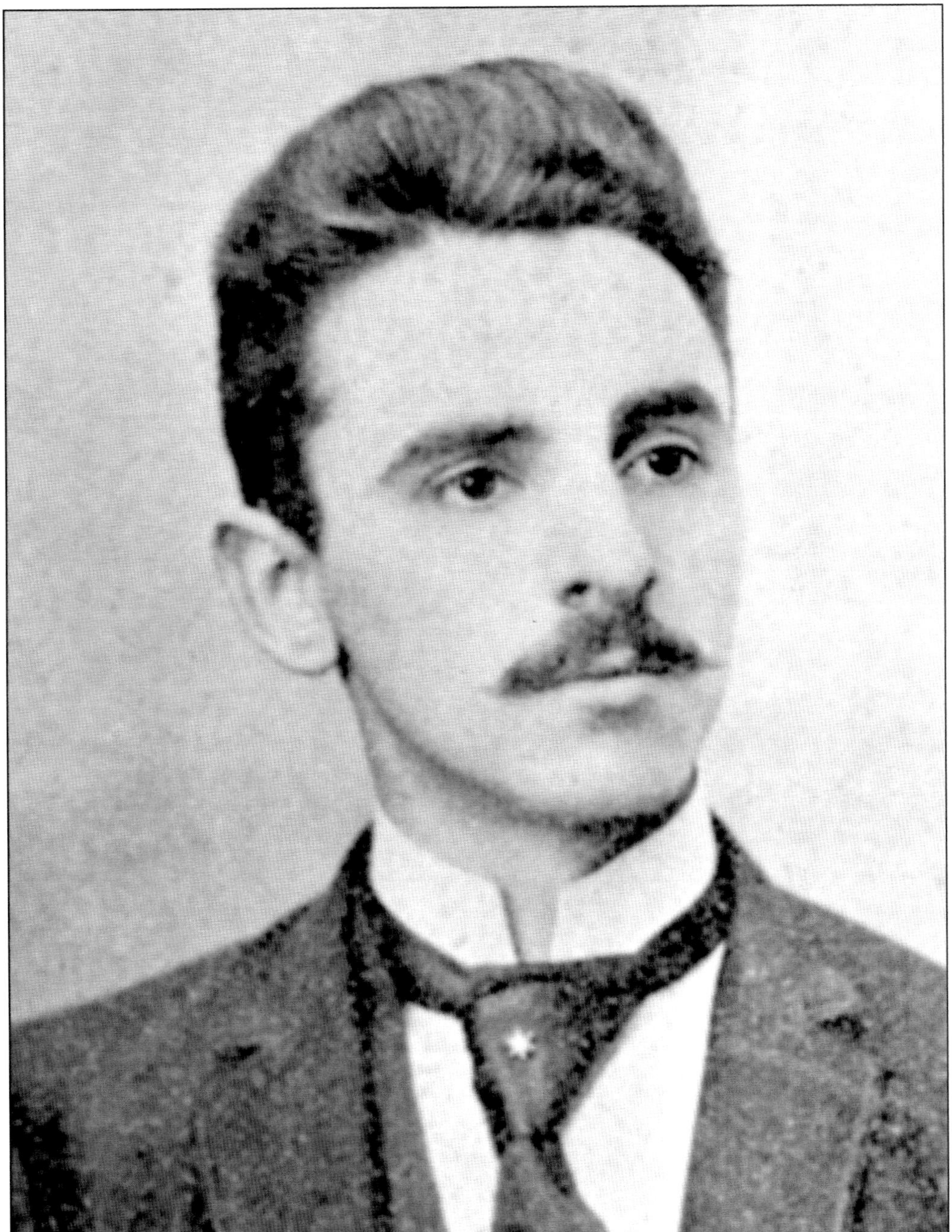

The Becker family brought great distinction to the musical community. Carl Becker remembered the 1880s as the "golden age" when his father, brothers, and sisters played before a variety of audiences. Carl Becker, the youngest of the family, was given his first violin at age five. His father, Daniel Becker Sr., emigrated from Germany, raised a family of musicians, and tutored many young musicians in Washington County. Playing music was an expectation for the family. Traditionally, the men played stringed instruments while Louisa and Anna played the piano. The family had a gift for horn instruments as well as the strings. Carl played the baritone horn. Daniel Becker Jr. was known nationally for his mastery of the flute. (Courtesy of Marietta College.)

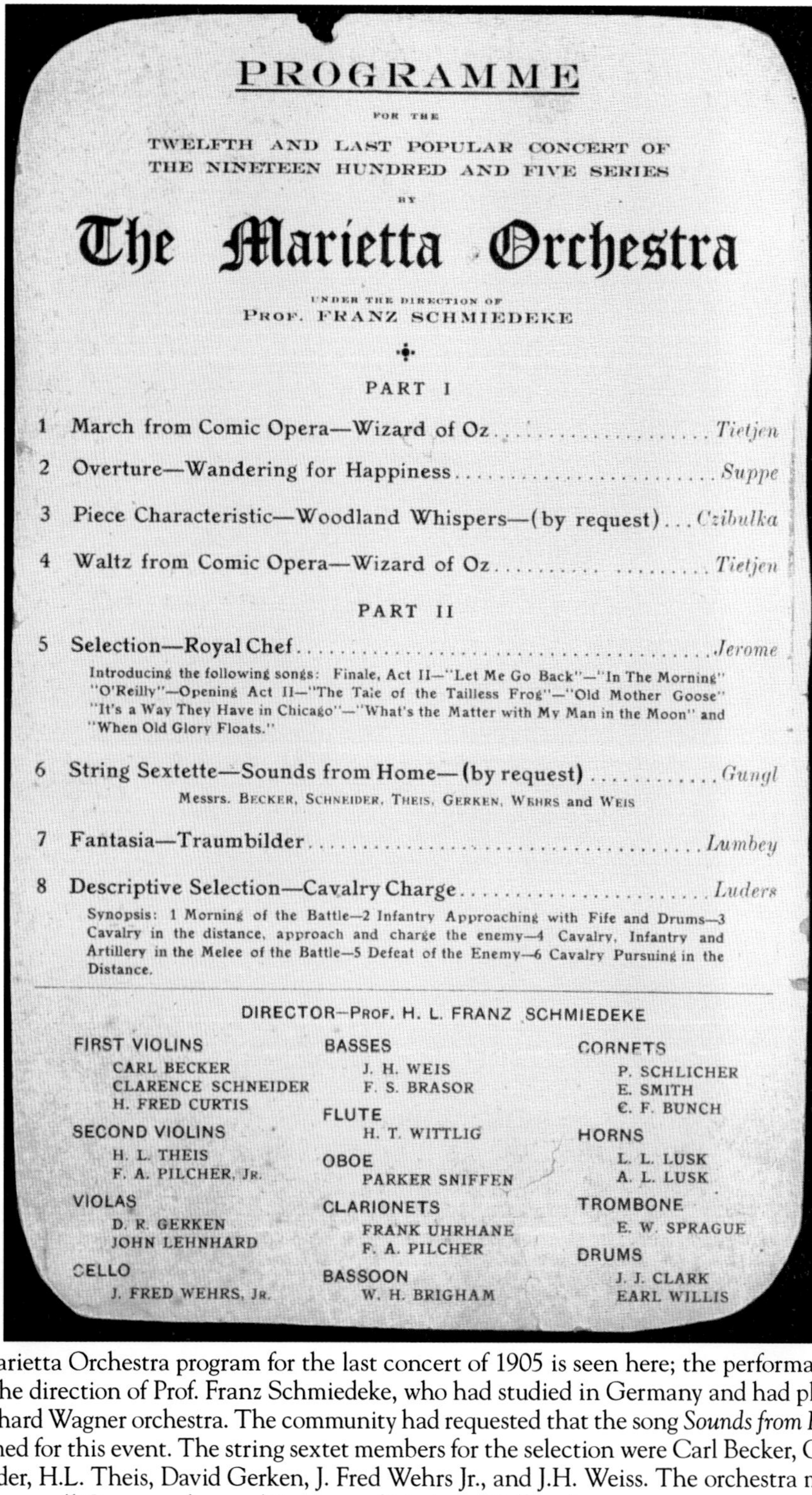

PROGRAMME

FOR THE

TWELFTH AND LAST POPULAR CONCERT OF
THE NINETEEN HUNDRED AND FIVE SERIES

BY

The Marietta Orchestra

UNDER THE DIRECTION OF
PROF. FRANZ SCHMIEDEKE

PART I

1 March from Comic Opera—Wizard of Oz . . . . *Tietjen*

2 Overture—Wandering for Happiness . . . . *Suppe*

3 Piece Characteristic—Woodland Whispers—(by request) . . . *Czibulka*

4 Waltz from Comic Opera—Wizard of Oz . . . . *Tietjen*

PART II

5 Selection—Royal Chef . . . . *Jerome*

Introducing the following songs: Finale, Act II—"Let Me Go Back"—"In The Morning" "O'Reilly"—Opening Act II—"The Tale of the Tailless Frog"—"Old Mother Goose" "It's a Way They Have in Chicago"—"What's the Matter with My Man in the Moon" and "When Old Glory Floats."

6 String Sextette—Sounds from Home—(by request) . . . . *Gungl*

Messrs. BECKER, SCHNEIDER, THEIS, GERKEN, WEHRS and WEIS

7 Fantasia—Traumbilder . . . . *Lumbey*

8 Descriptive Selection—Cavalry Charge . . . . *Luders*

Synopsis: 1 Morning of the Battle—2 Infantry Approaching with Fife and Drums—3 Cavalry in the distance, approach and charge the enemy—4 Cavalry, Infantry and Artillery in the Melee of the Battle—5 Defeat of the Enemy—6 Cavalry Pursuing in the Distance.

DIRECTOR—PROF. H. L. FRANZ SCHMIEDEKE

FIRST VIOLINS
CARL BECKER
CLARENCE SCHNEIDER
H. FRED CURTIS

SECOND VIOLINS
H. L. THEIS
F. A. PILCHER, JR.

VIOLAS
D. R. GERKEN
JOHN LEHNHARD

CELLO
J. FRED WEHRS, JR.

BASSES
J. H. WEIS
F. S. BRASOR

FLUTE
H. T. WITTLIG

OBOE
PARKER SNIFFEN

CLARIONETS
FRANK UHRHANE
F. A. PILCHER

BASSOON
W. H. BRIGHAM

CORNETS
P. SCHLICHER
E. SMITH
C. F. BUNCH

HORNS
L. L. LUSK
A. L. LUSK

TROMBONE
E. W. SPRAGUE

DRUMS
J. J. CLARK
EARL WILLIS

The Marietta Orchestra program for the last concert of 1905 is seen here; the performance was under the direction of Prof. Franz Schmiedeke, who had studied in Germany and had played for the Richard Wagner orchestra. The community had requested that the song *Sounds from Home* be performed for this event. The string sextet members for the selection were Carl Becker, Clarence Schneider, H.L. Theis, David Gerken, J. Fred Wehrs Jr., and J.H. Weiss. The orchestra members were almost all German players. (Courtesy of Marietta College.)

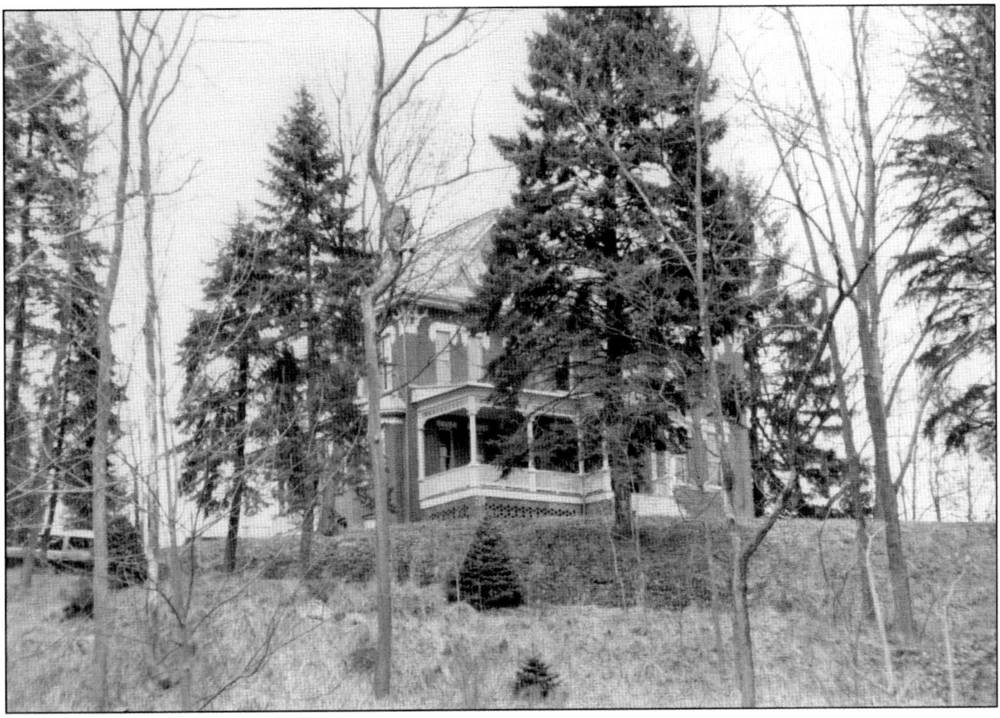

The love of music was shared with the community at the Cisler home. The Marietta Bach Society met in the home for the yearly performance of the music of Johann Sebastian Bach. Thomas Cisler formed the society about 1923. The society met each month to read and play music with the Cisler organ being a feature. Lillian Cisler, daughter of Thomas, continued the society after his death. (Courtesy of Washington County Historical Society.)

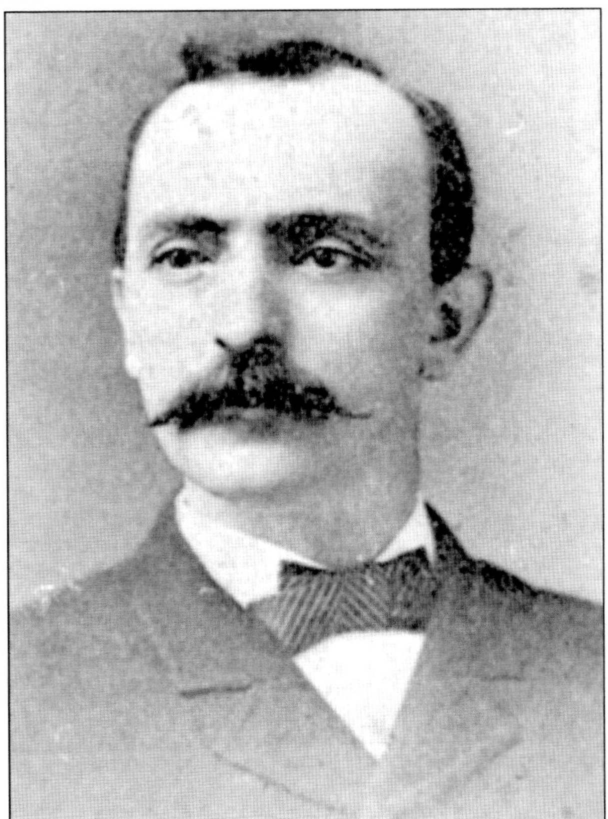

One of the most prominent players of music in Marietta was Henry L. Theis. He was a musician and a composer of musical literature for over 50 years. Theis was associated with both the Marietta Band and the Marietta Orchestra. In composing, Theis focused on the violin and guitar. Corinne Theis, his daughter, was well known for writing "Orange and Black" for Marietta High School. (Courtesy of Marietta College.)

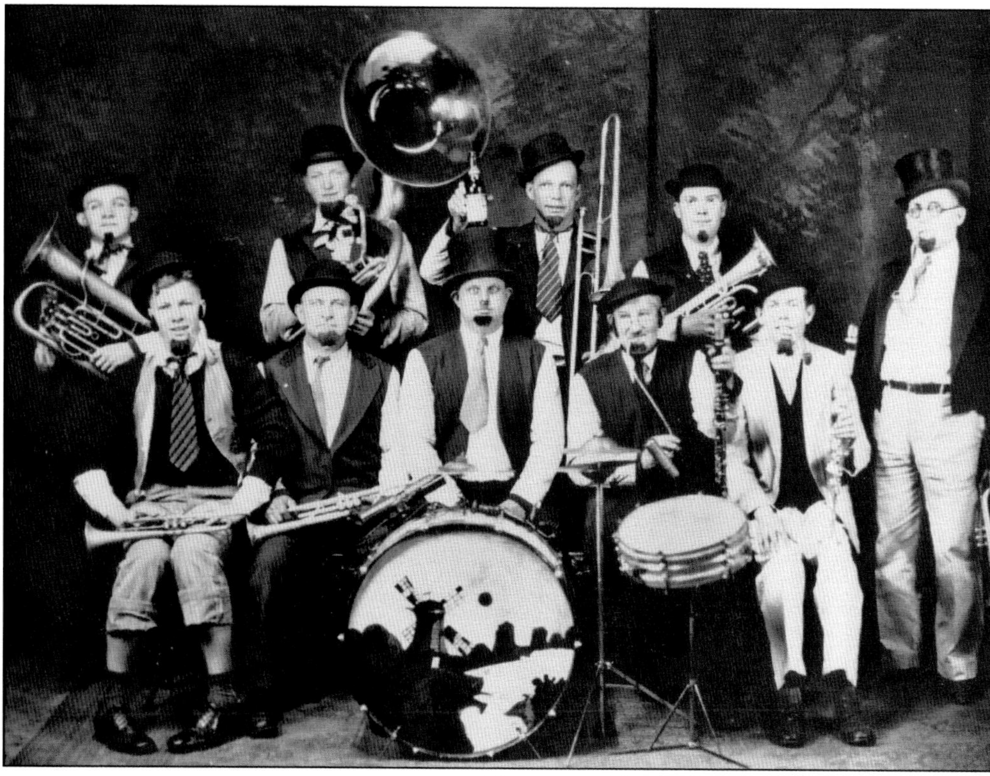

The original Little German Band first formed when a musical group led Washington County recruits in parade as they departed for the Civil War in 1861. Over the years, the band had different players. Pictured here is a group who humorously posed in German costume to perform locally. Players were Vernon Miller (baritone horn), Herman Trautner (cornet and trumpet), Clarence Henniger (clarinet), and director Richard Miller (trumpet). (Courtesy of Washington County Historical Society.)

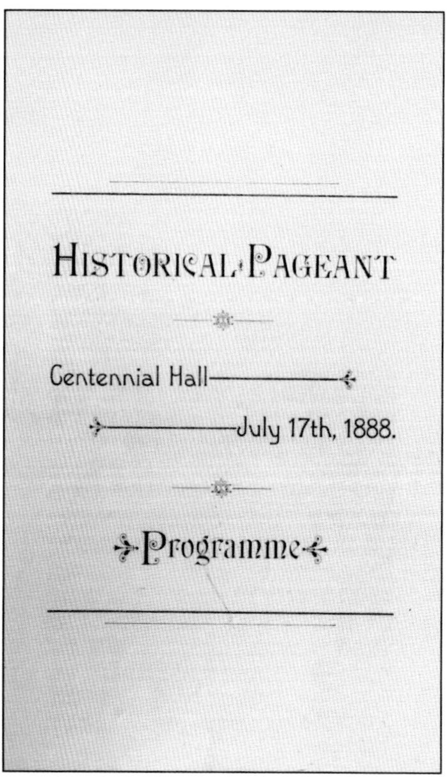

HISTORICAL PAGEANT

Centennial Hall

July 17th, 1888.

Programme

In 1888, Marietta held a celebration of the 100th anniversary of the landing of Marietta's first pioneers. Though the original pioneers were of Anglo-Saxon heritage, citizens of German descent took part in the historical pageant at Centennial Hall. Cornelia Wehrs, August Schmidt, William Ebinger, Leroy Protsman, and B.F. Strecker played the roles of people in early Marietta history. (Courtesy of Marietta College.)

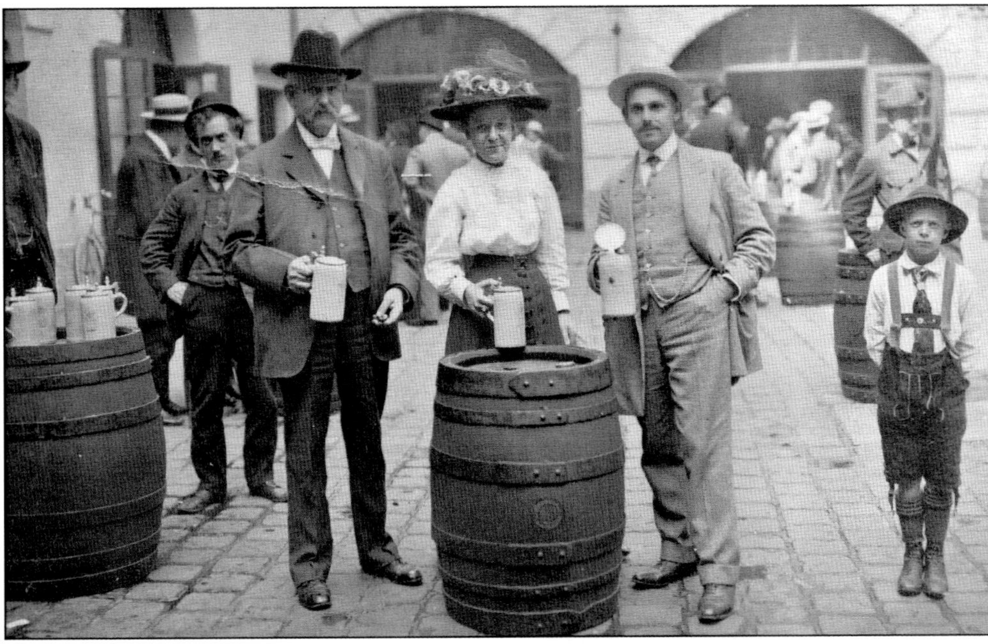

Some immigrants never looked back to the homeland, and some could never afford to return to Europe. Others lost touch with families. But some who could afford the passage did travel abroad to see relatives. August V. Kuehn and his daughter Marie enjoyed a stein of beer when they visited family in the Alsace-Lorraine region. (Courtesy of Norma Jean Kuehn Adams.)

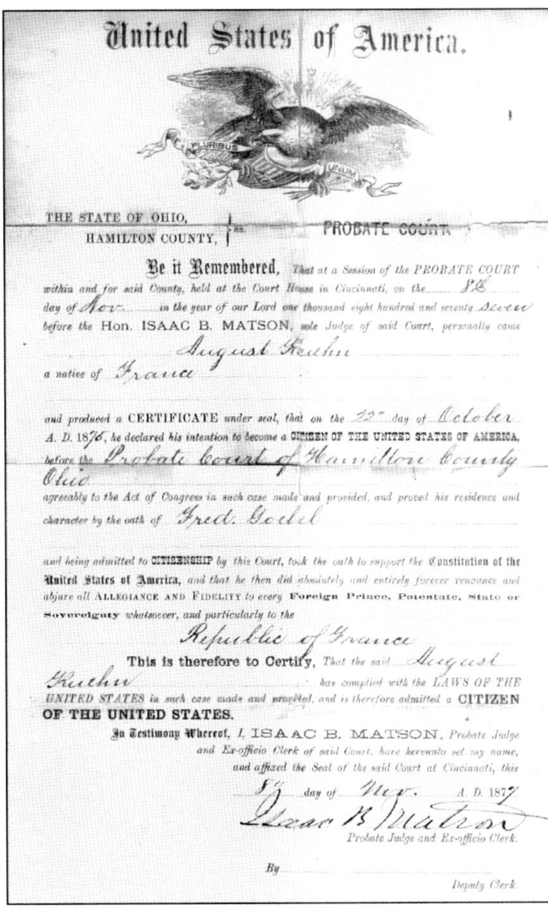

United States of America.

PLURIBUS UNUM

THE STATE OF OHIO, HAMILTON COUNTY, } ss. PROBATE COURT

Be it Remembered, That at a Session of the PROBATE COURT within and for said County, held at the Court House in Cincinnati, on the 8th day of Nov in the year of our Lord one thousand eight hundred and seventy Seven before the Hon. ISAAC B. MATSON, sole Judge of said Court, personally came August Kuehn a native of France

and produced a CERTIFICATE under seal, that on the 22nd day of October A. D. 1876, he declared his intention to become a CITIZEN OF THE UNITED STATES OF AMERICA, before the Probate Court of Hamilton County Ohio agreeably to the Act of Congress in such case made and provided, and proved his residence and character by the oath of Fred. Goebel

and being admitted to CITIZENSHIP by this Court, took the oath to support the Constitution of the United States of America, and that he then did absolutely and entirely forever renounce and abjure all ALLEGIANCE AND FIDELITY to every Foreign Prince, Potentate, State or Sovereignty whatsoever, and particularly to the Republic of France

This is therefore to Certify, That the said August Kuehn has complied with the LAWS OF THE UNITED STATES in such case made and provided, and is therefore admitted a CITIZEN OF THE UNITED STATES.

In Testimony Whereof, I, ISAAC B. MATSON, Probate Judge and Ex-officio Clerk of said Court, have hereunto set my name, and affixed the Seal of the said Court at Cincinnati, this 8th day of Nov. A. D. 1877

Isaac B Matson
Probate Judge and Ex-officio Clerk.

By
Deputy Clerk.

Germans were eager to gain citizenship with arrival to the United States. August V. Kuehn, a German who had come from the Alsace-Lorraine region, was listed as a native of France on the citizenship paper. For many Germans, Cincinnati was a destination, and Kuehn received his citizenship there in 1877. (Courtesy of Norma Jean Kuehn Adams.)

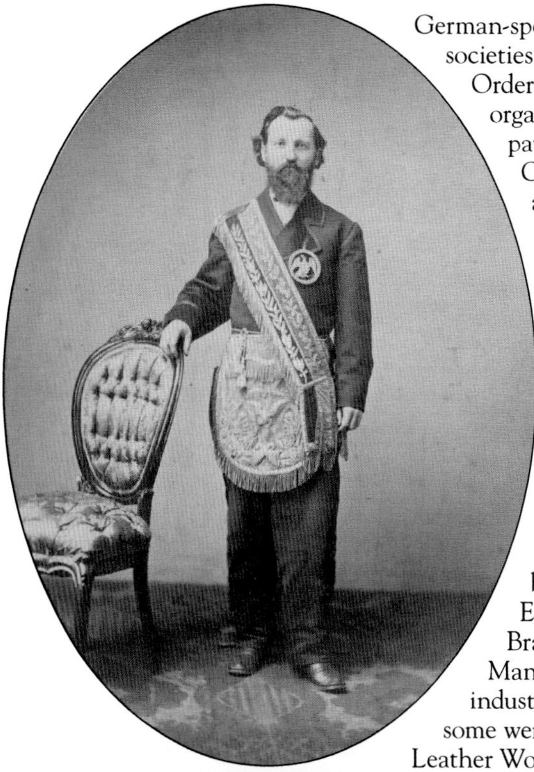

German-speaking men joined German-based secret societies. The Guttenberg Lodge and the Improved Order of Red Men attracted many members. Both organizations followed principles supporting patriotism and charitable programs. John G. Snyder is seen wearing the official attire of the Improved Order of the Red Men. (Courtesy of Washington County Historical Society.)

Marietta had a history of leather industries that were involved in the making of harnesses, saddles, straps, bridles, shoes, boots, and other accessories. Early German tanneries were the Jacob Brand Tannery and Meister's Tannery. Many of the tanneries and leatherworking industries employed German laborers, and some were members of the United Brotherhood of Leather Workers. (Courtesy of Marietta College.)

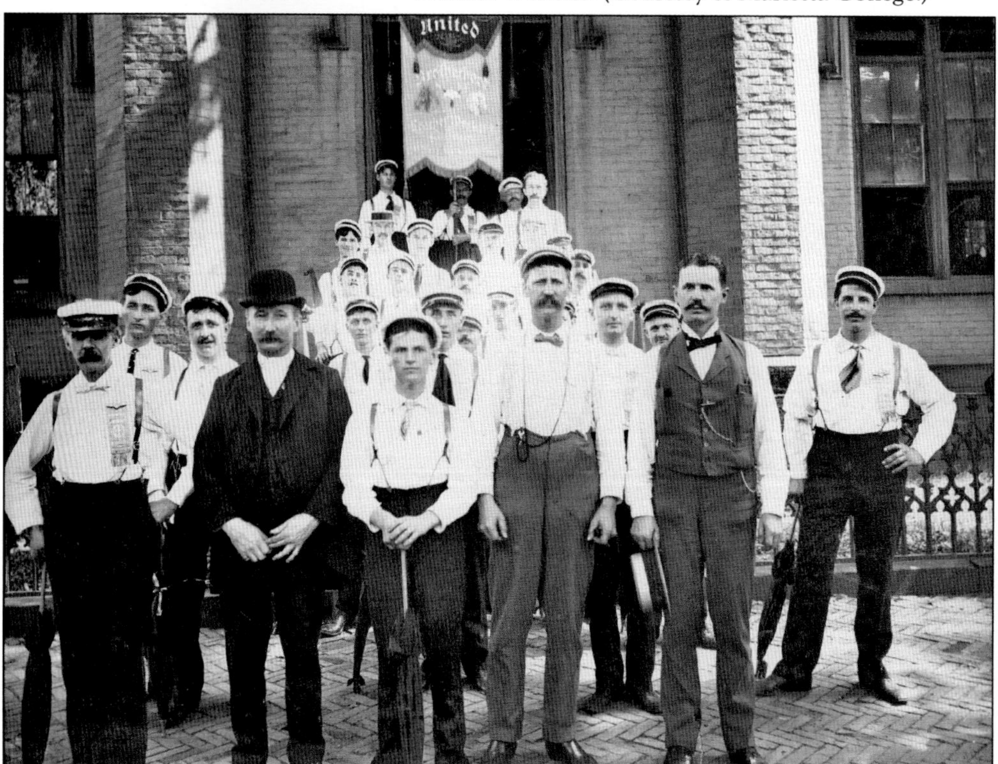

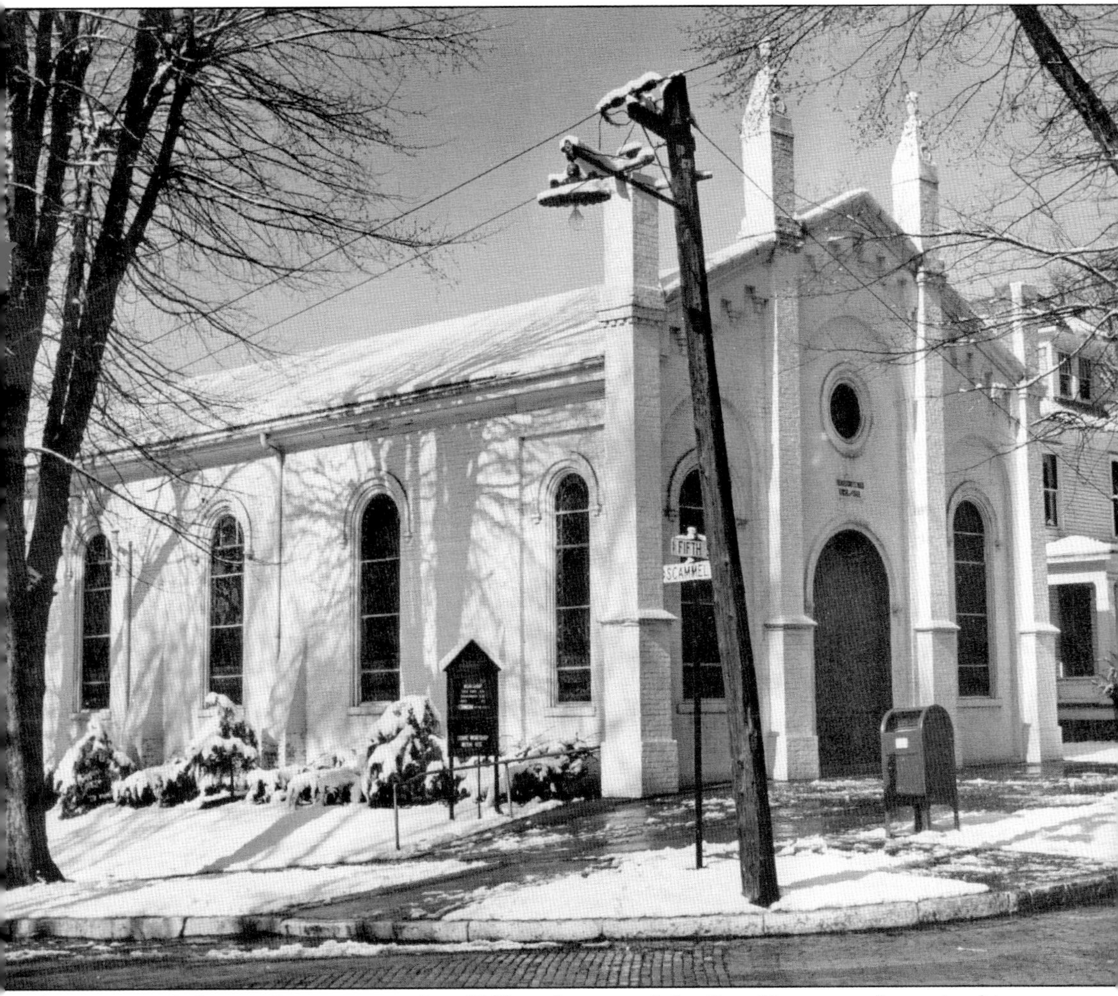

The German Religious Society started in 1838 with some of the first Germans who arrived in Marietta. It was chartered as the German Evangelical Church. They bought the lot at Fifth and Scammel Streets across the street from the Mound Cemetery in 1847 and erected a church building in 1849. The congregation was made up of a number of Protestant groups who arrived here from the German states. In 1872, the name was changed to St. Paul's Evangelical Church. The German word *kirche*, meaning "church," is still seen above the church door. Services were held in German until about 1919, when it changed to English. This congregation has gathered here since its inception. (Courtesy of Washington County Historical Society.)

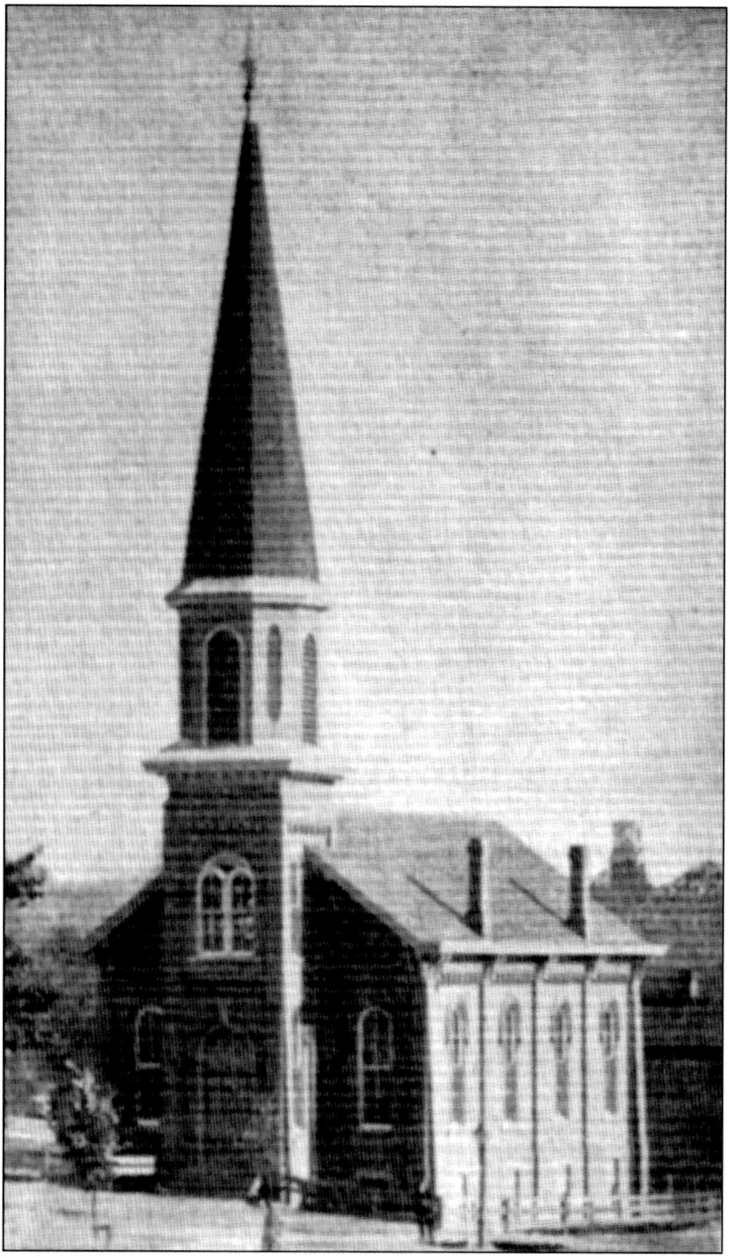

In 1839, Methodist circuit rider Carl Best was given the task of uniting the emerging German pioneers in Marietta. George Danker and J.H. Bahrenburg served as early ministers. As the membership flourished, a new Italianate-style German Methodist Episcopal Church was built at the corner of Third and Wooster Streets in 1878. The steeple was 110 feet high, and the church bell weighed 1,800 pounds. Later, the tall steeple was removed. Traditionally, services and hymns were given in the German language. As a new century began, some members asked for English services. For about 10 years, morning services were in German and evening services were in English. With the onset of World War I, all services were in English, and the building was renamed the Trinity Methodist Episcopal Church. In 1919, the Otto family donated the German-made Midmer reed organ. (Courtesy of Marietta College.)

The founding of St. Lucas Evangelical Lutheran Church in 1858 was recorded as Die Deutsche Evangelisch-Protestantiche St. Lucas Kirchen-Gemeinde. Church officers were Jacob Grossclas, Daniel Hashler, John Kuntz, John Pfaff, Henry Cisler, Peter Schlicher, John Peters, Jacob Hennemann, and Jacob Lorentz. The congregation was small until the 1890s, when the Reverend K.F. Thieme became pastor and introduced the English language into the evening church services. By the close of the 19th century, the congregation had outgrown the earlier building at Fourth and Scammel Streets and erected a new green fieldstone neo-Romanesque church in 1901 at the same location. The sanctuary holds an exquisite woodcarving of the Lord's Supper, completed by master woodcarver Alois Lang. The congregation offered a variety of activities for members, such as the *Frauenverein* (women' association) and *Jugend Verein* (youth association). (Right, courtesy of Marietta College; below, courtesy of Washington County Historical Society.)

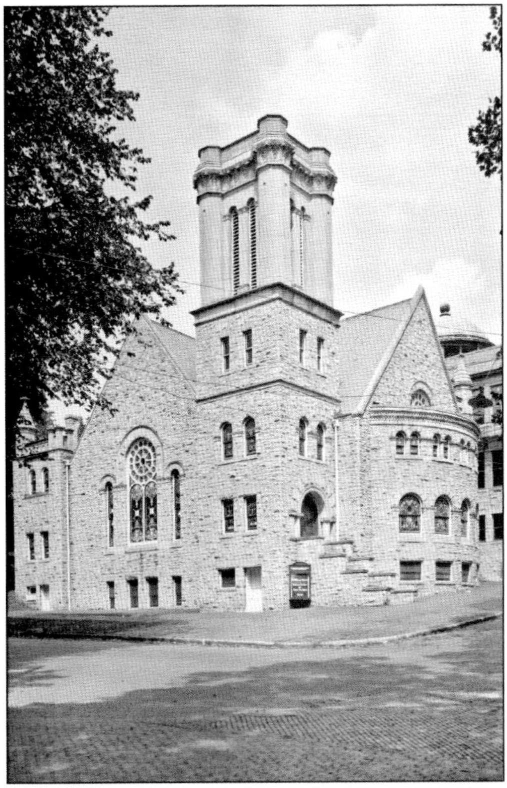

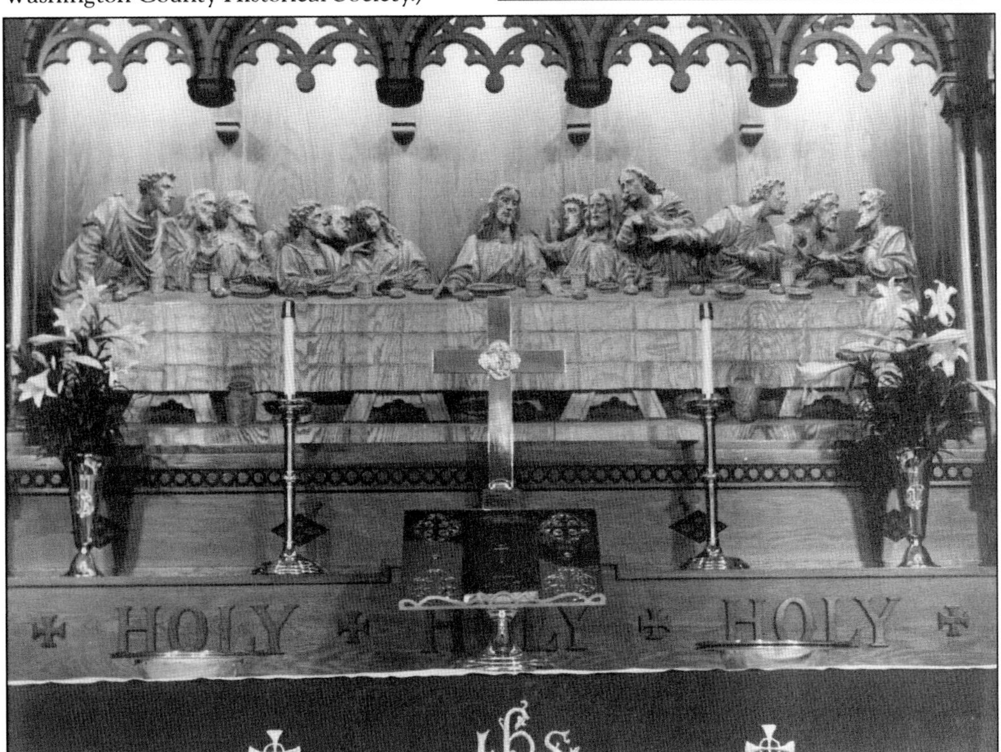

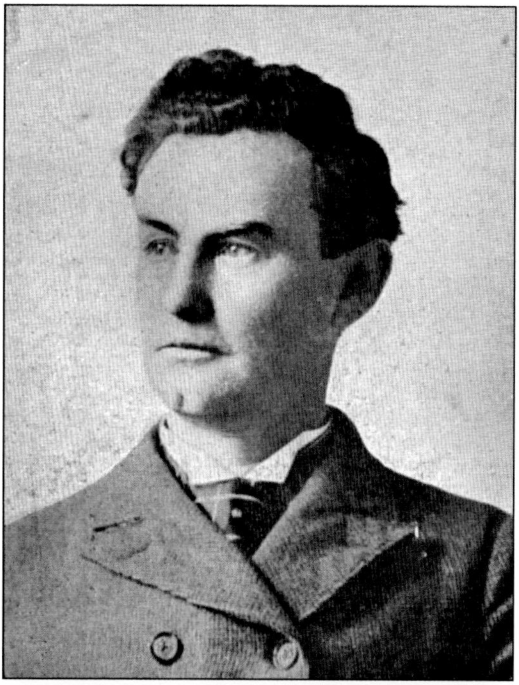

Edward Meisenhelder was a member of the first city council in 1889 and served as mayor in 1896. His list of achievements included the following: helped to form Marietta's first regular paid police and fire departments, promoted the first water plant and the old municipal electric plant, and helped to give Marietta its first paved streets. From 1911 to 1914, Meisenhelder was the city's first director of public service. (Courtesy of Marietta College.)

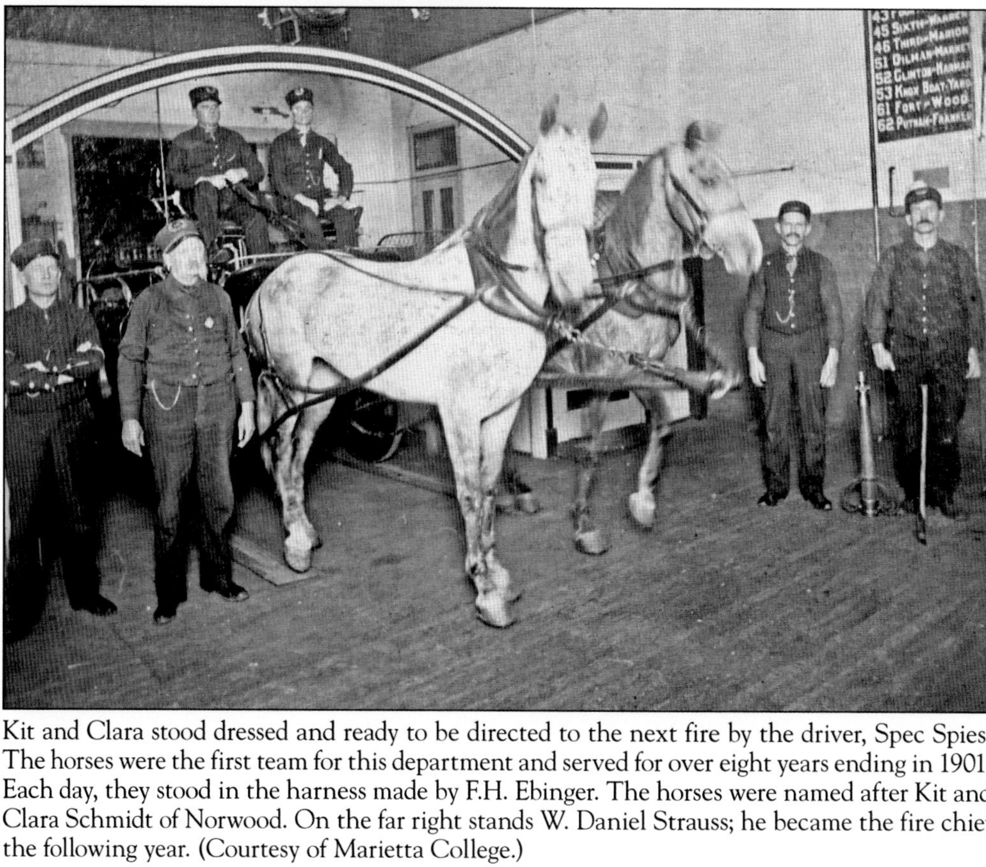

Kit and Clara stood dressed and ready to be directed to the next fire by the driver, Spec Spies. The horses were the first team for this department and served for over eight years ending in 1901. Each day, they stood in the harness made by F.H. Ebinger. The horses were named after Kit and Clara Schmidt of Norwood. On the far right stands W. Daniel Strauss; he became the fire chief the following year. (Courtesy of Marietta College.)

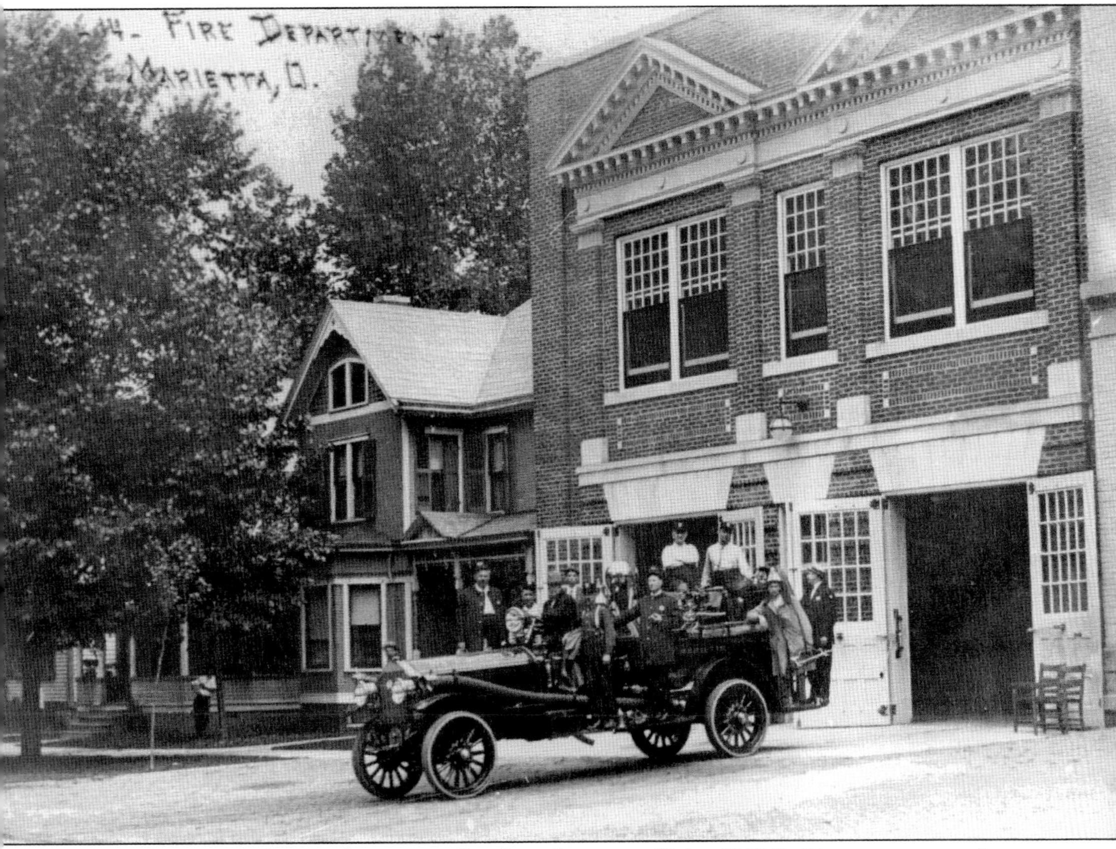

This 1914 photograph depicts firemen and police showing off the 1912 Robinson pumper that could shoot water to the tower of the courthouse. The purchase of the pumper occurred under the leadership of Chief George Holst, who is seated in the passenger seat. The 1890 photograph shows firemen as they returned victoriously from a firemen's tournament in Cincinnati with a broom, indicating they "swept" the competition. Most of the men were sons of parents born in a German state (indicated after name). Identified by their last names, from left to right are (first row) are Lancaster, Bernhart (Germany), Beck (Bavaria), Schlicher (Bavaria), Meagle (Bavaria), Schlicher (Germany), Otterbein (Prussia), Abicht, and Bacchus (Germany); (second row) Kexall (Bavaria), Beck (Bavaria), Weber (Germany), Danker, Biszantz (Germany), McClaren, and Campbell; (third row) Boeshar (Bavaria), Lorenz (Bavaria), and Congden. (Courtesy of Washington County Historical Society.)

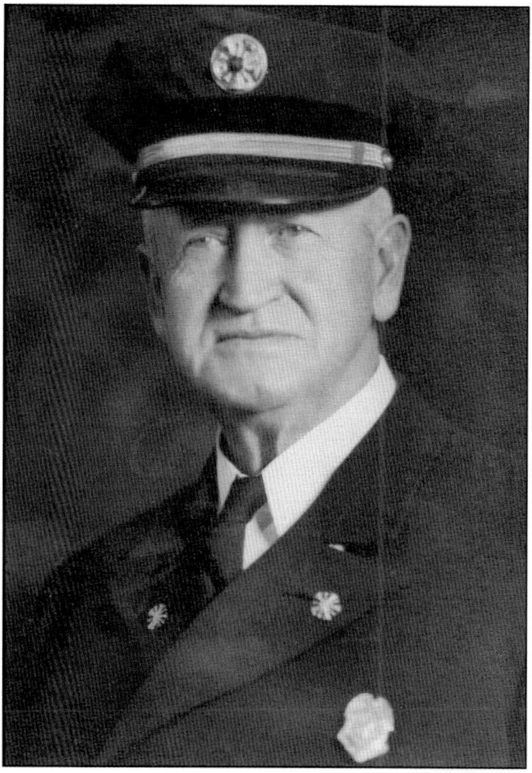

George B. Holst was the longest-serving chief in the history of the Marietta Fire Department. During those years, firefighters engaged in some of the city's worst fires, such as Union Station's in 1910, the Bellevue Hotel's in 1916, and city hall's in 1935. Holst saw the city move from horse-drawn pumper to the Robinson motorized pumper, the introduction of rubber coats, and acquisition of an aerial ladder truck and a fireboat. (Courtesy of Marietta Fire Department.)

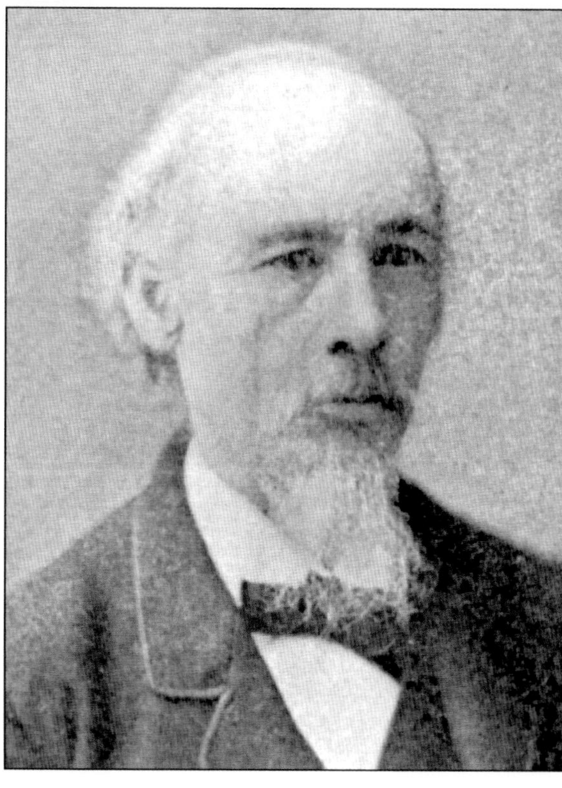

Active in the community, Leroy S. Protsman served as captain of the Harmar volunteer fire squad from 1890 to 1893 and played the role of Major Zeigler in the Centennial Pageant in 1888. His father, Daniel, was the first mayor of German descent in Marietta in 1854. He also served as Washington County's first marshal in 1826. (Courtesy of Marietta College.)

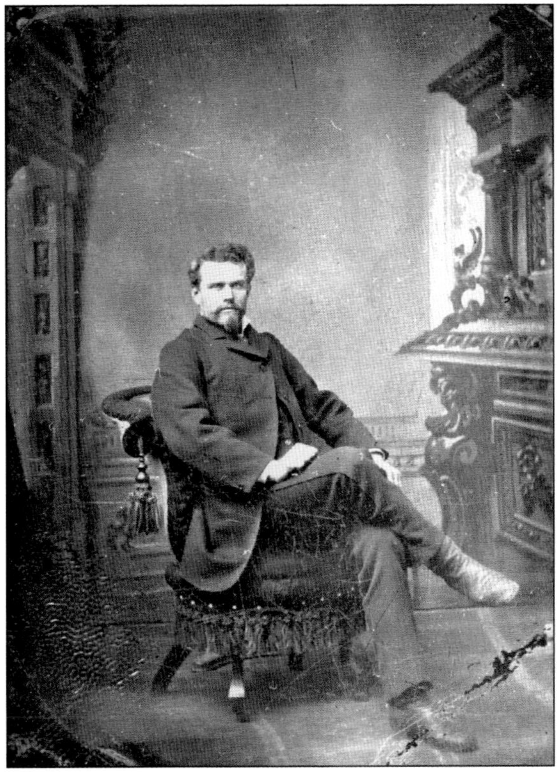

Frank S. Finkel became known as the only white survivor of Custer's Last Stand at the Battle of the Little Big Horn in 1876. Born in Marietta, Finkel enlisted in the Army under the name of August Finckle of Prussia. Much later in his life, Finkel told that he had been shot at the battle, his horse had bolted, and he had spent several months recovering before discovering the outcome of the battle. Fearing a court martial for desertion, he kept the incidence a secret. (Courtesy of Marietta College.)

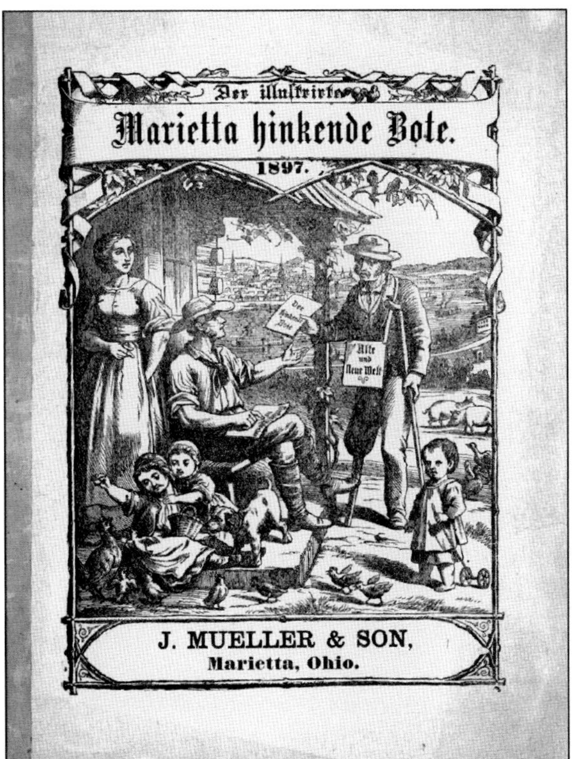

German American almanacs were published for German communities around the United States. The almanacs were printed in High German, the dialect of southern Germany, and included weather predictions and planting guides, short stories, news, humor, and jokes. Jacob Mueller, publisher of the *Marietta Zeitung*, ordered the *Cincinnatier hinkende Bote* for the local German community. (Courtesy of Marietta College.)

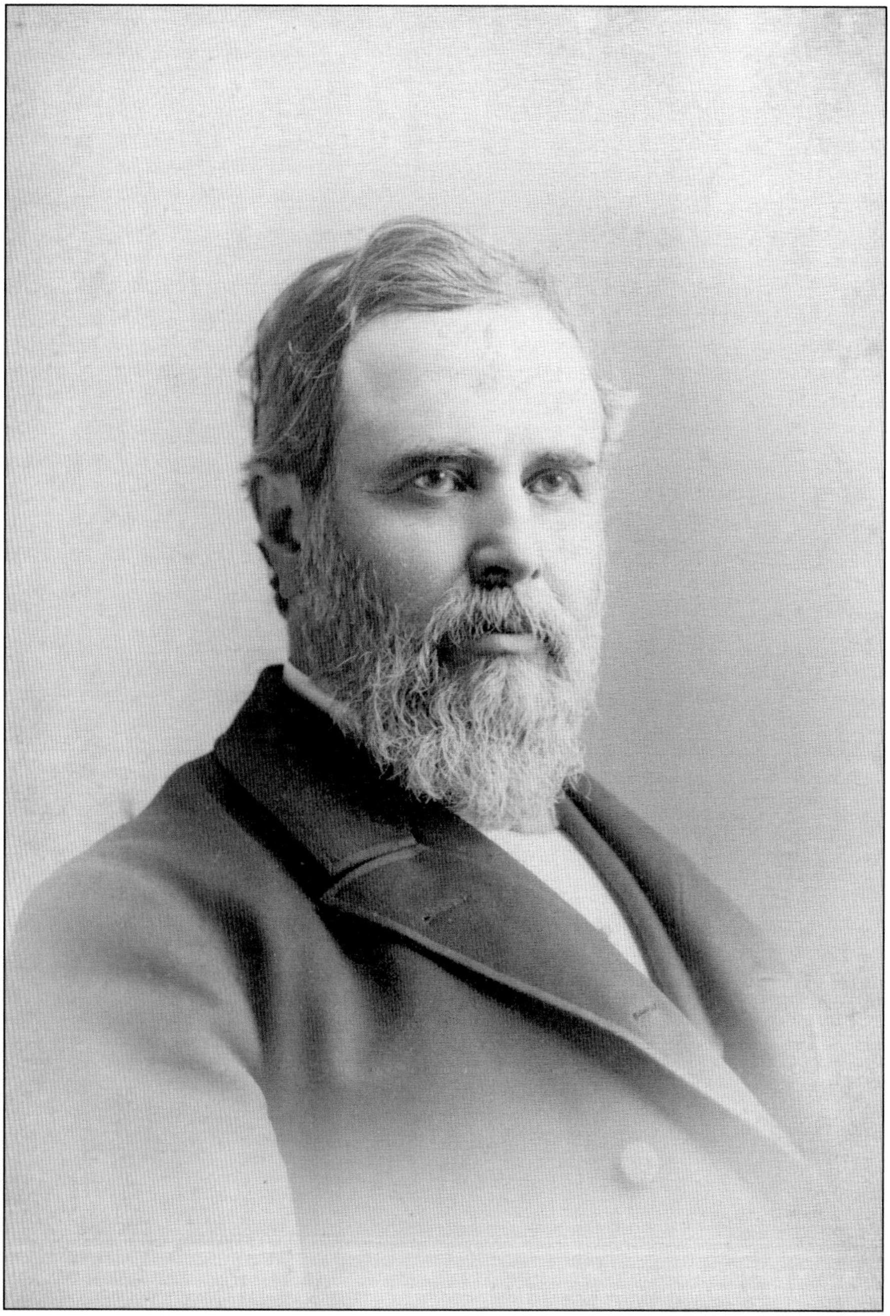

For the 1888 Marietta Centennial Celebration, Bernard Peters of Brooklyn, New York, was an honored speaker in town and was especially remembered for his oratory at city hall on April 7. He told the story of the first German pioneers who came to Washington County from the Rhein Palatinate in the summer of 1833. It was the story of brothers (and Bernard's uncles) Jacob and Charles Frederick Peters' struggle to find land in Ohio. Bernard Peters was the son of the youngest, John Philip Peters, who came in 1834. Bernard Peters was an ordained Universalist minister and worked in Brooklyn, New York, during the Civil War. Later, he was owner and editor of the *Brooklyn Times* until near his death in 1899. (Courtesy of Marietta College.)

Each year, the Marietta Board of Trade held an annual dinner meeting filled with speakers and food. This menu of 1910 shows a variety of specialty foods of the time. The entertainment was the Marietta Orchestra. W.H. Ebinger and Arch A. Schramm were both on the event's committee. The vice president of the board was B.F. Strecker. (Courtesy of Marietta College.)

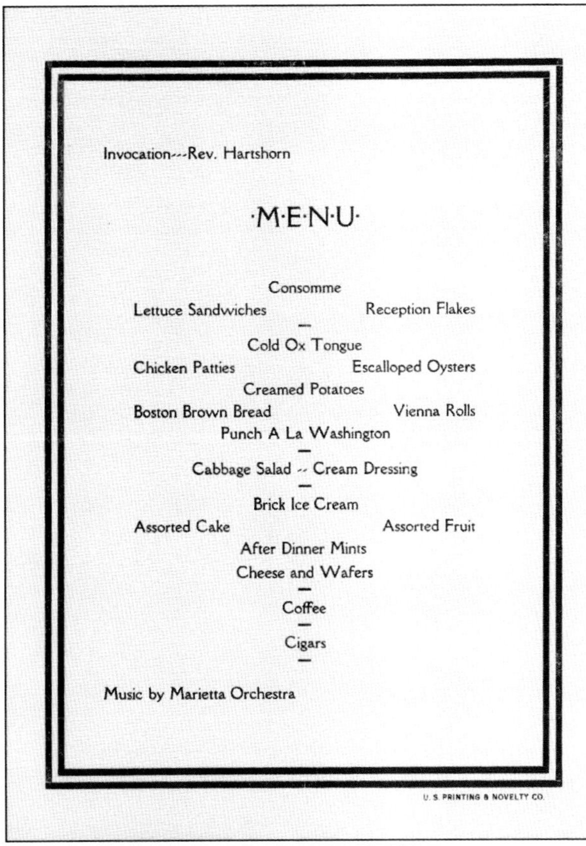

Invocation---Rev. Hartshorn

·M·E·N·U·

Consomme

Lettuce Sandwiches — Reception Flakes

Cold Ox Tongue

Chicken Patties — Escalloped Oysters

Creamed Potatoes

Boston Brown Bread — Vienna Rolls

Punch A La Washington

Cabbage Salad -- Cream Dressing

Brick Ice Cream

Assorted Cake — Assorted Fruit

After Dinner Mints

Cheese and Wafers

Coffee

Cigars

Music by Marietta Orchestra

U. S. PRINTING & NOVELTY CO.

In 1915, the Marietta Board of Trade was renamed the Marietta Chamber of Commerce. The first board members included, from left to right, W. Windsor, J. Dysle, C. Otto, L. Gruber (vice president), C. Speary, F. Hall, J. Warburton, and F. Brickwede. Dysle, Otto, Gruber, Speary, and Brickwede were of German descent. (Courtesy of Marietta College.)

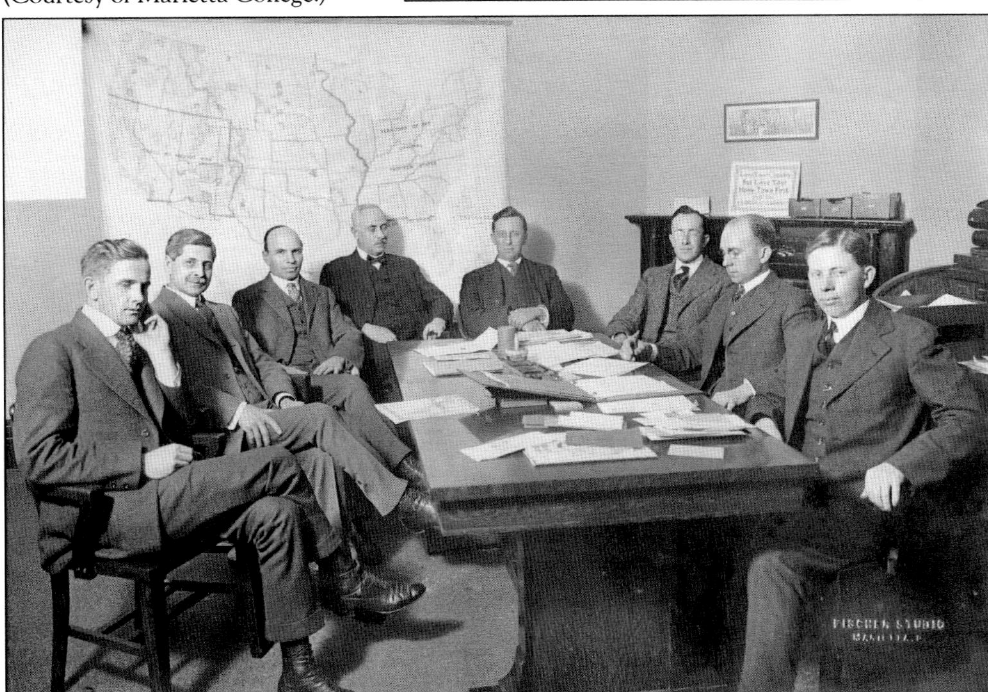

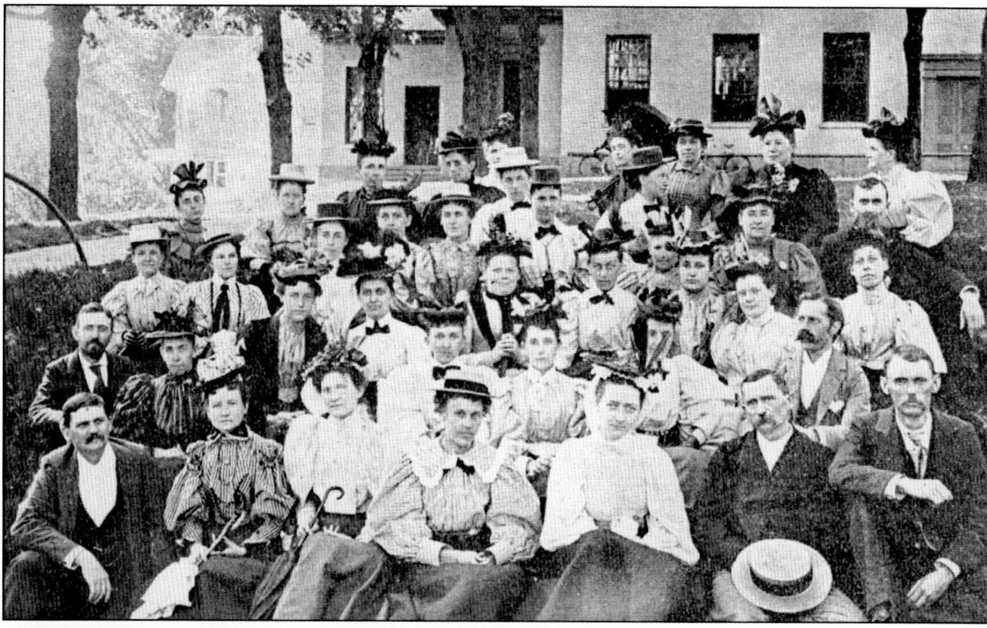

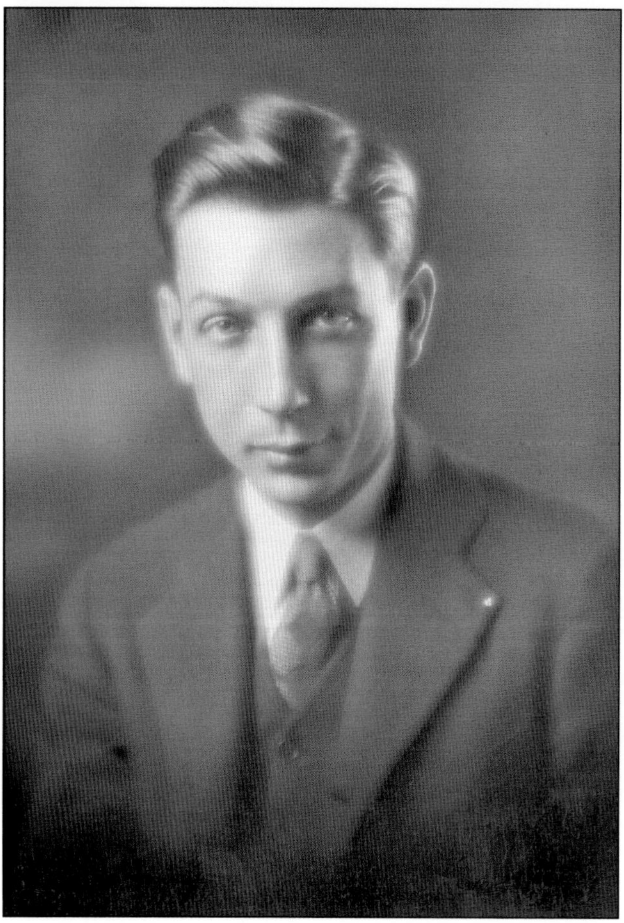

Because students of recent immigration were not fluent in English, there was a separate school for German pupils for a number of years. In 1901, there were 10 teachers of German descent. Carrie Strecker was the German teacher for all schools. Amela Weber was the principal at Marion School. During World War I, German was dropped from the curriculum and was returned in 1932. (Courtesy of Marietta College.)

During his 41 years in education, Allen Rupp served at Marietta High School as an instructor and debate coach, assistant principal, principal, and superintendent. He was superintendent in 1960 when a new site for the high school was needed, and he chose the Children's Home farm. Rupp was a prolific writer on educational topics. (Courtesy of Marietta College.)

This Catholic church was built around 1853 on South Fourth Street. In 1879, Father John B. Kuehn rallied enthusiasm from the parishioners to complete the church spire in 1883. In 1892, Rev. F.M. Woesman took charge of St. Mary's Parish, and the parochial school was erected in 1896. Nearly half of the donors for funding the school were German. Among the significant donors were Elizabeth Schneider, George Wieser, Louisa Strauss, and Amelia Weber. (Courtesy of Washington County Public Library.)

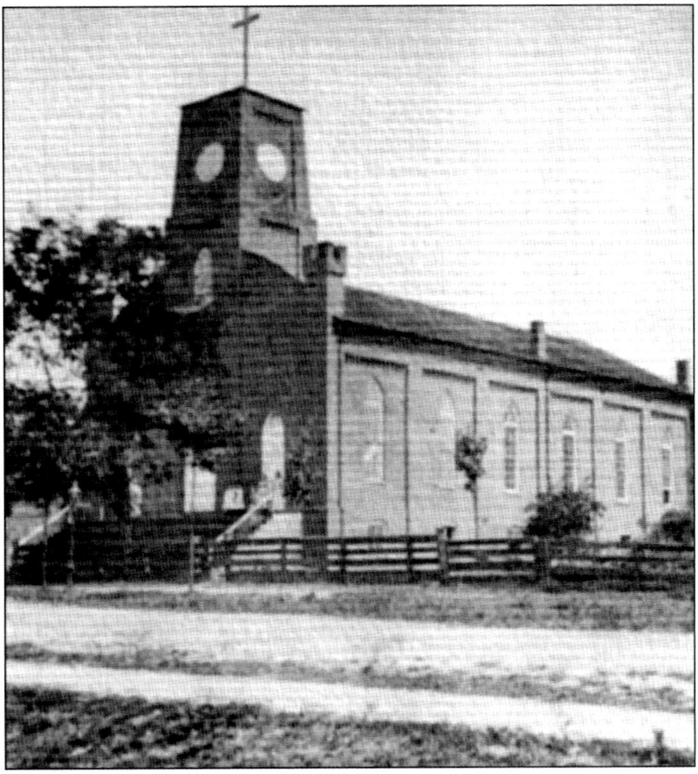

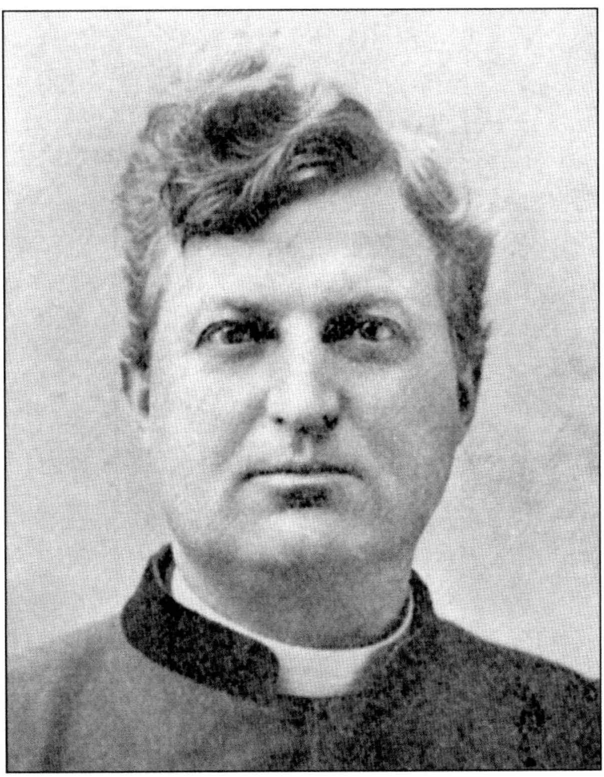

Rev. F.M. Woesman led the members of the Catholic church at a critical time of their history. In 1892, when he took charge, the church was faced with the question to relocate the aging church away from flood-prone lower Fourth Street to a site on higher ground. Woesman and an advisory board selected a Fourth Street and Wooster Street location for the new church. Two members of the board were Joseph S. Goebel and George Wieser. (Courtesy of Marietta College.)

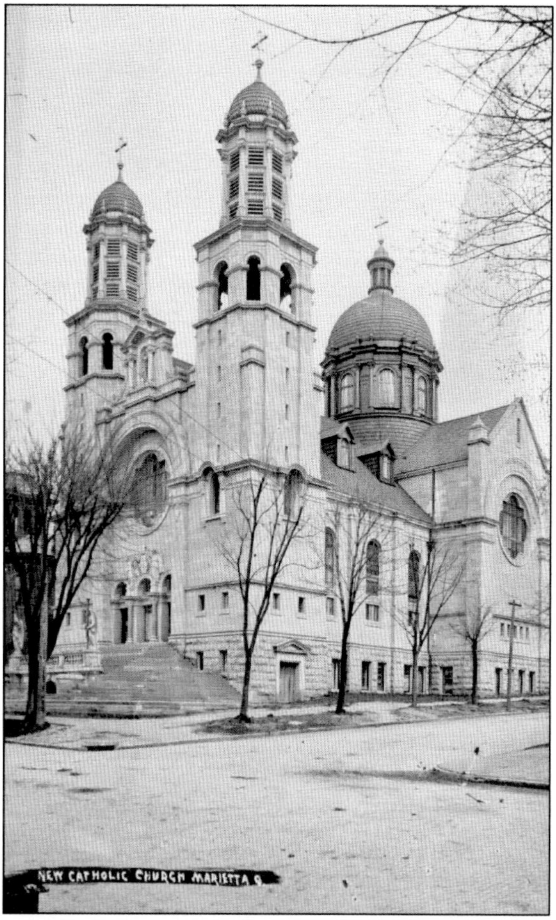

When it was decided in 1900 to build a new church at Fourth and Wooster Streets, the old Elizabeth College building was on the corner. Using oxen and logs, it was moved to the next lot to serve as a rectory. A large percentage of donors for the new church were native Germans or of German descent. In 1909, the Rev. Francis M. Woesman, of German descent, celebrated the first High Mass in Marietta. (Courtesy of Marietta College.)

With its bell towers and dome, St. Mary's Church highlights the landscape of Marietta. The architect, Emile Ulrich, a graduate of a Berlin art school and the Academy of Paris, described it as Spanish Renaissance style with a blend of Romanesque and Gothic. Huge pillars support the grand nave over a mosaic floor. The three large stained-glass windows were installed in 1916 from Munich, Germany. One of the windows commemorated Rev. J.B. Kuehn who served from 1879 to 1892. (Courtesy of Marietta College.)

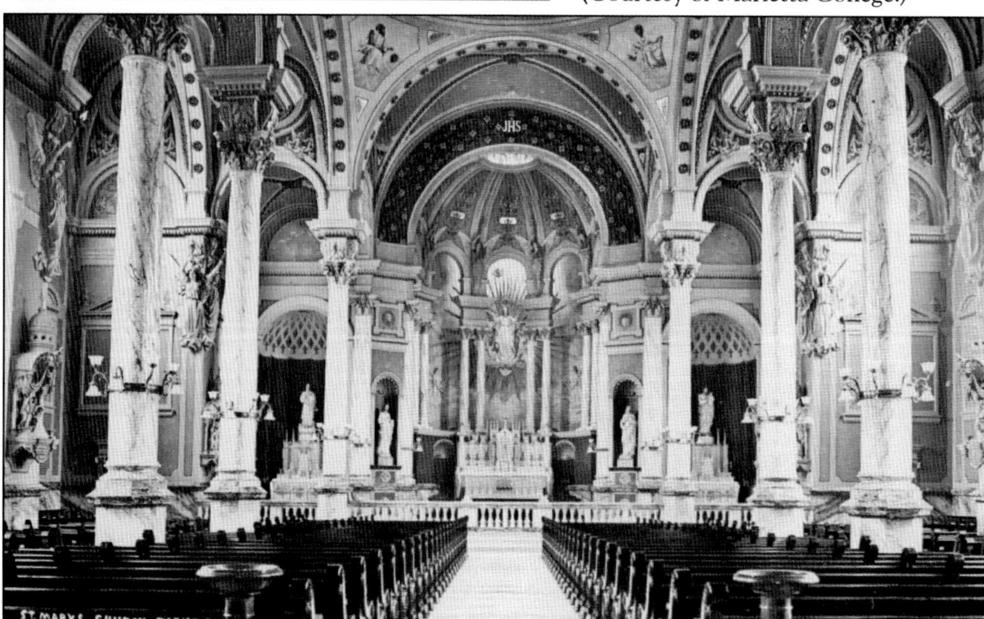

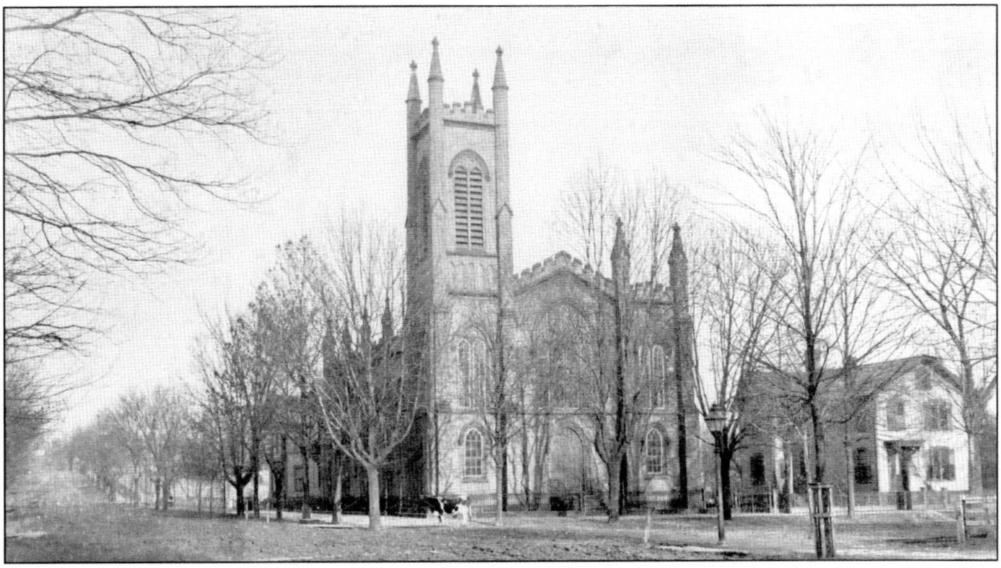

Some people of German heritage were drawn to attend the Unitarian Church that was dedicated in 1857 in the midst of heavy German migration. Both Fred Wehrs and Nora Gerken donated a set of large stained-glass windows in memory of their loved ones. The Von Gerichten stained-glass windows crafted in Germany hold the names of those departed. (Courtesy of Marietta College.)

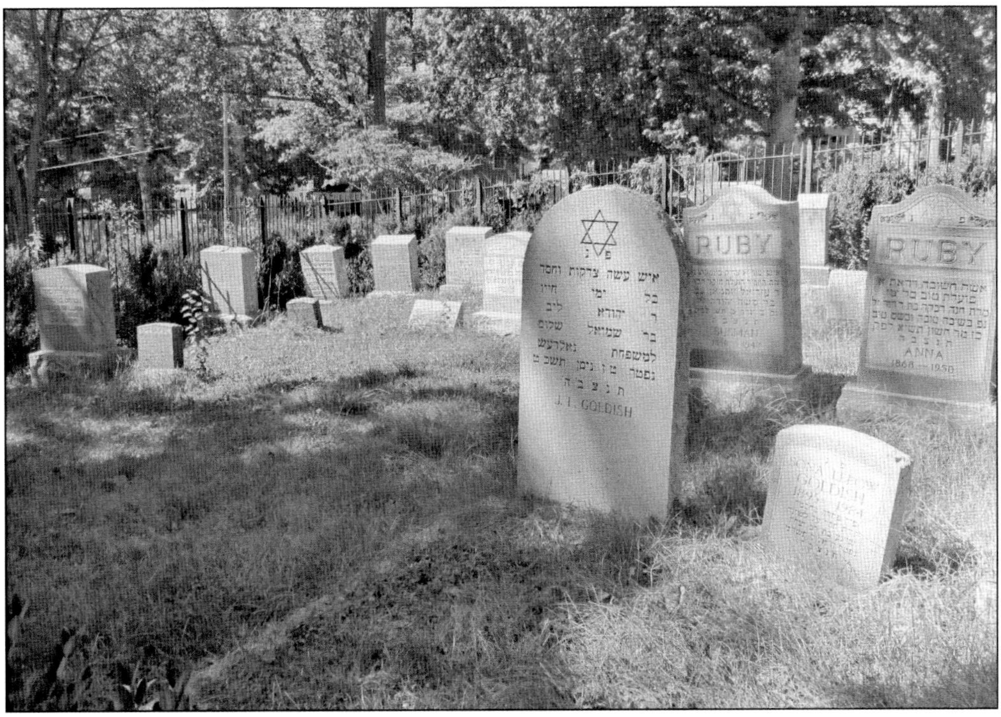

Two small Jewish cemeteries in Marietta leave a remembrance of this religious group in Marietta. The older Ginsberg Cemetery is located off Cisler Drive. In 1900, the Marietta Hebrew Church Society dedicated a fenced section in Oak Grove Cemetery. The Jewish Community, many German, reached a peak in the mid-1920s with nearly 35 families. By 1935, the Jewish population was in serious decline. (Courtesy of the author's collection.)

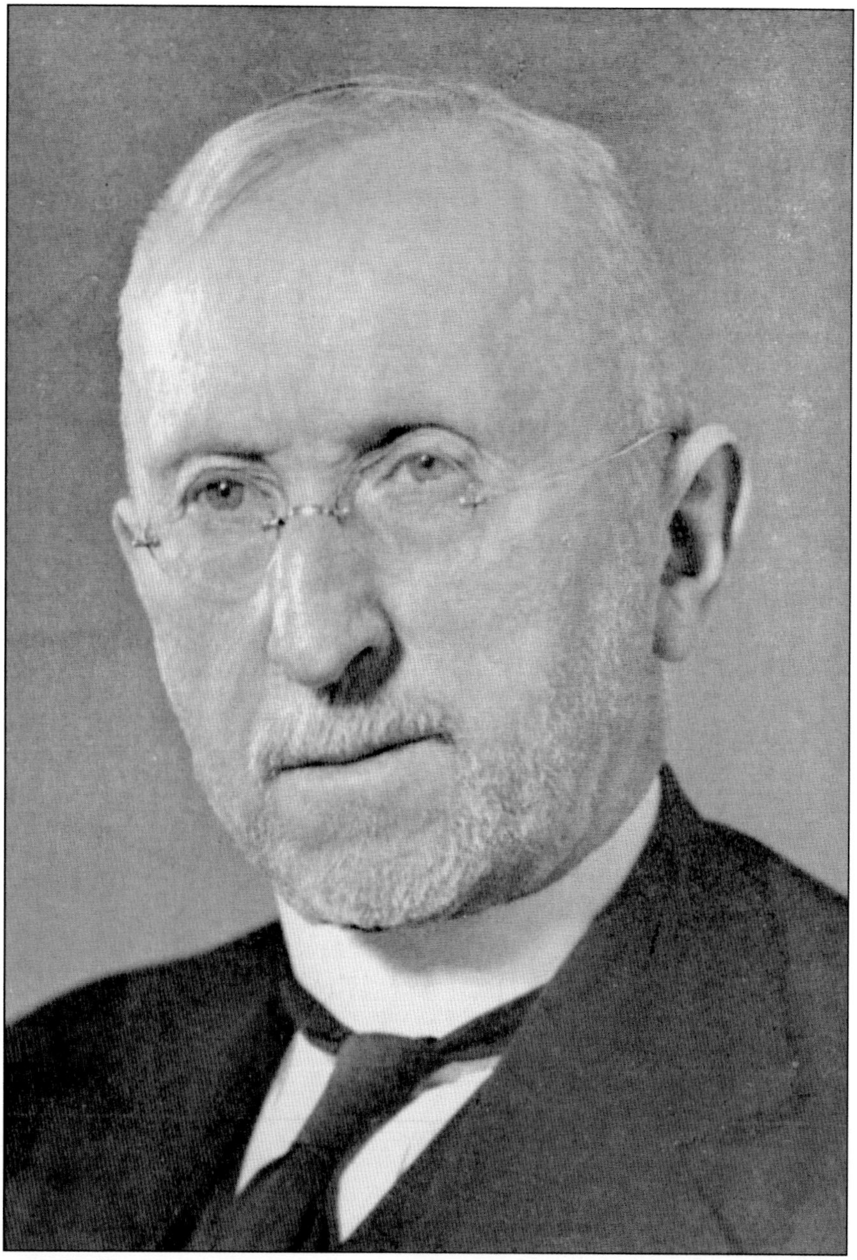

Thomas H. Cisler, son of Thomas and Caroline Schneider Cisler of the Cisler Brickyards, demonstrated business, civic, and cultural advancement in Marietta. After graduating from Marietta College in 1889, he expanded the company to include the making of shale brick. In 1900, he married Lillie Weiss and had two daughters, Grace and Lillian, whom he would raise following the early death of his wife. As a lover of classical music and a church organist/choirmaster for 26 years for St. Luke's Lutheran Church, Cisler founded the Marietta Bach Society. Cisler remained mindful of his alma mater by donating a site for the Marietta College Observatory and founded the Marietta Astronomical Society. He donated land to create Cisler Park, land for the development of Ephraim Cutler Street, and land for the building of the YMCA. (Courtesy of Marietta College.)

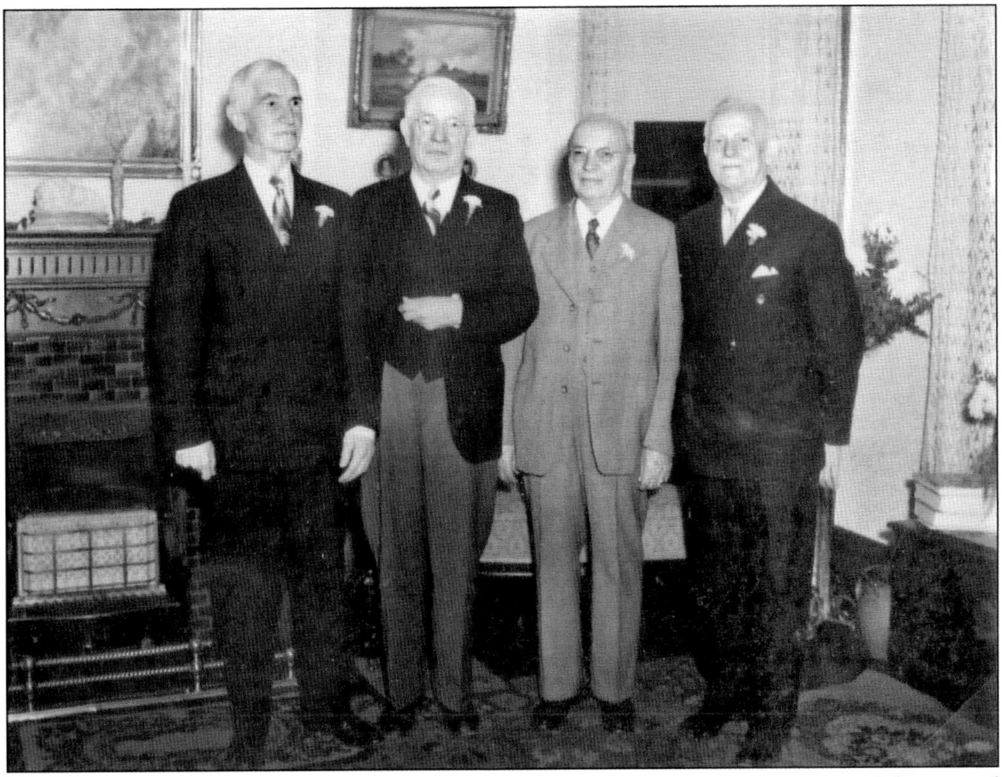

The Otto sons brought the American dream alive for their immigrant parents, Johann and Elizabeth Fischer Otto, who arrived in Marietta in 1857. Sons John Wesley (left center) and Charles W. Otto (right center) founded the Otto Brothers department store. John Christian Otto (far left) served as the auditor. Harry Otto (far right) worked at the store for 68 years. (Courtesy of Gretchen Otto.)

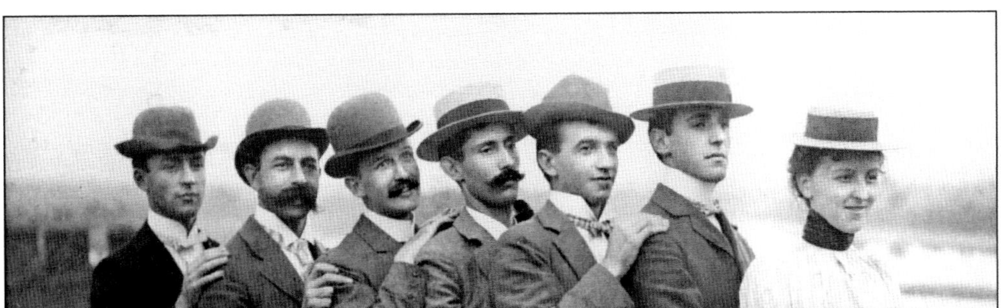

The Gay Nineties brought city lights, streetcars, bicycles, and money into the pocket for young people working in a variety of businesses. In 1895, the First National Bank employed this group. Shown are, from left to right, G. Knox, J. Goebel, H. Hart, R. Payne, J. Otto, J. Lehnhard, and L. Best. Four of these happy-looking young people were first-generation Germans. (Courtesy of Marietta College.)

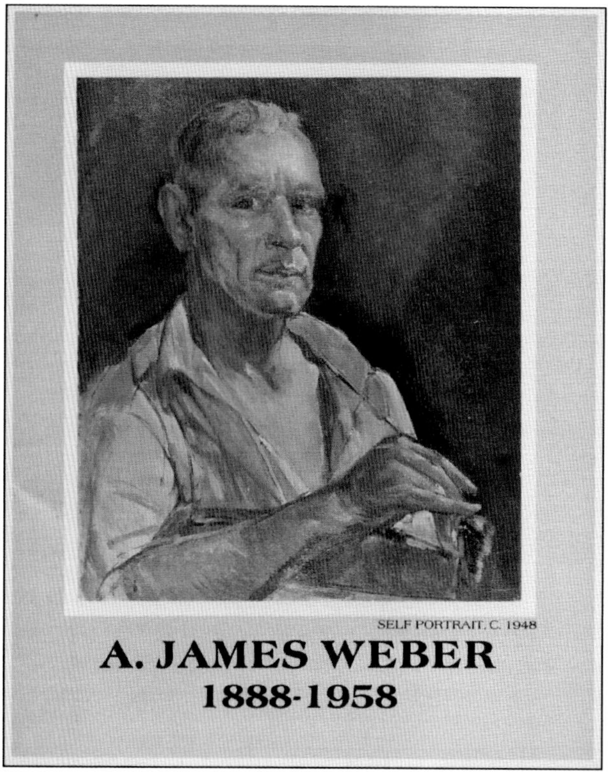

August James Weber, a fine-art painter, was a son of the owners of the August Weber Grocery. He attended art school in Cincinnati and became part of the art colony where he was a dedicated impressionist from 1907 to the 1930s. Unfortunately, James Weber fell on hard times when a fire in his studio in 1917 destroyed most of his work. In 1936, his mother was in poor health, and the family wanted his return to Marietta. Though disheartened, Weber returned and taught art classes. (Courtesy of Betty Boersma.)

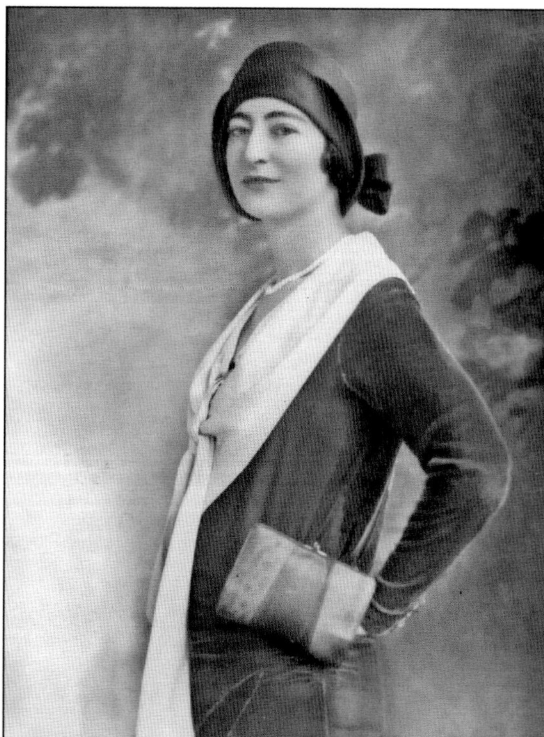

Helen Josephy, daughter of German Jewish businessman Jules Josephy, published a bestselling travel book with and Margaret McBride titled *Paris is a Woman's Town* in 1929. After graduating from Smith College in 1921, Josephy briefly worked for the *Marietta Times* and then lived in Paris while working for *Vogue*. The two women also wrote *London is a Man's Town, But Women Go There*, *Beer and Skittles: A Friendly Guide to Modern Germany*, and *New York is Everybody's Town*. (Courtesy of Margaret Espinola.)

As a young man, Harry P. Fischer worked in his father's shoe store on Front Street, but his love was photography. In 1901, he opened a photography shop on the second floor and was known as a studio photographer. Harry P. Fischer's photographs of street scenes, architecture, portraits, floods, and other Marietta sights are a part of the Special Collections at Marietta College. (Courtesy of Marietta College.)

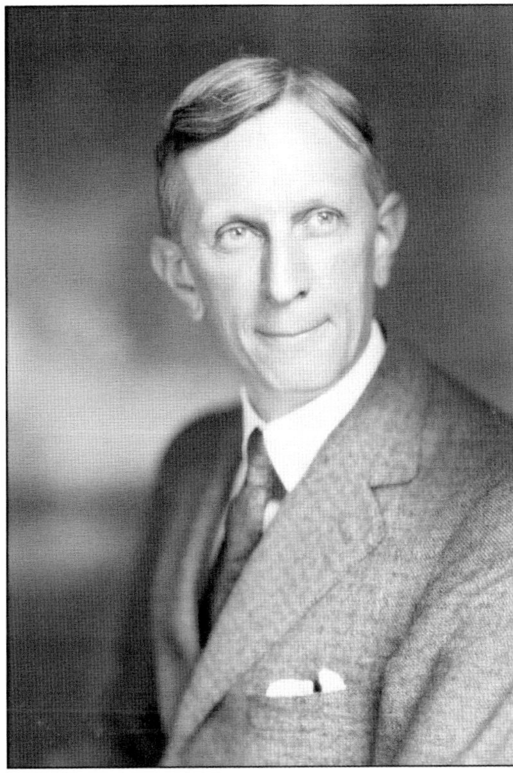

Marietta native Col. Dean Hess talked with Rock Hudson about the film *Battle Hymn,* shown at Marietta's Colony Theatre in 1957. Hudson depicted Hess as a hero during the Korean War when Hess helped to rescue 950 orphans and 80 orphanage staff from the invading Chinese. In 1956, he wrote an autobiography and used the royalties to fund a new orphanage in Seoul. (Courtesy of Marietta College.)

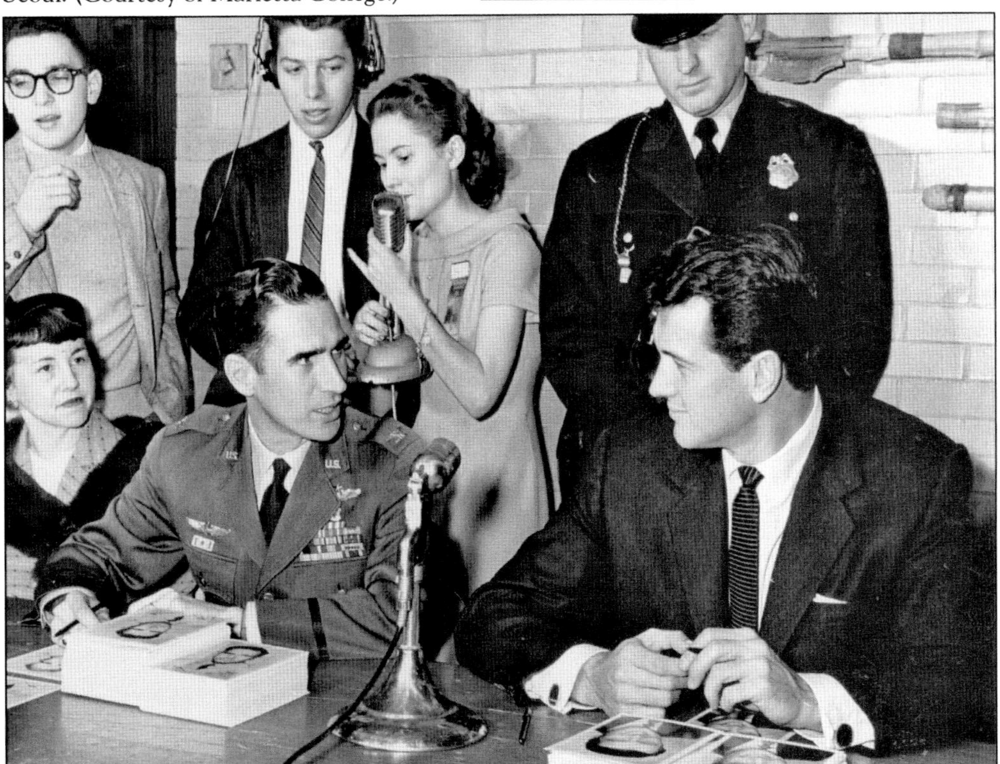

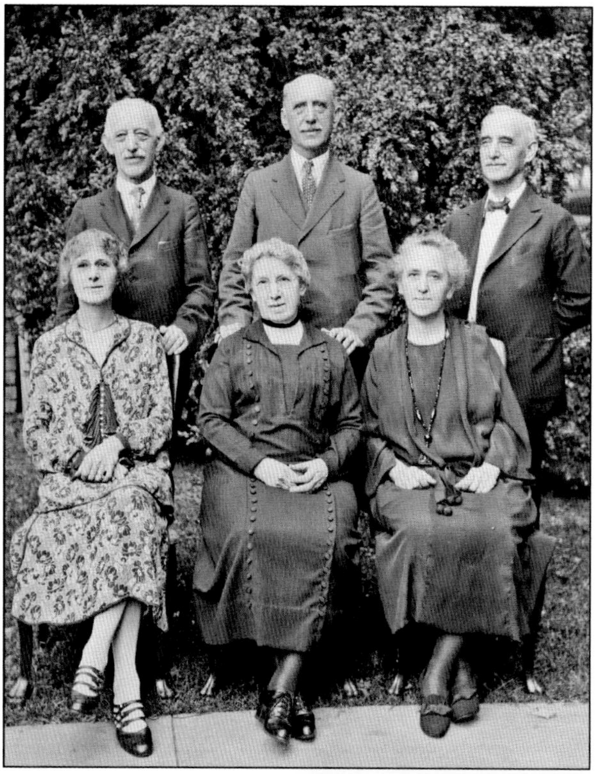

The Ebinger family was involved in the dry goods business for decades. Henry Ebinger became a partner at Turner & Ebinger in 1881. He and his wife, Anna Meister, had sons, Harry and William, who followed in the Turner & Ebinger Company. Following the death of Fred Turner, Henry J. Ebinger became president of the firm. William Ebinger, brother to Henry, and then Harry Ebinger followed in leadership until it closed in 1956. (Courtesy of Marietta College.)

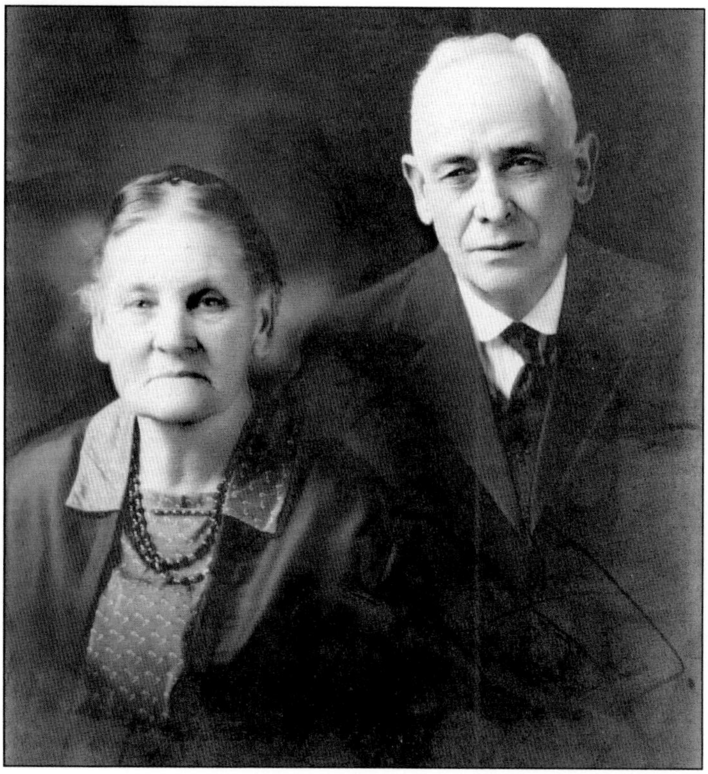

Louis Gruber (pictured here with his wife, Sarah) was the founder and head of L. Gruber and Sons Department Store at 155–157 Front Street and was considered one of Marietta's leading citizens by the *Marietta Times*. Born in Germantown in Liberty Township, he later took over his father's store in Whipple. Gruber founded his department store in Marietta in 1903. Gruber served as the director for the Peoples Banking and Trust Company for 34 years. He remained active until 1937 at the age of 82. (Courtesy of Vera Gruber descendants.)

Women sometimes ran their own businesses, many assisted their husbands, and some worked as domestic servants before marriage. Young Minnie Seyerle of Plochingen, Germany, would not have guessed that after raising her family, she would become the vice president of the Marietta Brewing Company when her husband, Jacob Epple, became president of the firm. Luella Schneider took up the livery business after her husband, George, suffered an early death in 1895. They had operated the livery and stable at 223 Second Street since the 1880s. Ideally located across from the train station, the Schneiders also sold feed, boarded horses, and leased horses and buggies. Interestingly, Luella Schneider used her own name in the advertisement instead of the customary Mrs. George Schneider. (Right, courtesy of William R. Marshall; below, courtesy of Washington County Historical Society.)

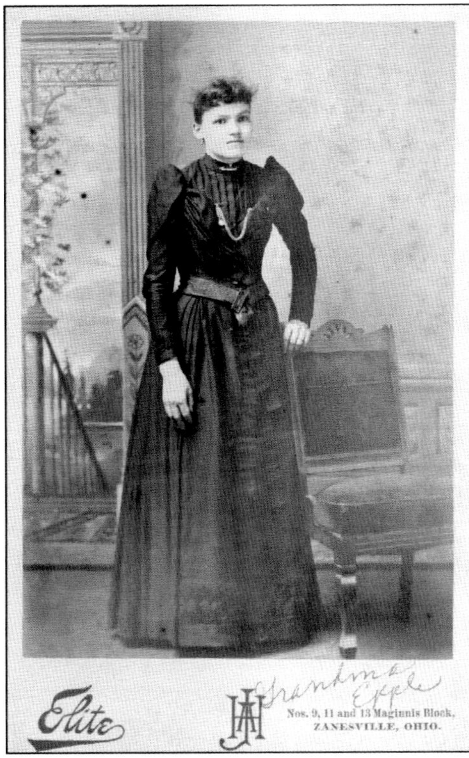

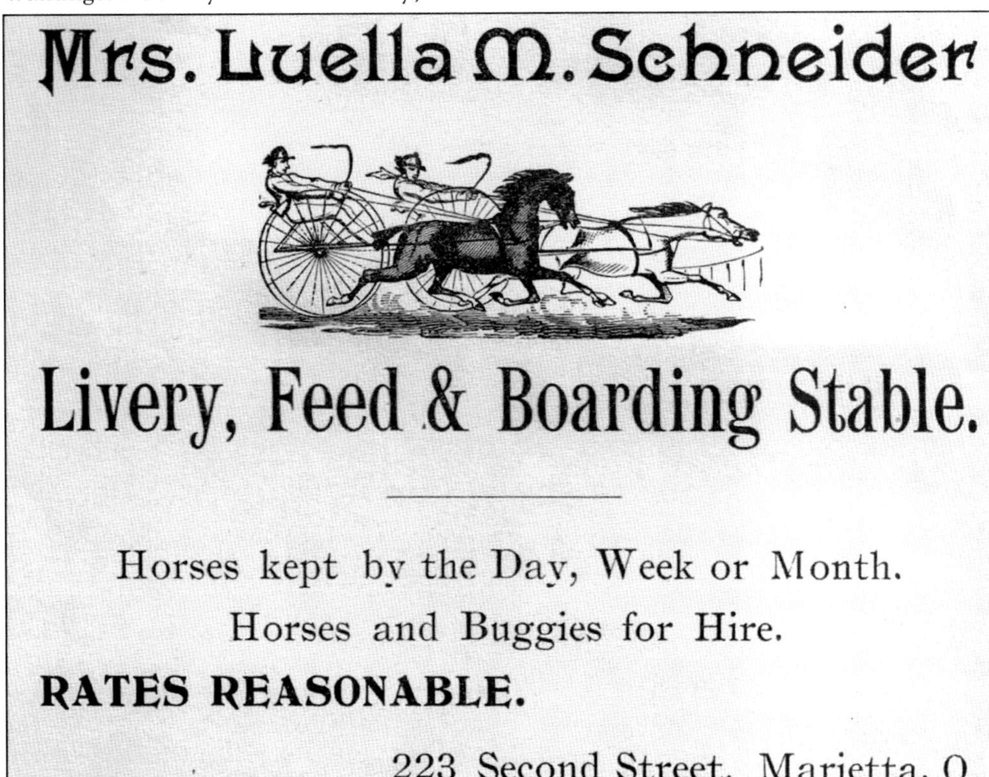

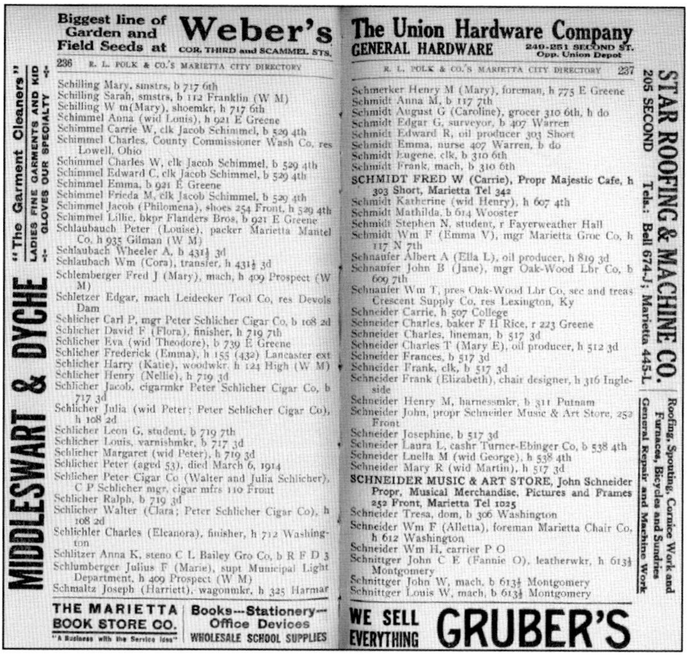

Biggest line of Garden and Field Seeds at **Weber's** COR. THIRD and SCAMMEL STS.

"The Garment Cleaners" LADIES FINE GARMENTS AND KID GLOVES OUR SPECIALTY MIDDLESWART & DYCHE

236 R. L. POLK & CO.'S MARIETTA CITY DIRECTORY

Schilling Mary, smstrs, b 717 6th
Schilling Sarah, smstrs, b 112 Franklin (W M)
Schilling W m(Mary), shoemkr, h 717 6th
Schimmel Anna (wid Louis), h 921 E Greene
Schimmel Carrie W, clk Jacob Schimmel, b 529 4th
Schimmel Charles, County Commissioner Wash Co, res Lowell, Ohio
Schimmel Charles W, clk Jacob Schimmel, b 529 4th
Schimmel Edward C, clk Jacob Schimmel, b 529 4th
Schimmel Emma, b 921 E Greene
Schimmel Frieda M, clk Jacob Schimmel, b 529 4th
Schimmel Jacob (Philomena), shoes 254 Front, h 529 4th
Schimmel Lillie, bkpr Flanders Bros, b 921 E Greene
Schlaubauch Peter (Louise), packer Marietta Mantel Co, h 935 Gilman (W M)
Schlaubach Wheeler A, b 431½ 3d
Schlaubach Wm (Cora), transfer, h 431½ 3d
Schlemberger Fred J (Mary), mach, h 409 Prospect (W M)
Schletzer Edgar, mach Leidecker Tool Co, res Devols Dam
Schlicher Carl P, mgr Peter Schlicher Cigar Co, b 108 2d
Schlicher David F (Flora), finisher, h 719 7th
Schlicher Eva (wid Theodore), b 739 E Greene
Schlicher Frederick (Emma), h 155 (432) Lancaster ext
Schlicher Harry (Katie), woodwkr, h 124 High (W M)
Schlicher Henry (Nellie), h 719 3d
Schlicher Jacob, cigarmkr Peter Schlicher Cigar Co, b 717 3d
Schlicher Julia (wid Peter; Peter Schlicher Cigar Co), h 108 2d
Schlicher Leon G, student, b 719 7th
Schlicher Louis, varnishmkr, b 717 3d
Schlicher Margaret (wid Peter), h 719 3d
Schlicher Peter (aged 53), died March 6, 1914
Schlicher Peter Cigar Co (Walter and Julia Schlicher), C P Schlicher mgr, cigar mfrs 110 Front
Schlicher Ralph, b 719 3d
Schlicher Walter (Clara; Peter Schlicher Cigar Co), h 108 2d
Schlichler Charles (Eleanora), finisher, h 712 Washington
Schlitzer Anna K, steno C L Bailey Gro Co, b R F D 3
Schlumberger Julius F (Marie), supt Municipal Light Department, h 409 Prospect (W M)
Schmaltz Joseph (Harriett), wagonmkr, h 325 Harmar

THE MARIETTA BOOK STORE CO. "A Business with the Service Idea" Books—Stationery—Office Devices WHOLESALE SCHOOL SUPPLIES

The Union Hardware Company GENERAL HARDWARE 249-251 SECOND ST. Opp. Union Depot

R. L. POLK & CO.'S MARIETTA CITY DIRECTORY 237

Schmerker Henry M (Mary), foreman, h 775 E Greene
Schmidt Anna M, b 117 7th
Schmidt August G (Caroline), grocer 310 6th, h do
Schmidt Edgar G, surveyor, b 407 Warren
Schmidt Edward R, oil producer 303 Short
Schmidt Emma, nurse 407 Warren, b do
Schmidt Eugene, clk, b 310 6th
Schmidt Frank, mach, b 310 6th
SCHMIDT FRED W (Carrie), Propr Majestic Cafe, h 303 Short, Marietta Tel 342
Schmidt Katherine (wid Henry), h 607 4th
Schmidt Mathilda, b 614 Wooster
Schmidt Stephen N, student, r Fayerweather Hall
Schmidt Wm F (Emma V), mgr Marietta Groc Co, h 117 N 7th
Schnaufer Albert A (Ella L), oil producer, h 819 3d
Schnaufer John B (Jane), mgr Oak-Wood Lbr Co, b 609 7th
Schnaufer Wm T, pres Oak-Wood Lbr Co, sec and treas Crescent Supply Co, res Lexington, Ky
Schneider Carrie, h 507 College
Schneider Charles, baker F H Rice, r 223 Greene
Schneider Charles, lineman, b 517 3d
Schneider Charles T (Mary E), oil producer, h 512 3d
Schneider Frances, b 517 3d
Schneider Frank, clk, b 517 3d
Schneider Frank (Elizabeth), chair designer, h 316 Ingleside
Schneider Henry M, harnessmkr, b 311 Putnam
Schneider John, propr Schneider Music & Art Store, 252 Front
Schneider Josephine, b 517 3d
Schneider Laura L, cashr Turner-Ebinger Co, b 538 4th
Schneider Luella M (wid George), h 538 4th
Schneider Mary R (wid Martin), h 517 3d
SCHNEIDER MUSIC & ART STORE, John Schneider Propr, Musical Merchandise, Pictures and Frames 252 Front, Marietta Tel 1025
Schneider Tresa, dom, b 306 Washington
Schneider Wm F (Alletta), foreman Marietta Chair Co, h 612 Washington
Schneider Wm H, carrier P O
Schnittger John C E (Fannie O), leatherwkr, h 613½ Montgomery
Schnittger John W, mach, b 613½ Montgomery
Schnittger Louis W, mach, b 613½ Montgomery

STAR ROOFING & MACHINE CO. 205 SECOND Tels.: Bell 674-J; Marietta 445-L Roofing, Spouting, Cornice Work and Furnaces, Bicycles and Sundries General Repair and Machine Work

WE SELL EVERYTHING GRUBER'S

Native and first-generation Germans made Marietta their home. The 1914–1915 Polk City Directory for Marietta showed an overwhelming amount of German surnames. It is difficult to account for the number of people who were offspring of their German mothers who married non-Germans. In 1910, the US Bureau of Census indicated that Marietta had a foreign-born population of 544 with 316 of these being native Germans. (Courtesy of Washington County Public Library.)

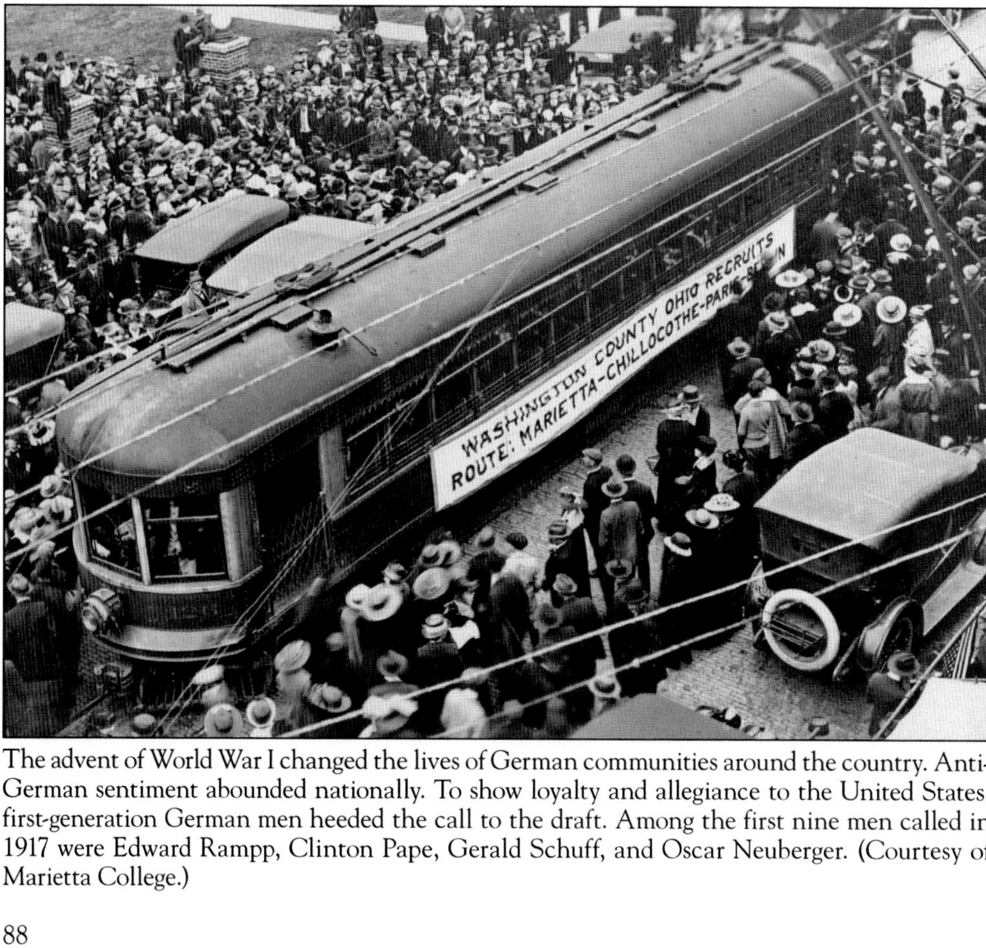

The advent of World War I changed the lives of German communities around the country. Anti-German sentiment abounded nationally. To show loyalty and allegiance to the United States, first-generation German men heeded the call to the draft. Among the first nine men called in 1917 were Edward Rampp, Clinton Pape, Gerald Schuff, and Oscar Neuberger. (Courtesy of Marietta College.)

Four

Around the County

The lure of acres of land with arable soil provided the incentive for thousands of Germans to leave family in Europe, endure the long ocean voyage, and arrive in a land devoid of their language and customs. Farmers disembarked from boats along the Ohio River and flooded through small cities like Matamoras, Newport, and Marietta to inquire about suitable land in the interior. All ethnic groups had a tendency to settle where they shared a common language and customs of their kinsmen. People from Scotland, Ireland, and England tended to cluster in the western portion of Washington County. Though Germans were speckled around the county, the greatest portion of them settled in the center and eastern townships. Fearing, Adams, Salem, Liberty, Marietta, Muskingum, Lawrence, and Grandview Townships had significant German colonies.

Township Germans broke the ground not only by farming, but also in establishing pockets of Germans who improved the land and established stores in concert with civic participation. Fearing Township attracted the earliest German pioneers as the first group came in the early 1830s. Early Germans in Fearing had the surnames of Peters, Dankers, Seylers, Zimmers, Biszantz, Pape, Boseshar, Biehl, and Leonhardts. Muskingum Township was formed from parts of Fearing, Marietta, and Union Townships in 1861 and was heavily German. The Ahrendts family settled on the ridge separating the Muskingum River and Duck Creek. The ridge road connecting State Routes 60 and 821 bears their name today. *Williams' History of Washington County*, published in 1881, noted the following about Adams Township: "The population of the hill districts is, at the present time, more than 80 percent German, and it is to the people of this nationality that the township owes a large proportion of its wealth." The Reverend Theodore Schreiner, a German immigrant, was the first mayor of Lowell.

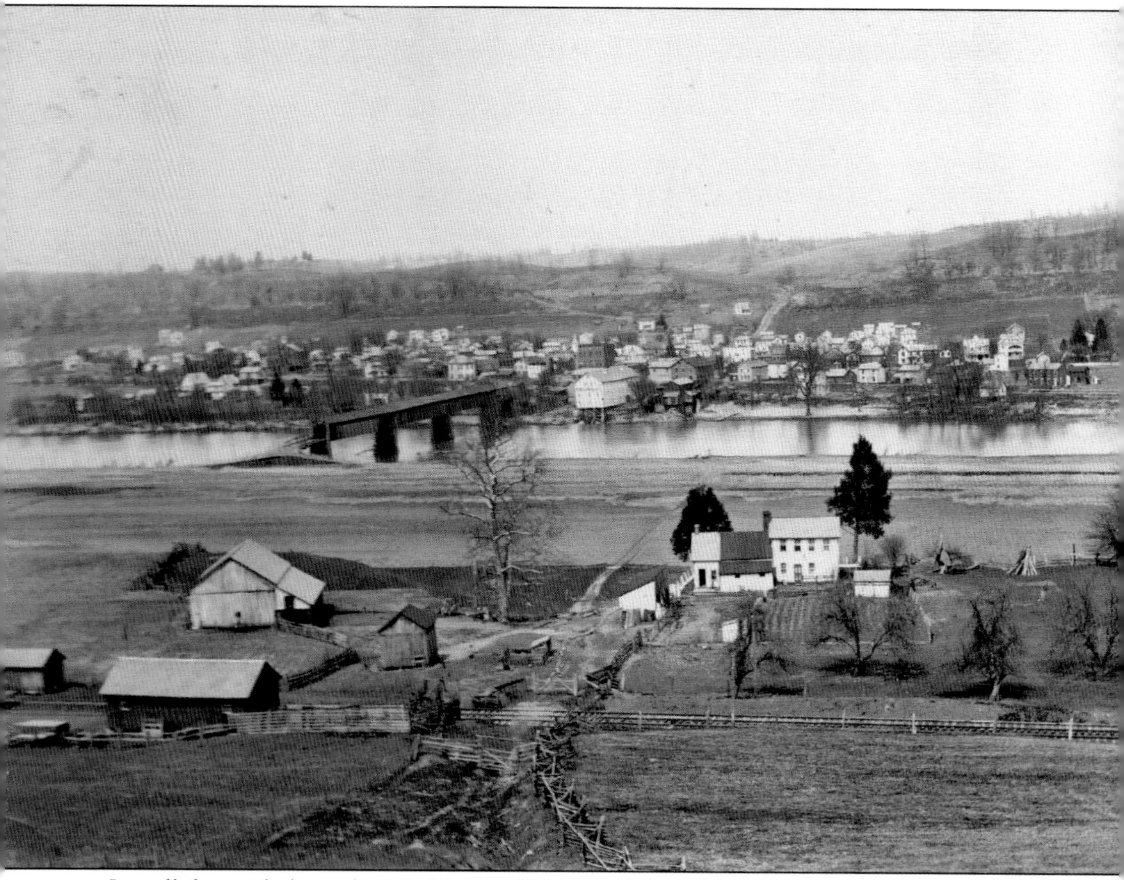

Lowell, located along the Muskingum River in Adams Township, had a significant German population. This 1906 photograph features a pronounced image of the ill-fated covered bridge. Local residents on both sides of the river were excited by the bridge when it was first built in 1880, but they were soon dismayed when it was blown off its piers by a violent storm the following year. The bridge was rebuilt a year later by Hall, Becker, and Bailey. In 1884, a flood left residents again without a bridge, but it was rebuilt by Daniel Wilking and would last for 29 more years. Another noted structure in the photograph is the flour mill, built about 1844 and owned by Harold Rechstiener and Alva Born. The flood of 1913 took out the covered bridge and devastated downtown Lowell. On the opposite side of the river, J.A. Schwendeman moved his newly formed contracting business to higher ground on Lowell Hill after the flood destroyed its river location. J.A. Schwendeman & Sons is still in business today. (Courtesy of Steven Weber.)

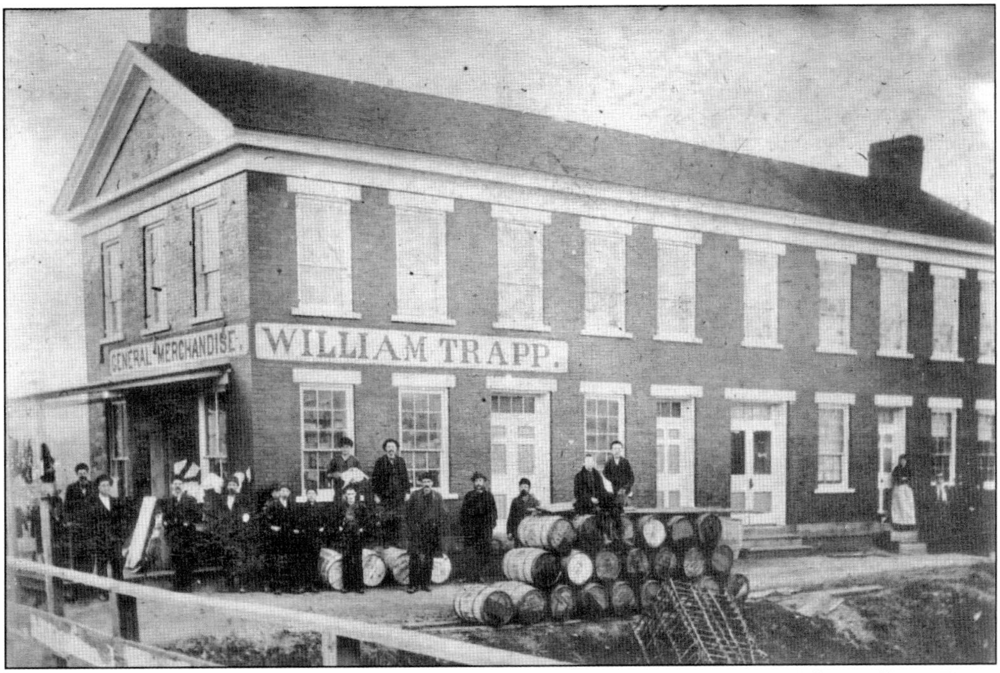

General merchandise stores were vital to villages and towns. The building of the William Trapp General Merchandise Store in Lowell was later the home of the Riecker General Store, which was in operation for many years. It was located on Buell Island next to the canal. The Knights of Pythia used the upstairs. (Courtesy of Everett Yarnell.)

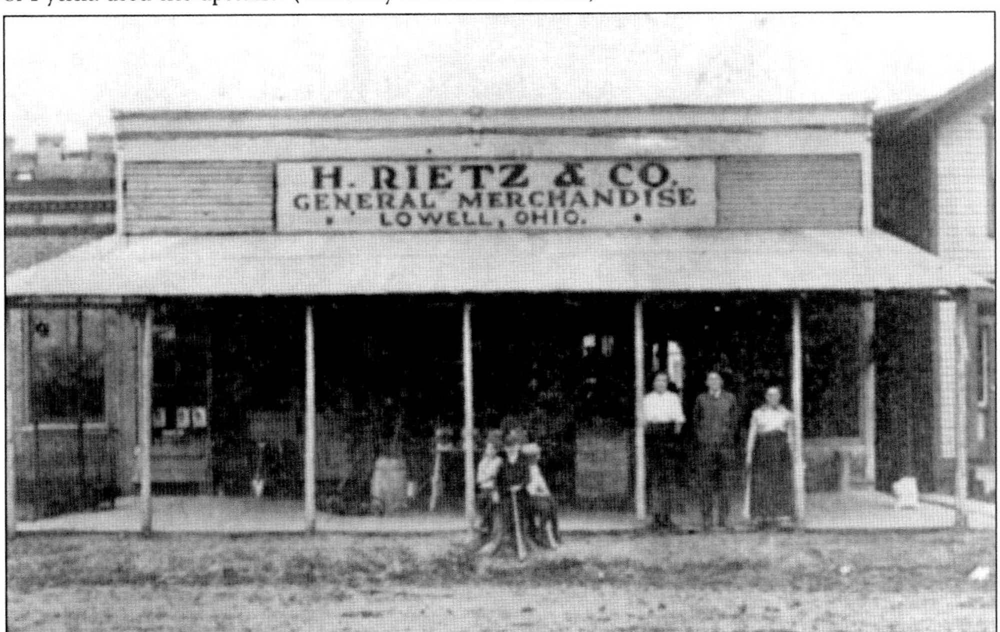

The H. Rietz and Company general merchandise store in Lowell carried not only the staples for the kitchen, but also selected clothing goods and needs for the household. This was the store's second location after a fire destroyed a previous store. The photograph shows store owners Harry and Nora Rietz Young with Phoebe Rietz. (Courtesy of Everett Yarnell.)

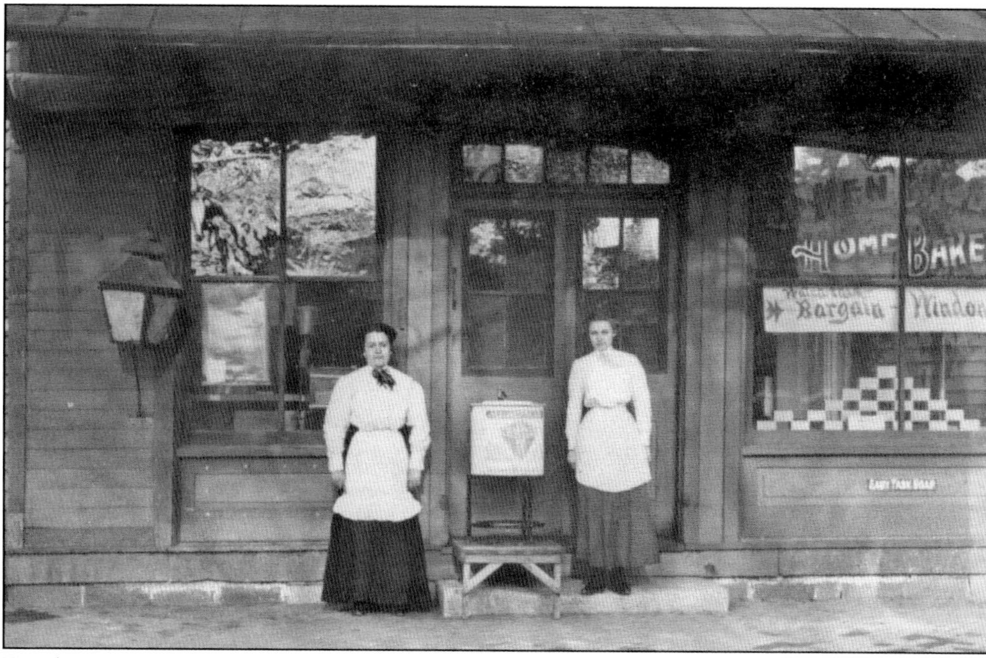

For about 15 years, Otto and Matilda Henniger operated a bakery on Main Street in Lowell in Adams Township. Later, Otto gave up the business to work as a rural mail carrier. Both sets of their parents were born in Prussia, where Otto Henniger's father had been a tanner. (Courtesy of Jane Anne Rauch.)

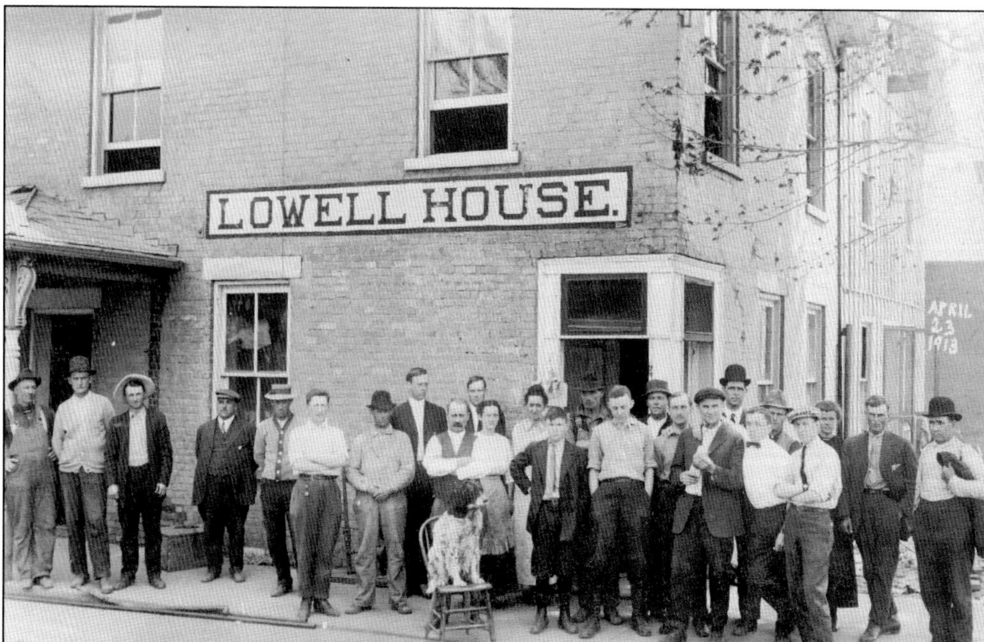

Lowell was a thriving community in the decades around the turn of the 20th century. In 1875, Franz Wilking opened the Lowell Hotel beside the canal at Walnut Street. William and Sarah Gheen made it a leading hotel in 1889. John Eck provided accommodations at the Lowell House, which opened in 1900. (Courtesy of Steven Weber.)

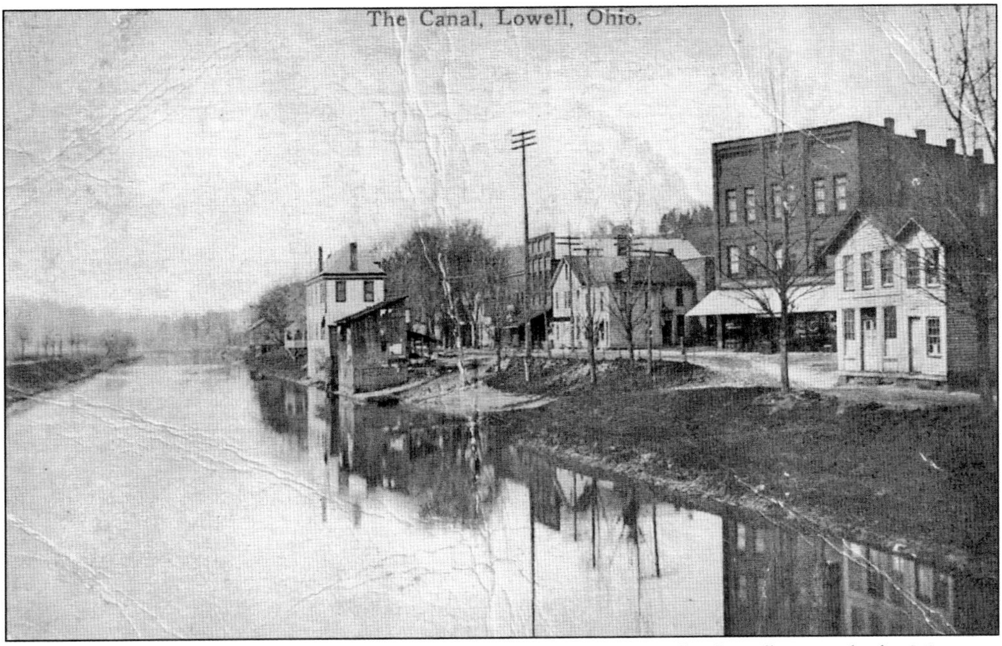

The large three-story brick building held Wolfram's Grocery on the first floor with the Masonic Lodge on the upper stories. To the left of the store were the telephone office and the two-story brick building of the Rietz General Store. The second story held the opera house. During the 1913 flood, a fire burned both structures to the waterline. Along the canal was a small bandstand where many German musicians performed. (Courtesy of Everett Yarnell.)

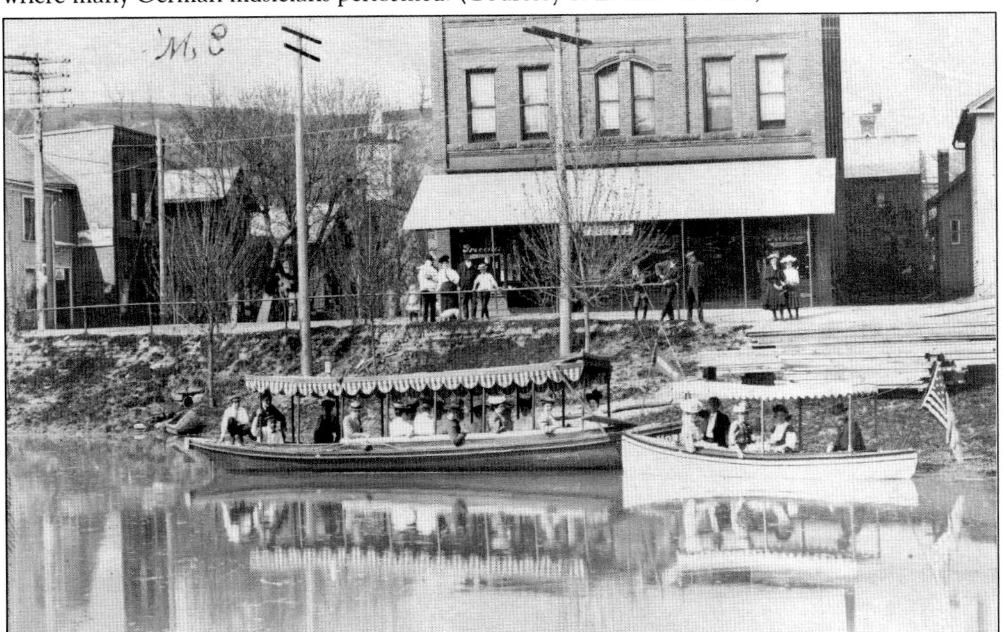

Lowell's wharf at Main and Walnut Streets was a busy area. Cargo was loaded and unloaded from boats on the canal. But the wharf also served pleasure craft. The *Lenora* on the left was a motorized launch boat, owned by the Rietz family. The boats would take people dressed in their Sunday best to a picnic site on the Muskingum River. (Courtesy of Steven Weber.)

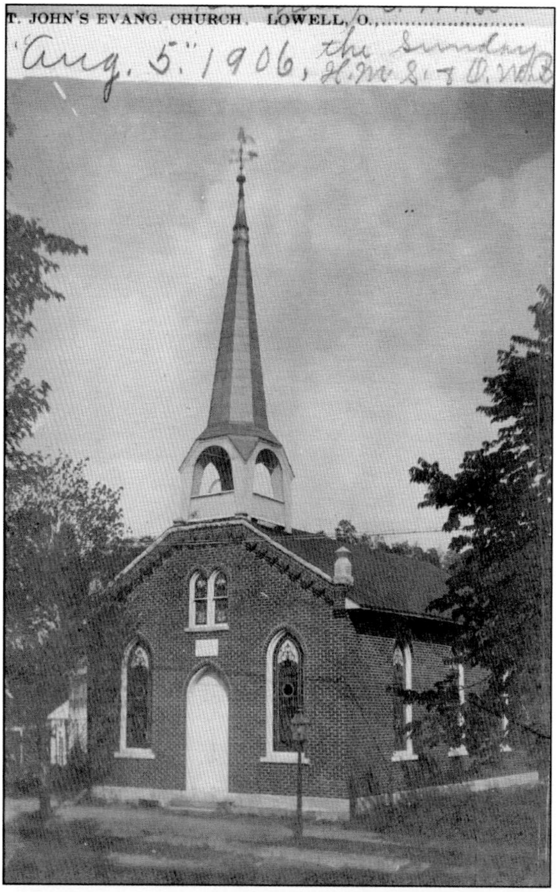

In 1858, the German Evangelical Protestant St. John's Church was formed by a group of Germans who had earlier attended service at a Methodist church on Third Street. At this time, the women of the church immediately formed a *Frauenverein*. Early ministers of the church were German with surnames of Juergens, Kretschmar, Eschenfeld, Friedrich, and Fuenfstueck. Around the time of the Civil War, the community dedicated a new church building on Walnut Street and later added the steeple with the rooster weather vane. At the turn of the century, Rev. Otto Breuhaus initiated English evening services. All of Lowell, including the church, suffered severe damaged in the 1913 flood. The property was sold to make a new town hall, and a new church was dedicated in 1916 on Fourth Street. St. John's Evangelical Church Cemetery, identified as the Old German Cemetery, can be found on County Road 76 (Cats Creek Road) just north of Lowell. (Left, courtesy of Steven Weber; below, courtesy of Theresa R. Thomas.)

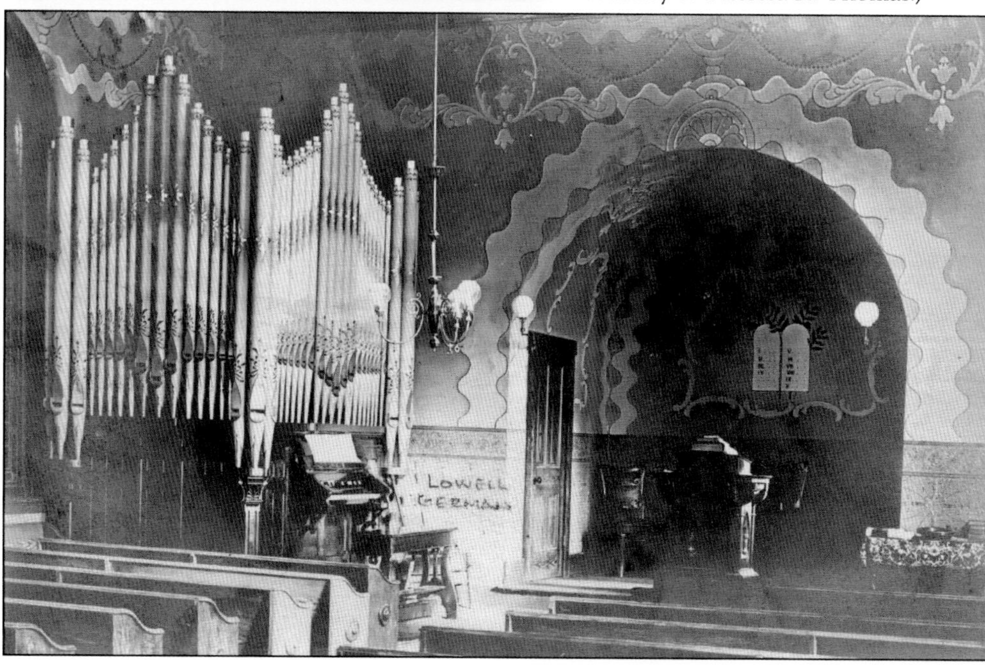

For decades, German churches held services in the German language. Church attendance was part of the fabric of the German culture. The German language could be heard in hymns and sermons. Here, they could gather in a group of peers to share stories and fellowship in the fashion of the homeland. After the service, German food was laid out on tables and information shared of relatives and friends in Europe. As the congregations had young people coming of age in an English-speaking world, they realized that their churches needed to address the changing times and offer English services. To meet everyone's needs, services in English and German were offered. (Courtesy of Steven Weber.)

GOTTESDIENST-KALENDER,

1907.

	Morgen:	Nachmittag:	Abend:
1. Jan.	*Watert'n.		
6. "	Hill.		*Lowell
13. "	Lowell,	Watertown,	
20. "	Hill.		*Lowell
27. "	Lowell.	*Watertown,	
3. Feb.	Hill,		*Lowell
10. "	Lowell,	Watertown,	
17. "	Hill.		*Lowell
24. "	Lowell.	*Watertown,	
3. Marz	Hill		*Lowell
10. "	Lowell,	Watertown,	
17. "	Hill,		*Lowell
24. "	Lowell,	*Watertown,	
29. "	Hill.		Lowell
31. "	Hill.		*Lowell
1. April	Watert'n.		
7 "	Lowell.	*Watertown,	
14. "	Hill.		*Lowell
21. "	Lowell.	Watertown	
28. "	Hill.		*Lowell
5. Mai	Lowell,	*Watertown,	
9. "	Hill.		
12. "	Hill.		*Lowell
19. "	Watert'n,	Lowell,	
20. "	Hill,		
26. "	Hill.		*Lowell
2. Juni	Lowell.	*Watertown.	
9. "	Hill,		*Lowell
16. "	Lowell.	Watertown,	
23. "	Hill.		*Lowell
30. "	Lowell,	*Watertown,	

	Morgen:	Nachmittag:	Abend:
7. Juli	Hill,		*Lowell
14. "	Lowell,	Watertown,	
21. "	Hill.		*Lowell
28. "	Lowell,	*Watertown.	
4. Aug	Hill.		*Lowell
11 "	Lowell.	Watertown,	
18 "	Hill,		*Lowell
25. "	Lowell,	*Watertown,	
1. Sept	Hill.		*Lowell
8. "	Lowell.	Watertown,	
15. "	Hill.		*Lowell
22. "	Lowell,	*Watertown.	
29. "	Hill.		*Lowell
6. Okt.	Lowell	Watertown,	
13 "	Hill.		*Lowell
20. "	Lowell.	*Watertown,	
27 "	Hill.		*Lowell
3. Nov.	Watert'n.	Lowell.	
10. "	Hill.		*Lowell
17 "	Lowell.	*Watertown,	
24 "	Hill.		Lowell
28. "	Lowell.		
1. Dez	Lowell,	Watertown.	
8. "	Hill.		*Lowell
15. "	Lowell.	*Watertown,	
22. "	Hill.		*Lowell
25. "	Lowell.		
26. "	Hill.		
29. "	Lowell.	Watertown,	
1. Jan.	*Watert'n,		

Services marked (*) English, all others German.

KONFIRMATION: Lowell am 24 Mærz; Hill am 9 Mai.

ABENDMAHLSFEIERN; Lowell am 7 April, 25 Sept., und 25 Dez: Hill am 12 Mai, und 29 Sept; Watertown am 19 Mai and 3 November.

OTTO W. BREUHAUS, Pastor.

Lowell, Ohio.

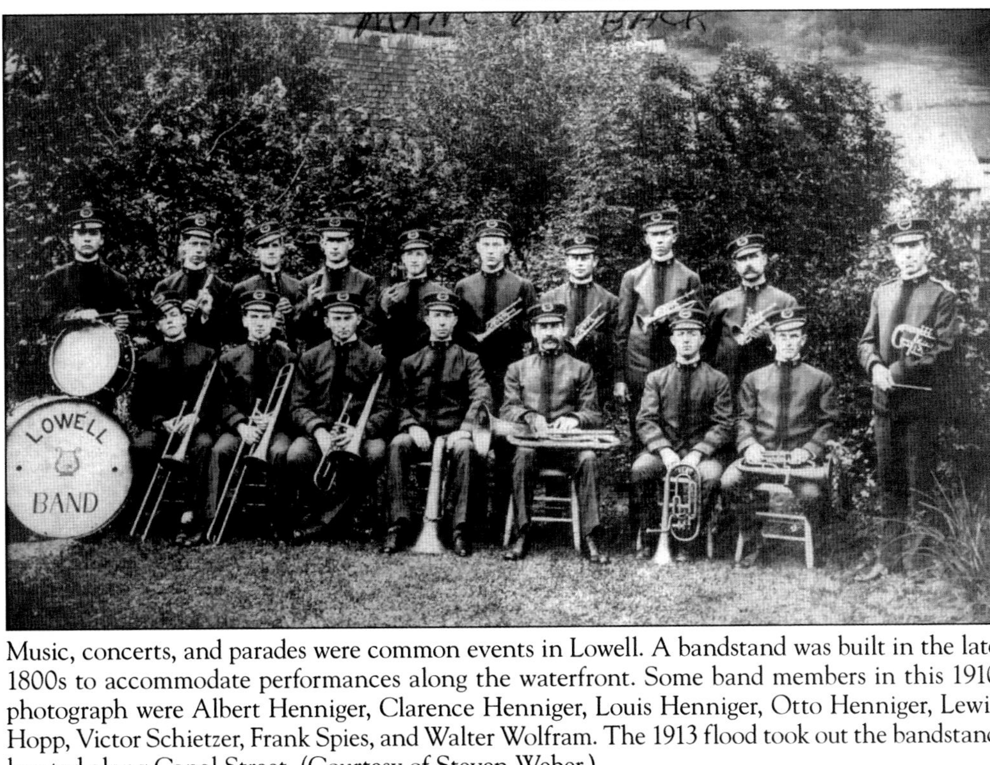

Music, concerts, and parades were common events in Lowell. A bandstand was built in the late 1800s to accommodate performances along the waterfront. Some band members in this 1910 photograph were Albert Henniger, Clarence Henniger, Louis Henniger, Otto Henniger, Lewis Hopp, Victor Schietzer, Frank Spies, and Walter Wolfram. The 1913 flood took out the bandstand located along Canal Street. (Courtesy of Steven Weber.)

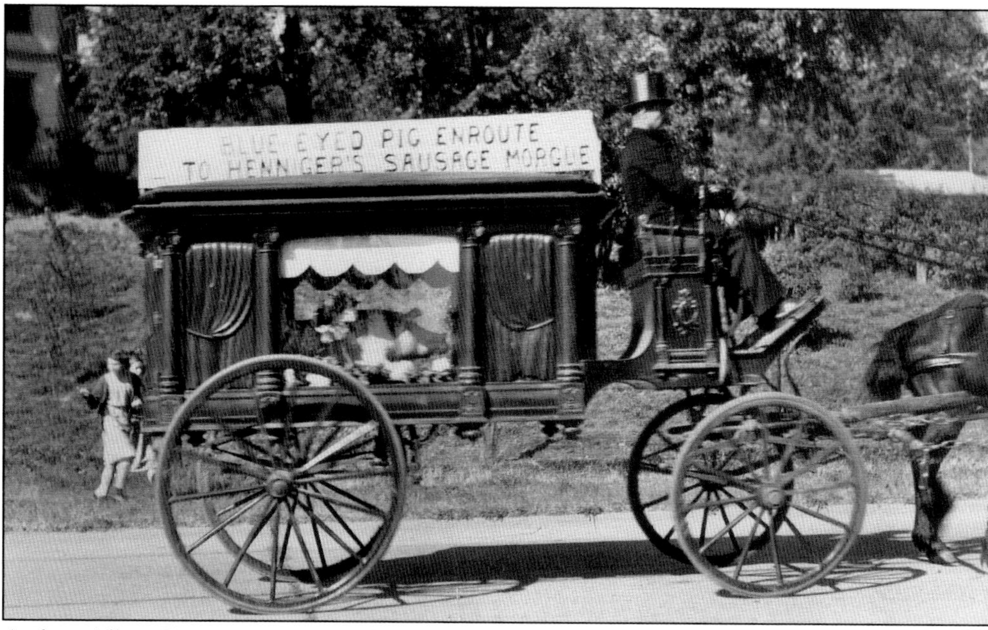

At first, Albert Henniger went into business with H. Rietz who had a general store. Albert was a butcher and provided meats. Later, he opened his own store, the Henniger Meat Market. In the photograph, Rietz advertises his business in a humorous way. A horse-drawn hearse carries a pig to market and the "sausage morgue." (Courtesy of Jane Anne Rauch.)

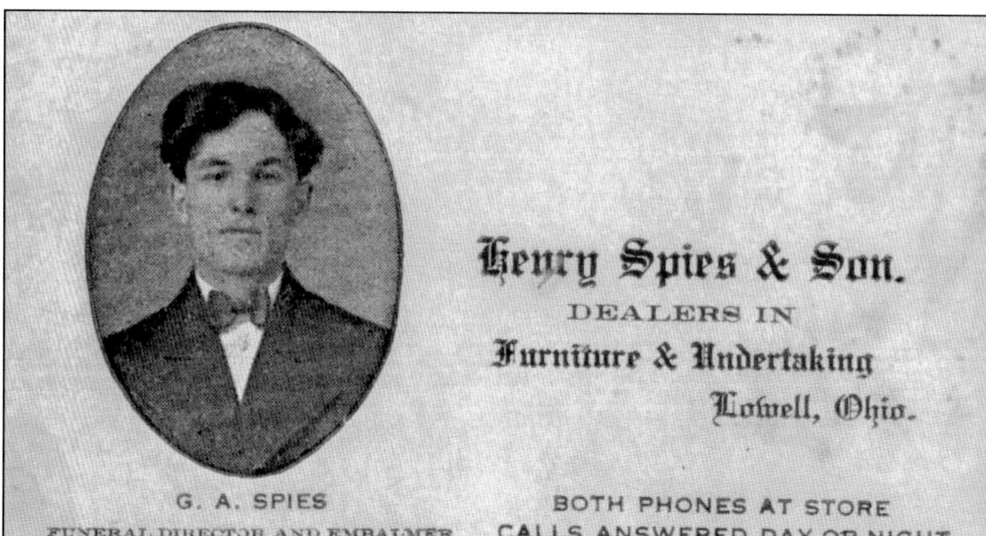

In 1913, Henry Spies purchased Schneider Undertaking on Main Street and moved the business across the street. He and his son George operated the undertaking and furniture business until 1947, when Robert Peoples acquired the business. In 1980, Robert's son William built a new funeral home in the location of the Schneider business. (Courtesy of Steven Weber.)

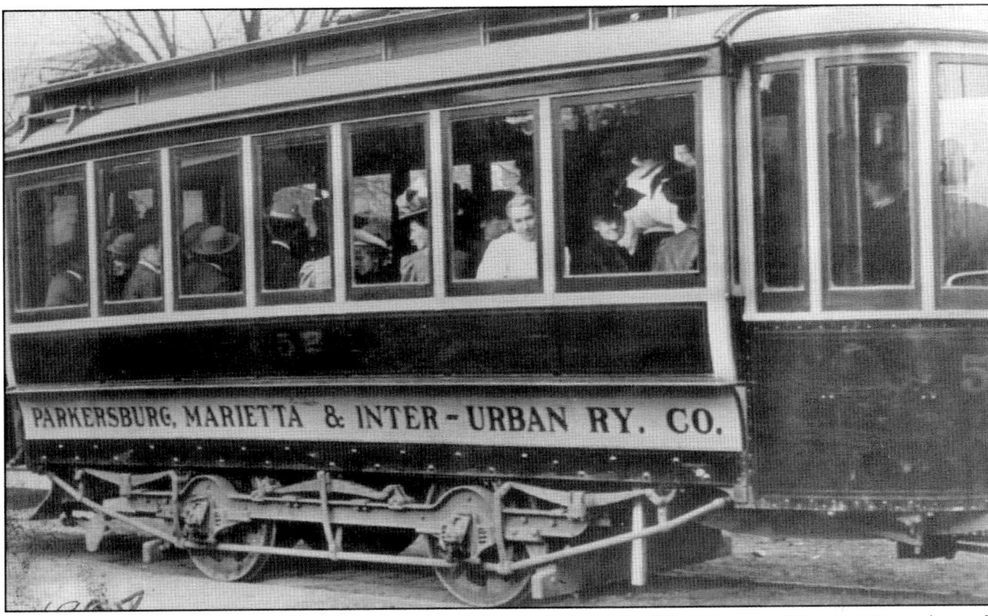

By 1908, the passenger and freight service was extended up the Muskingum River to Beverly with many stops along the way. Each car had an occupancy of 48 and room for cargo. Unfortunately, in 1914, there was a head-on collision of two interurbans near Lowell, resulting in the death of motorman Christian Noe. (Courtesy of Steven Weber.)

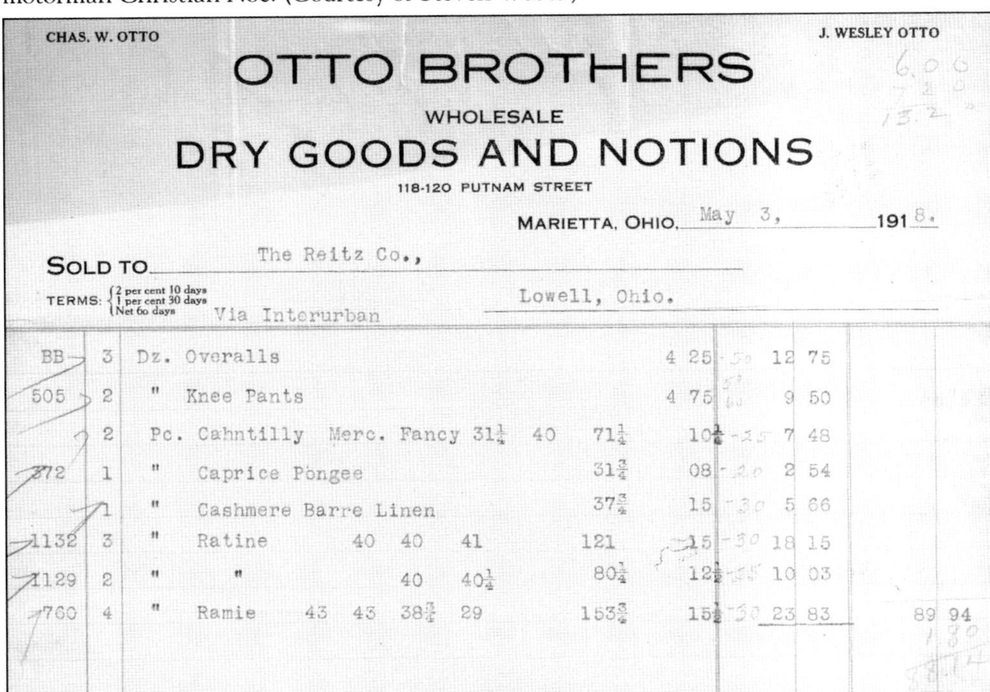

CHAS. W. OTTO | J. WESLEY OTTO

OTTO BROTHERS

WHOLESALE

DRY GOODS AND NOTIONS

118-120 PUTNAM STREET

MARIETTA, OHIO, May 3, 1918.

SOLD TO The Reitz Co., Lowell, Ohio.

TERMS: 2 per cent 10 days, 1 per cent 30 days, Net 60 days — Via Interurban

BB	3	Dz. Overalls	4 25	12 75	
505	2	" Knee Pants	4 75	9 50	
	2	Pc. Cahntilly Merc. Fancy 31¼ 40 71¼	10½	7 48	
372	1	" Caprice Pongee 31¾	08	2 54	
	1	" Cashmere Barre Linen 37¾	15	5 66	
1132	3	" Ratine 40 40 41 121	15	18 15	
1129	2	" " 40 40¼ 80¼	12½	10 03	
760	4	" Ramie 43 43 38¾ 29 153¾	15½	23 83	89 94

The interurban rail system allowed people of the villages, small towns, and rural areas to have easier access to shopping, visiting, entertainment, and nightlife in places along the line. The receipt showed that the Rietz Company in Lowell ordered goods from Marietta's Otto Brothers to be delivered via the interurban. (Courtesy of Steven Weber.)

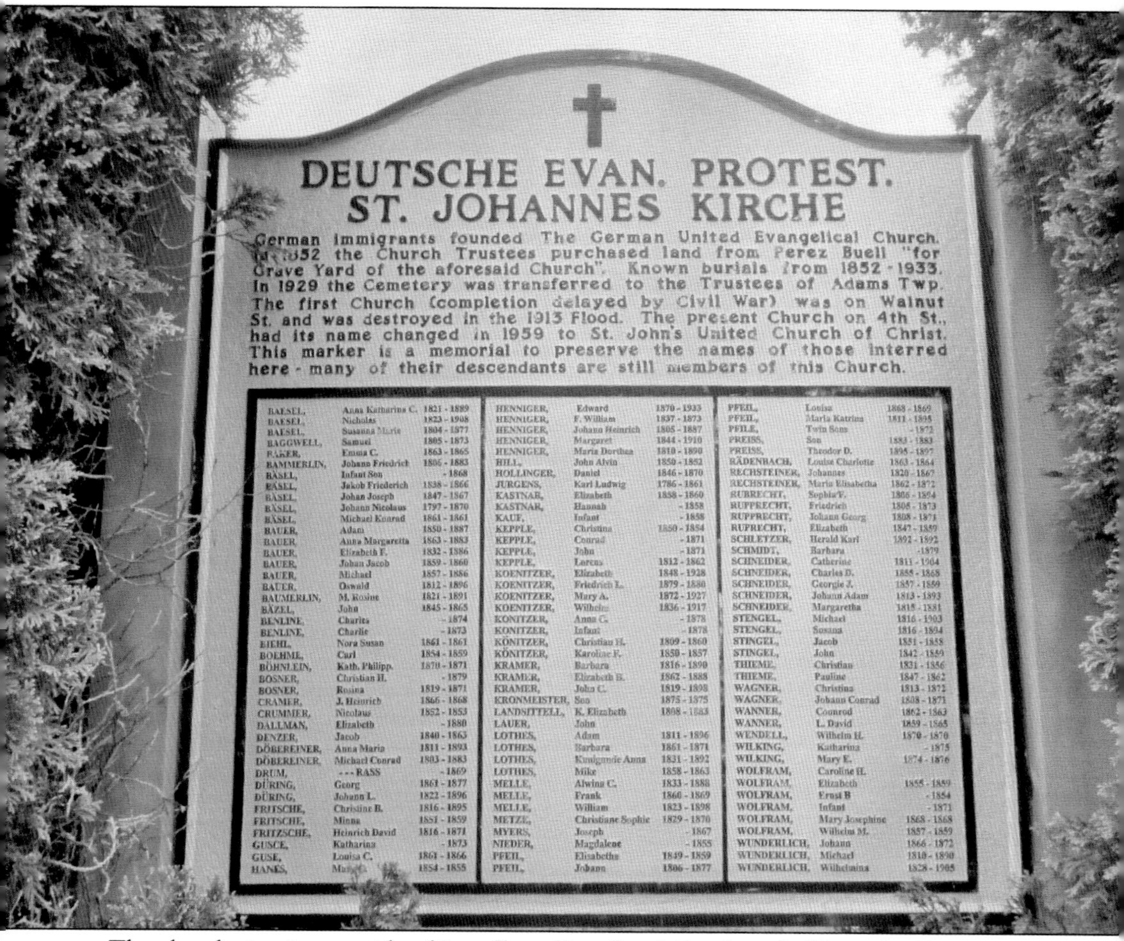

The church sign just outside of Lowell on Cats Creek Road reads "Deutsche Evan. Protest. St. Johannes Kirche," translated in English as "German Evangelical Protestant St. John's Church." The dates on the cemetery headstones indicate that the burial ground was in use from 1852 to 1933. Some of the earliest headstones have the names of Boehme, Nieder, Lothes, Crummer, Fritsche, Konitzer, Kaut, Pfeil, Hanes, Schneider, Wolfram, and Stingel. The cemetery is now maintained by Adams Township. (Courtesy of author's collection.)

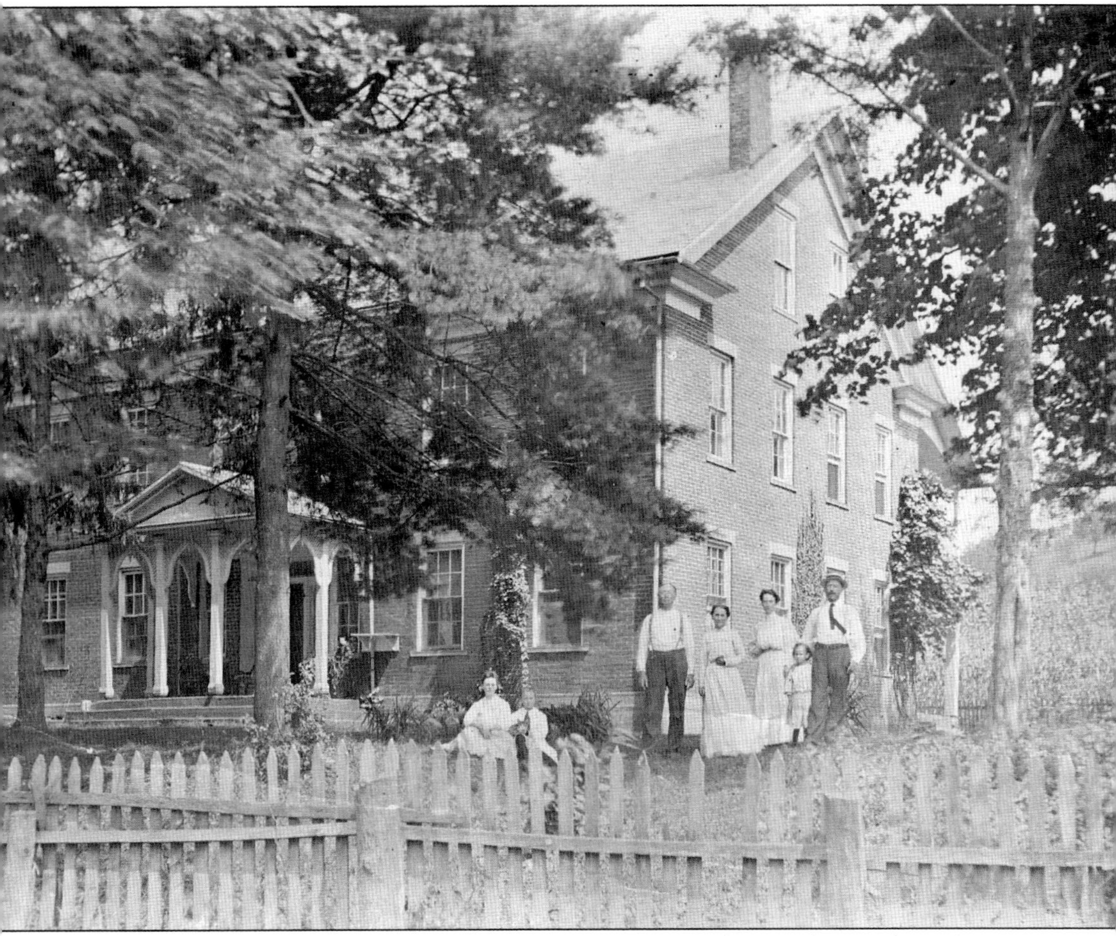

Ernest Waerniche started a tobacco farm in the 1850s along Archers Fork in Independence Township. The brick house was built in 1865 and was recorded as the first brick house in the township. The 1870 federal census indicated that Waerniche, wife Kate, his mother, son, domestic workers, and clerks lived on the property. One boarder was Augustus Hille who was learning the tobacco trade. In 1879, Augustus Hille, who had immigrated from Frankenburg, Hesse, with his mother in 1854, acquired the farm after the death of Waernicke. Hille married Theresa M. Vaupel in 1878, and they had four children. After Augustus Hille was named the postmaster of the Archers Fork community, he opened a general store on the property that also housed the post office. He was the postmaster until his death in 1918. Later, their daughter Ida was postmistress of Archers Fork. Augustus Hille's grandson Dr. Richard Hille and Richard's wife, Sally, were the last of the family to live in the house. (Courtesy of Washington County Historical Society.)

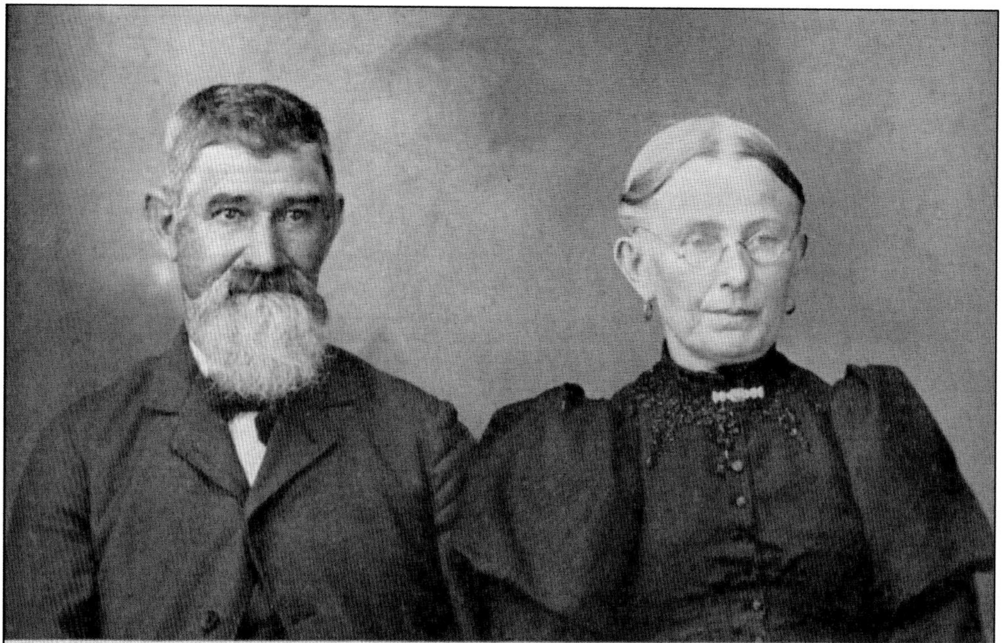

MR. AND MRS. CHARLES SCHIMMEL.

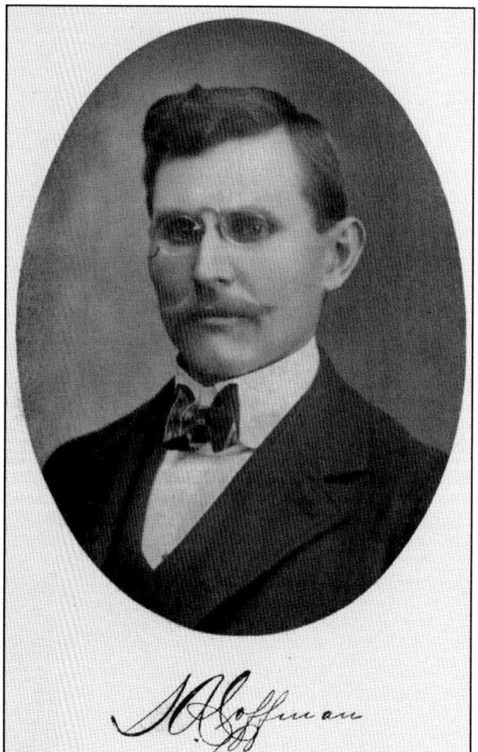

Charles Schimmel, the son of early German pioneers, was born in Fearing Township in 1842. He and his wife acquired 325 acres of rich farmland in Aurelius Township. When the county experienced an oil boom in the 1890s, Schimmel secured at least six producing wells making him a leading oil producer. He served as trustee of Aurelius Township. (Courtesy of Washington County Public Library.)

Born in Warren Township, S. Austin Coffman was an influential businessman. He worked for the Baltimore and Ohio Railroad, US Exchange Company, opened a general store at Fleming in Barlow Township, had an insurance and real estate business in Marietta, and developed interests in oil wells near Tunnel and other nearby fields. In 1922, Coffman and his brother bought the St. Cloud Hotel. (Courtesy of Washington County Public Library.)

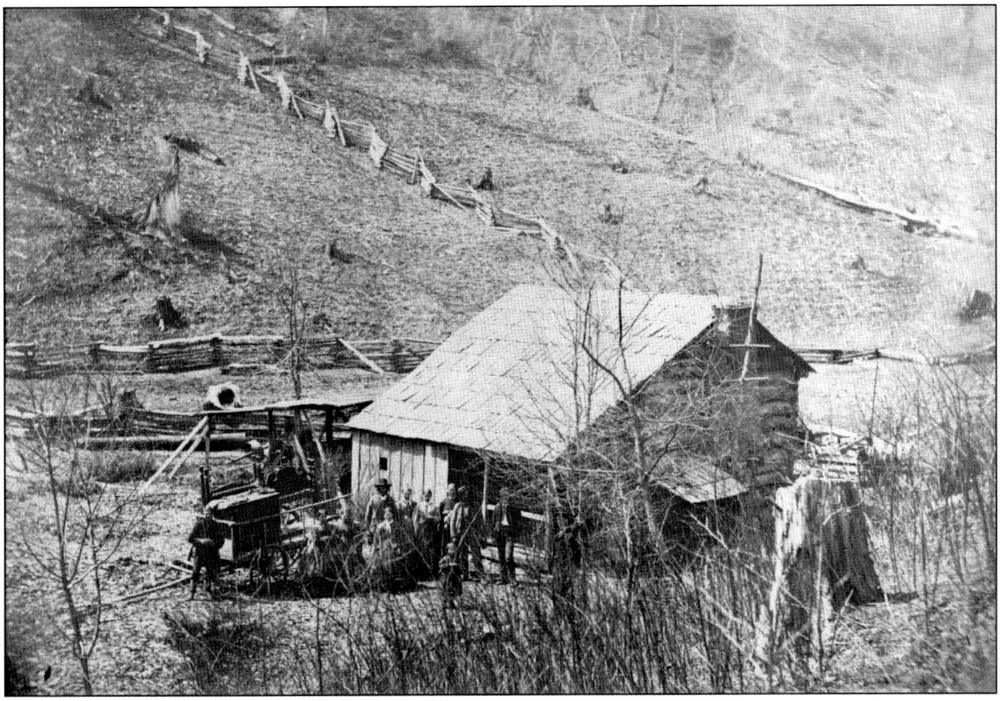

In 1838, early pioneer David Hendershot was chosen as the clerk for the newly formed Liberty Township. Germantown was established in 1852 making it the oldest village in the township. Hendershot, a teacher, designed the layout for Germantown. By 1880, this rural community along Paw Paw Creek had established a store, a mill, a blacksmith shop, a shoe shop, and a saloon. (Courtesy of Marietta College.)

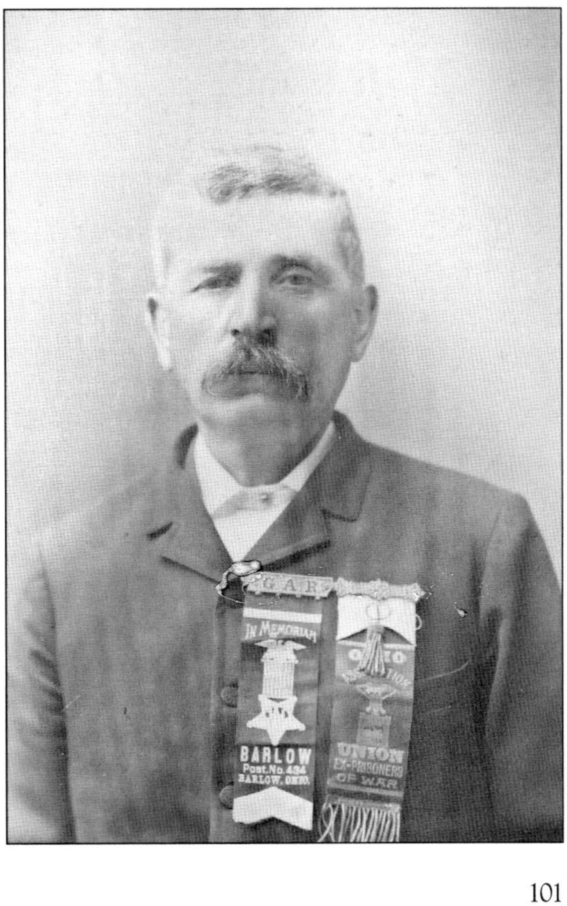

Former prisoner-of-war Jacob Bower bears the GAR Post No. 434 memorial ribbon and Ohio Association of Union ex-prisoners of war. Born in Baden in 1845, Bower joined the service in 1862 from Fairfield Township. He was wounded in Gettysburg and captured in 1864 and sent to Georgia's Andersonville prison. After his discharge in 1865, records show he was a farmer in Fearing Township and, later, a saloon keeper in Athens County. (Courtesy of Washington County Library.)

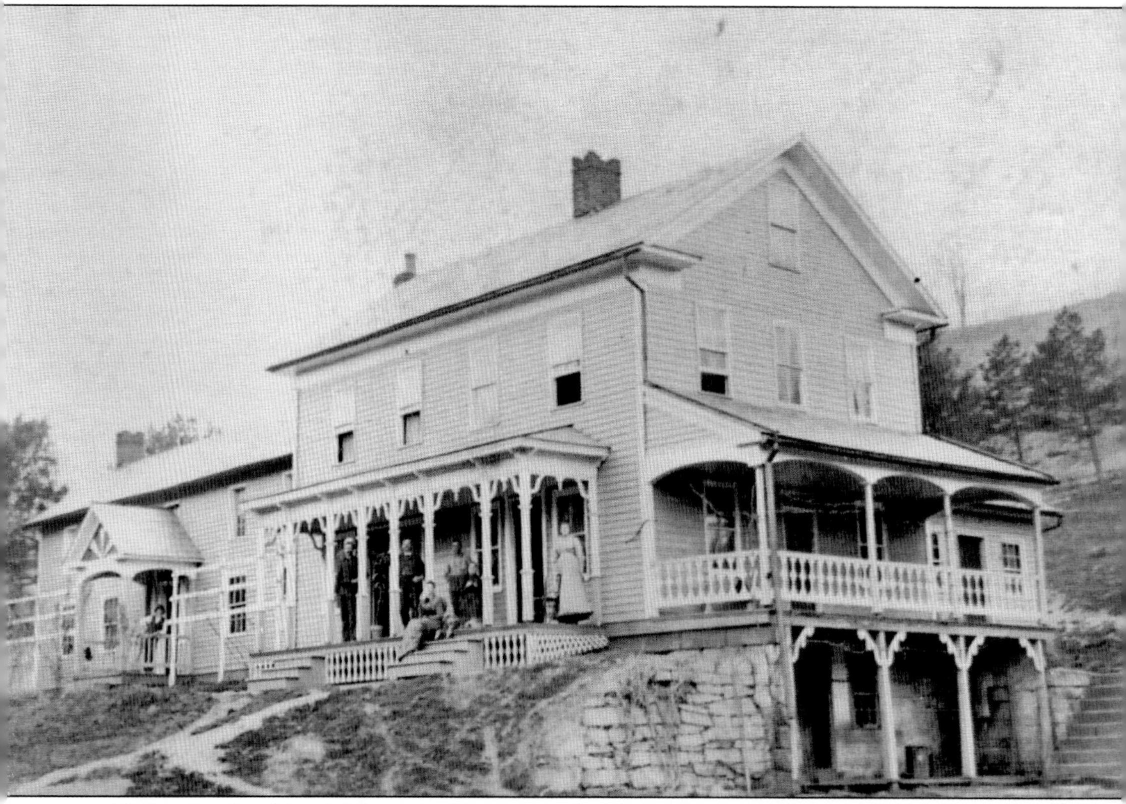

With a family of 12 children, the Hune household had outgrown the original log house. William Hune built a new house, but by the 1890s a second home was built next to the first. Later, the two houses were joined together. With 12 huge rooms, the pink-painted house was 90 feet long with eight entry doors. The stone basement of one of the sections served as a kitchen equipped with a fireplace for preparing food that would be carried upstairs to the dining room. At one time, it served as a boardinghouse and was known as the Hune Inn. This huge home welcomed friends by hosting dances and musicals in the hall between the house and the barn. The home served as the Lawrence Township post office as William Hune served as postmaster from 1849 to 1861. From 1893 to 1912, Carrie Hune ran the post office. (Courtesy of Washington County Historical Society.)

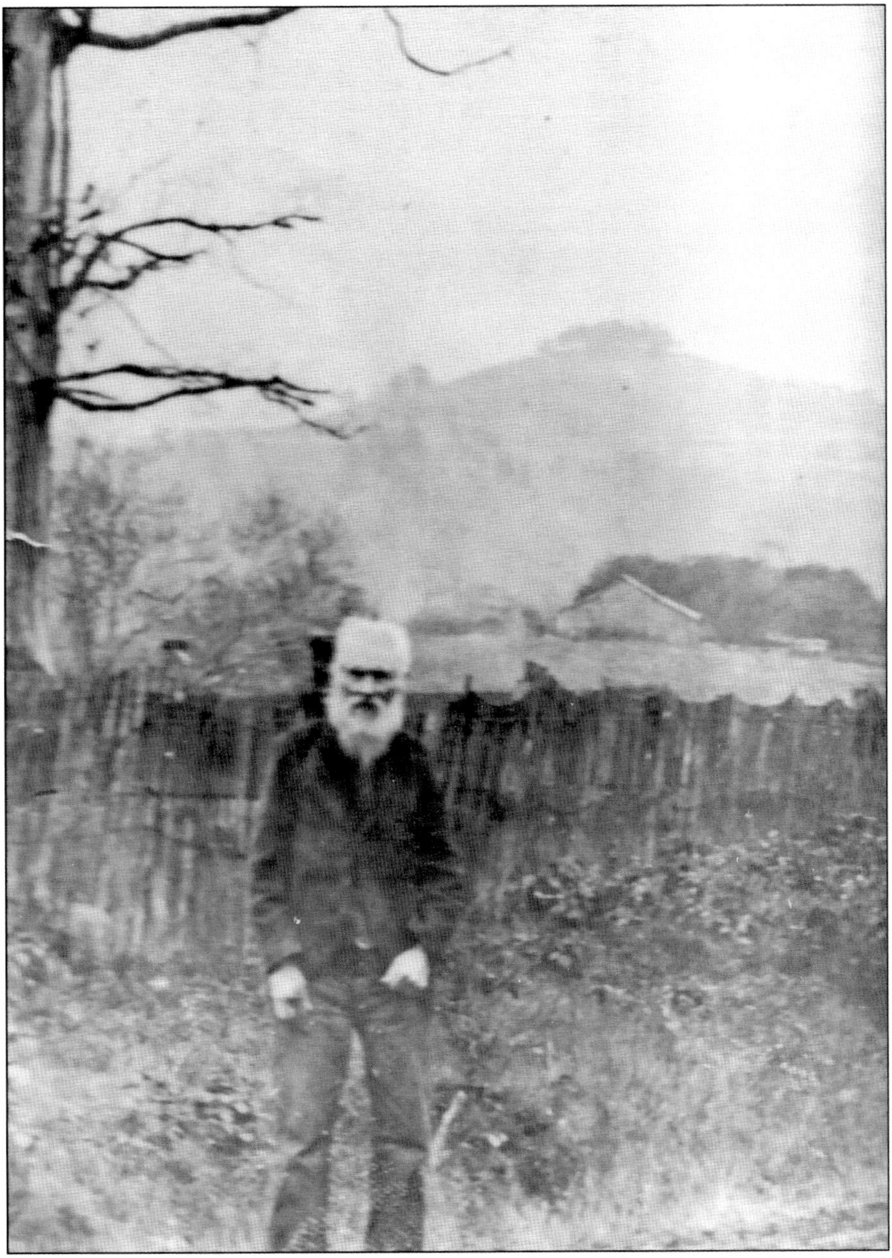

Wilhelm Heinrich Theodor Hune was a man with ambitious ideas that kept him busy during his 88 years. Hune immigrated to Baltimore with his parents in 1832. Leaving his family, he came to Ohio and eventually settled in Lawrence Township, where he served as the postmaster from 1849 to 1861. In an old log house, he started a store and a log tobacco-firing house that he later developed into a tobacco-packing house. William Hune started a blacksmith shop, sawmill, gristmill, tan shop, and sorghum-making factory. He employed other settlers in the area, which enabled him to ship tobacco products, sorghum, apple butter, and wool to eastern markets. Hune also built a schoolhouse and a covered bridge. Hune shared his talents in music with the family and community. In the home, there was a flute, guitars, violins, a mandolin, and a baby grand piano. (Courtesy of Judith Weber.)

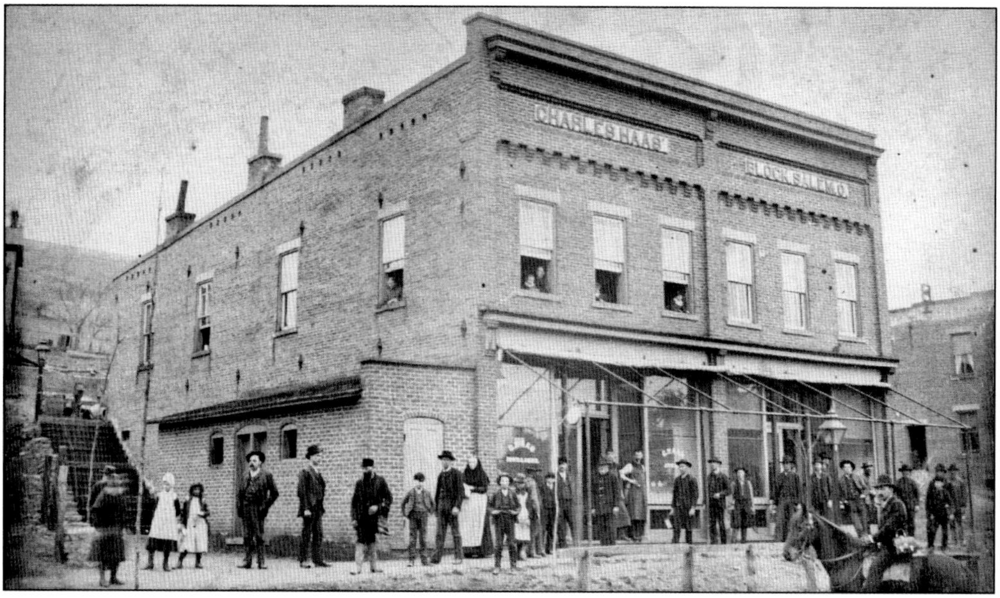

Charles Haas was born in 1852 to Valentine and Joanna Boger Haas in Salem Township. His father immigrated to America in 1840 after he served as a soldier for Napoleon's army for four years and took part in the Battle of Waterloo. In 1841, he married Joanna Boger of Wurtemburg and had six children, including Charles. Though Valentine was a farmer, Charles took up shoemaking as a trade by 1880. In 1879, he married Magdelena Lauer whose parents were natives of Bavaria and had settled in Salem. By 1890, he had this large store in Lower Salem where he was a jewelry, boot, and shoe dealer. (Courtesy of Marietta College.)

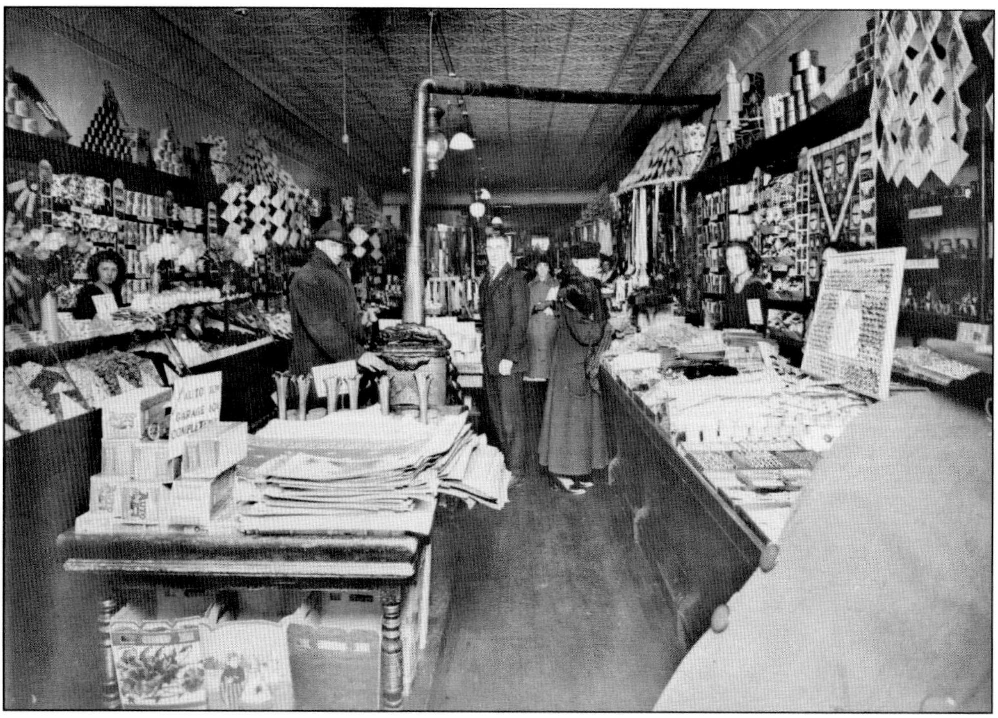

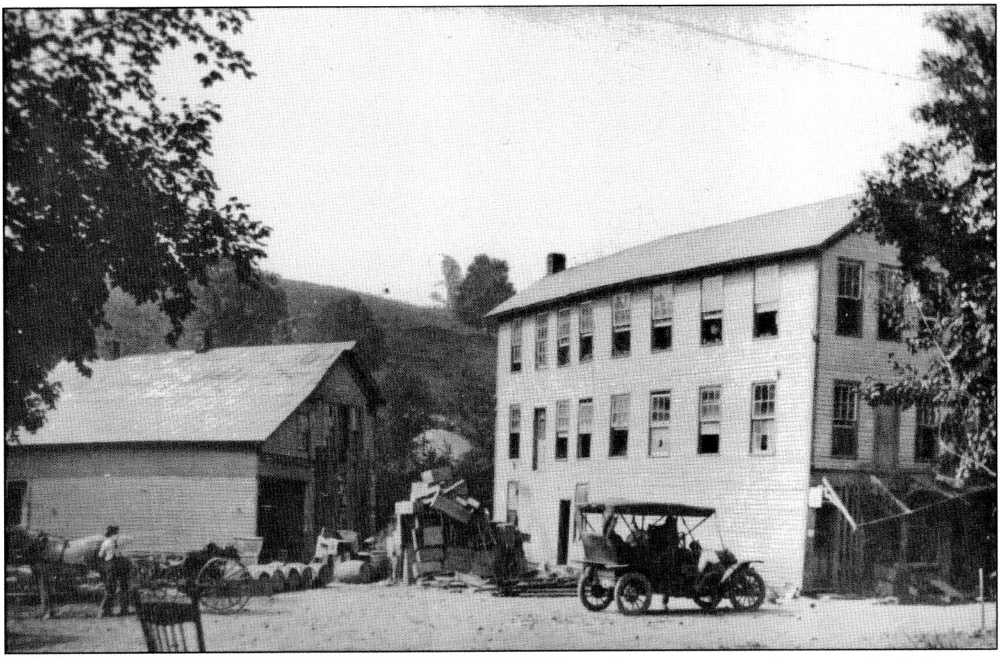

When referring to the two George Lauers of Lower Salem, the community distinguished the men by their nicknames. The older George "Nosy" Lauer operated a general store in Lower Salem. Nearby, George "Shoemaker" Lauer was a boot and shoe dealer. Lower Salem was incorporated in 1890. First jail and bank formed in 1911 with George Lauer as president. (Courtesy of Washington County Historical Society.)

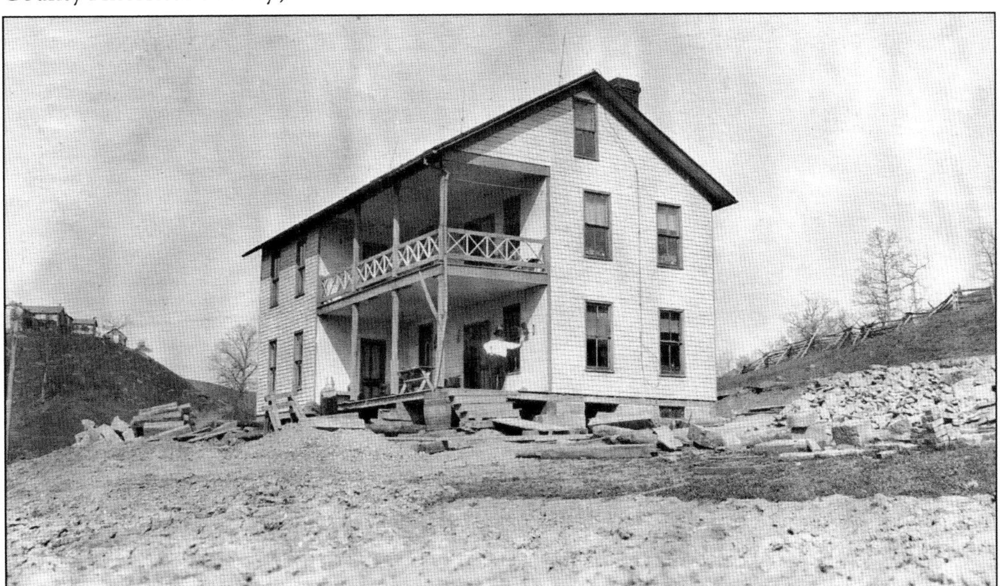

Christian Scherber came to America in 1833 with a group of families from Bavaria and reached Salem Township in 1834. Christian and Elisabetha Scherber acquired over 300 acres of land in Salem Township near Whipple. In this photograph, the house, owned by George Scherber, had just been moved to higher ground to avoid the often flash flooding of Duck Creek. (Courtesy of Lila Hill.)

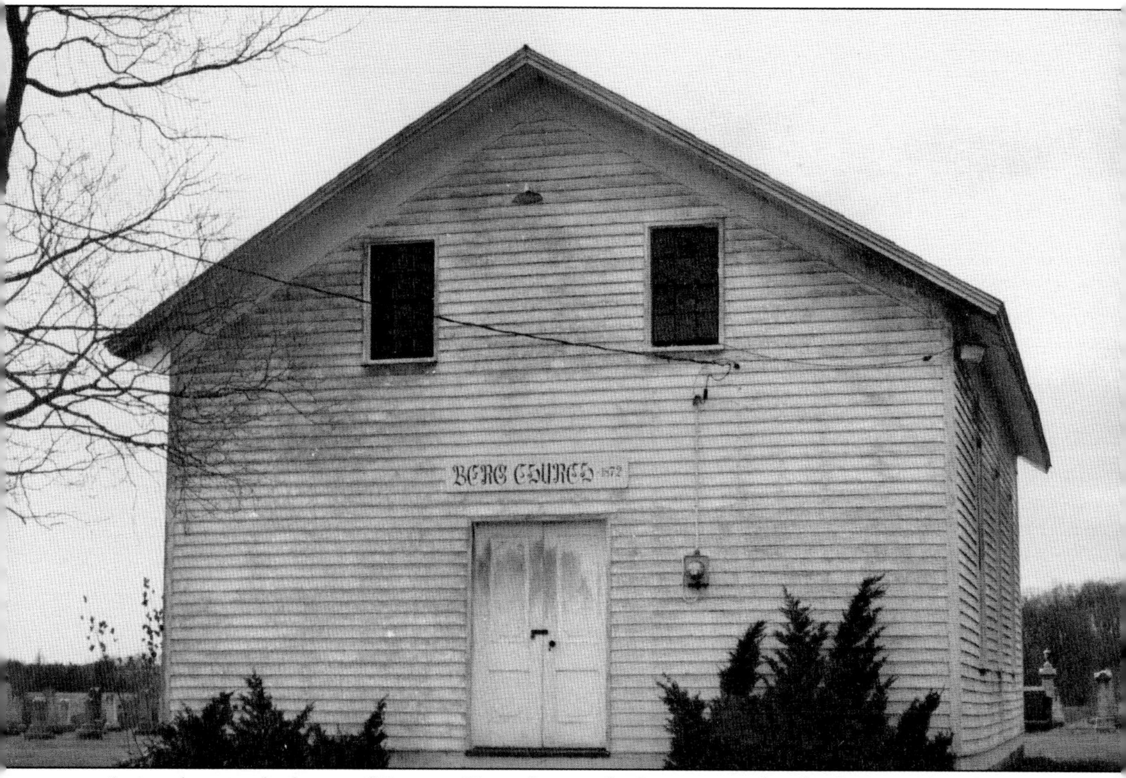

Lying deep in the heart of Fearing Township, early German settlers built Berg Church as a center for community worship. At first, the pioneers attended the church on Highland Ridge but were dismayed with the distance and lack of accessibility when the waters of Duck Creek flooded. In 1846, with land from Peter Berg, they chose to build a log structure church and cemetery in the highlands near their farms. The first minister was Rev. Theodore Schreiner who had taken a leadership role with the early German settlers of 1833. Time and increasing church attendance deemed the need to build a new church in 1872. Nearby land was purchased from Daniel Biehl for a new structure that served the community until it closed in 1955. Interestingly, for the nearly 100-year history of the congregation, records show the church had many names, including First Great Evangelical Reformed Church, First German Protestant Evangelical Church, Second Protestant Evangelical Church, and St. Peter's Church, but everyone referred to it as the Berg Church. (Courtesy of Washington County Historical Society.)

The German-language book of hymns was produced in 1882 and used in church services of Berg Church. The title was *Liederbuch fur Sonntags Schulen*, which translates as "Song Book for Sunday School." The hymn is "Almighty Fortress Is Our God." The book was published in St. Louis, Missouri, from the Eden Publishing House. (Courtesy of Donna Berg Betts.)

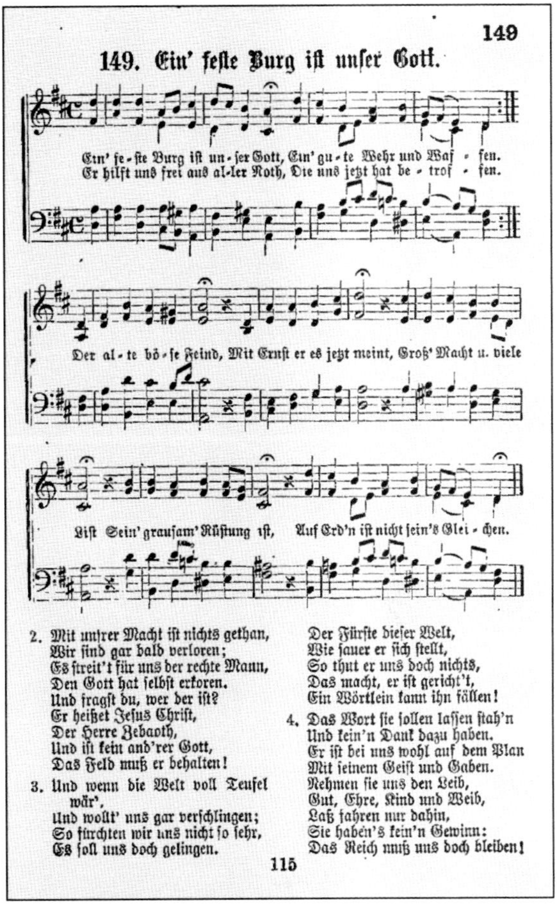

149

149. Ein' feste Burg ist unser Gott.

Ein' fe - ste Burg ist un - ser Gott, Ein' gu - te Wehr und Waf - fen.
Er hilft uns frei aus al-ler Noth, Die uns jetzt hat be - trof - fen.

Der al - te bö - se Feind, Mit Ernst er es jetzt meint, Groß' Macht u. viele

List Sein' grausam' Rüstung ist, Auf Erd'n ist nicht sein's Glei - chen.

2. Mit unsrer Macht ist nichts gethan,
Wir sind gar bald verloren;
Es streit't für uns der rechte Mann,
Den Gott hat selbst erkoren.
Und fragst du, wer der ist?
Er heißet Jesus Christ,
Der Herre Zebaoth,
Und ist kein and'rer Gott,
Das Feld muß er behalten!

3. Und wenn die Welt voll Teufel wär',
Und wollt' uns gar verschlingen;
So fürchten wir uns nicht so sehr,
Es soll uns doch gelingen.
Der Fürste dieser Welt,
Wie sauer er sich stellt,
So thut er uns doch nichts,
Das macht, er ist gericht't,
Ein Wörtlein kann ihn fällen!

4. Das Wort sie sollen lassen stah'n
Und kein'n Dank dazu haben.
Er ist bei uns wohl auf dem Plan
Mit seinem Geist und Gaben.
Nehmen sie uns den Leib,
Gut, Ehre, Kind und Weib,
Laß fahren nur dahin,
Sie haben's kein'n Gewinn:
Das Reich muß uns doch bleiben!

115

The Stanleyville Band was organized after World War I. The players used their uniforms as band attire. Players of German descent were Gilbert Born, Edwin and Edward Trautner, Louis and Charlie Pfaff, and George Zimmer. They played for any public gathering, Berg Church activities, church monthly potlucks, family events, and christenings. (Courtesy of Donna Berg Betts.)

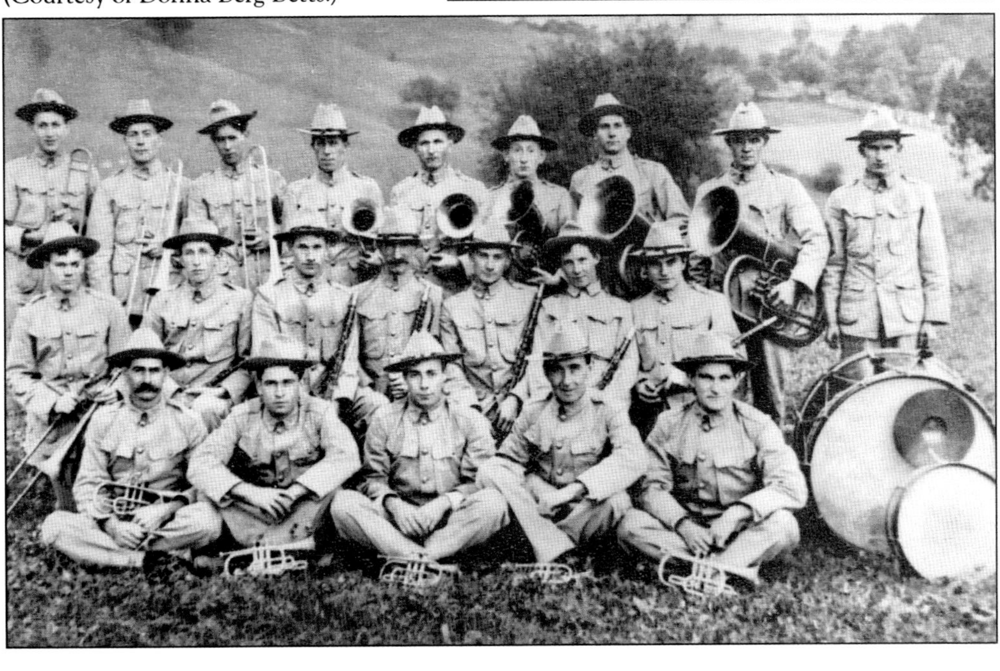

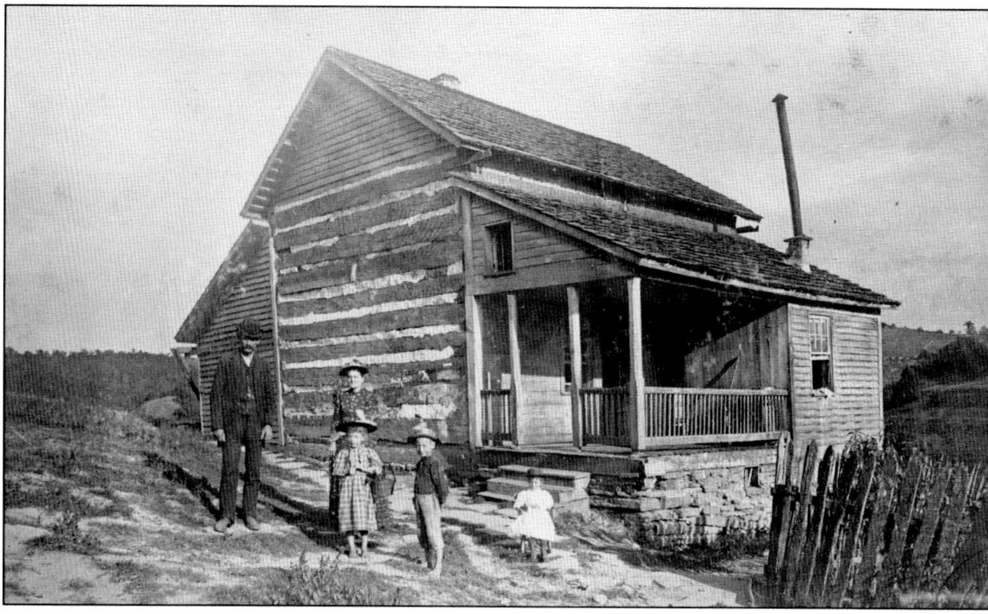

Martin Gerhold, from Hesse, arrived in Fearing Township in 1844. He and his wife, Carolina, built this log house on the land that they farmed. Early structures of hand-hewn logs from the virgin forests were often the first houses where families would live. Later, additions could be made to accommodate a growing family. (Courtesy of Washington County Historical Society.)

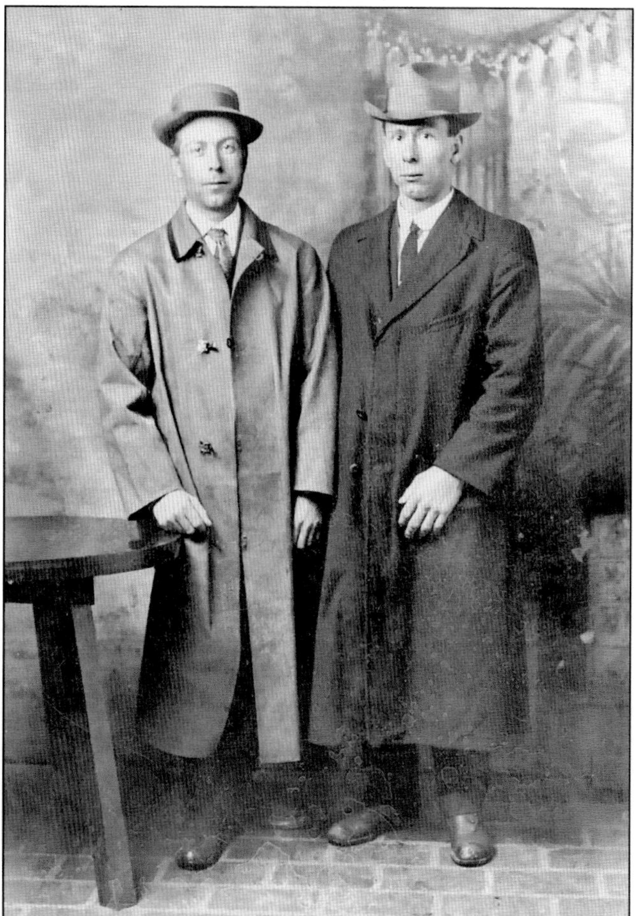

As young men, Robert (left) and Albert Schneider traveled to Missouri to claim an inheritance. They were raised on the farm in Fearing Township by paternal grandparents, Christian and Elenora Grosz Schneider, both German immigrants. Robert Schneider's son Norman served as clerk of the township for 23 years. (Courtesy of Karen J. Schneider.)

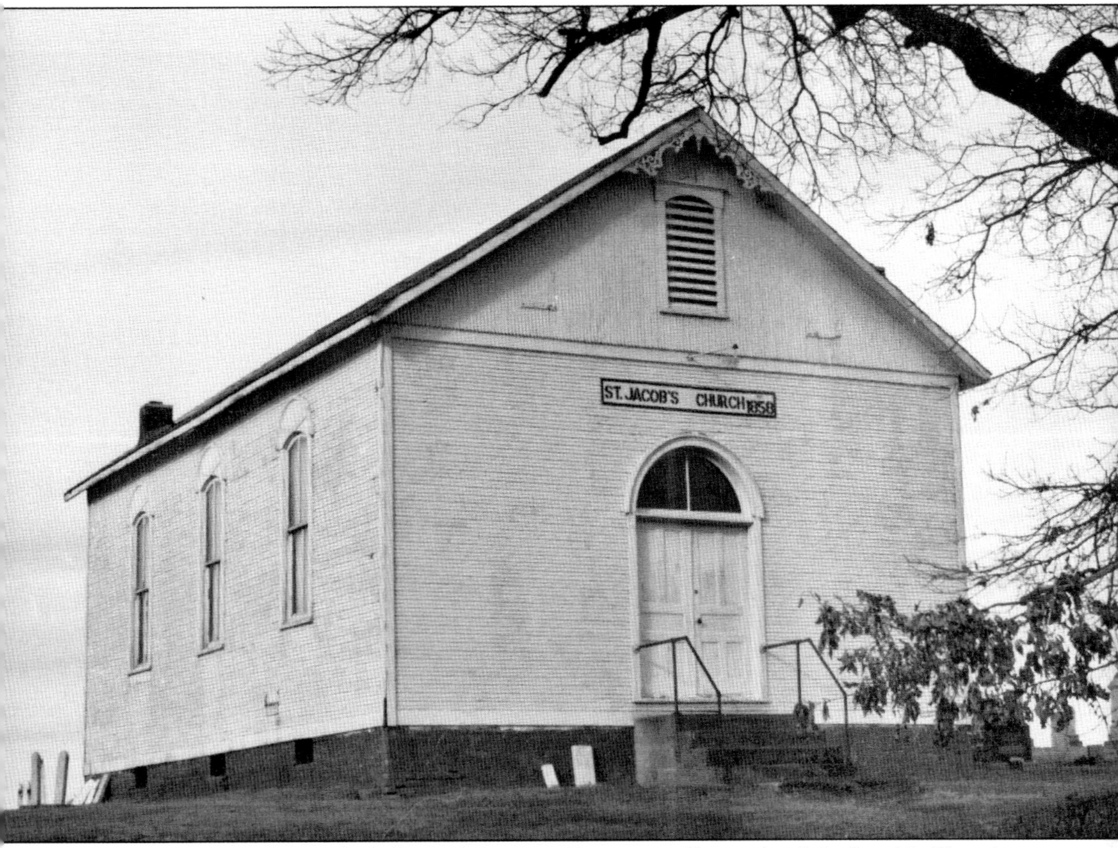

In 1859, the Rev. Daniel Hirsch dedicated German Protestant Evangelical St. Jacob's Church, which is now located on County Road 375. This hilltop church and cemetery overlooked the valley where the village of Stanleyville served as a center for the surrounding community of farmers. Early families in the church were several branches of the Trautners, Barths, Wagners, Knochs, and Millers. At some point in time, the building suffered a fire, and a new church was built in the 1870s. (Courtesy of Washington County Historical Society.)

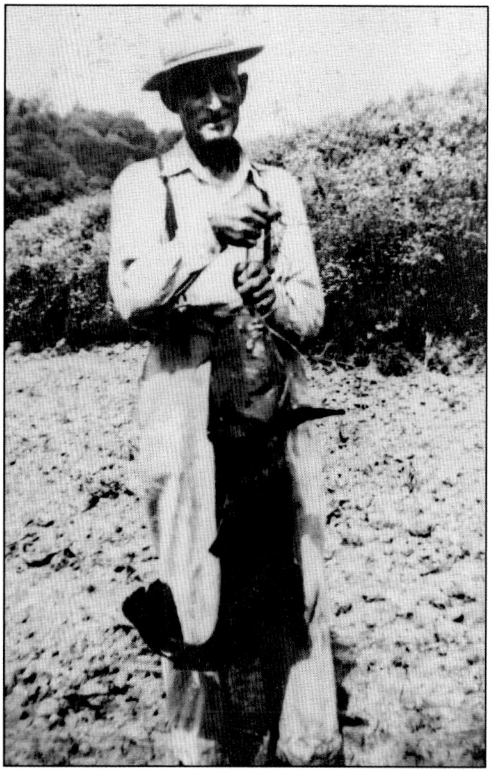

Local Germans would fish in Duck Creek. This photograph shows a large catch by Charlie Pfaff. Large catfish and other fish were plentiful before the 1960s. Many farms in the area were diversified, and products such as cream, eggs, butter, and milk were sold in Marietta. The Trautners were the last of the butter-and-egg people to take products to Marietta. (Courtesy of Donna Berg Betts.)

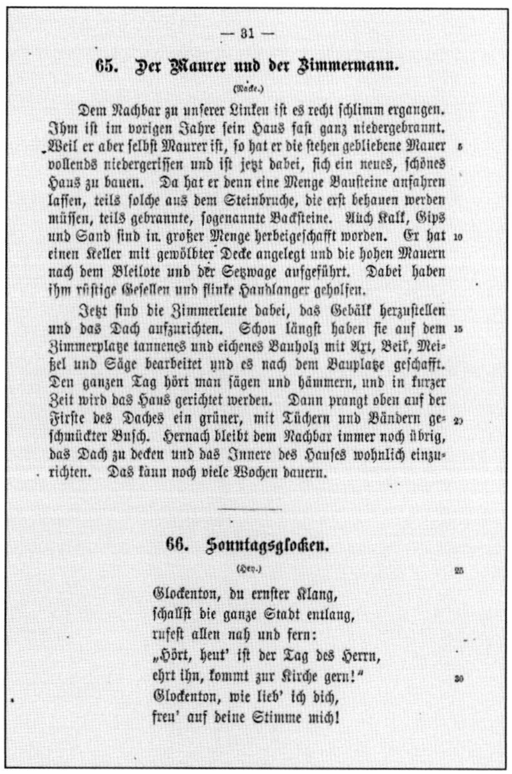

— 31 —

65. Der Maurer und der Zimmermann.

(Mäcke.)

Dem Nachbar zu unserer Linken ist es recht schlimm ergangen. Ihm ist im vorigen Jahre sein Haus fast ganz niedergebrannt. Weil er aber selbst Maurer ist, so hat er die stehen gebliebene Mauer vollends niedergerissen und ist jetzt dabei, sich ein neues, schönes Haus zu bauen. Da hat er denn eine Menge Bausteine anfahren lassen, teils solche aus dem Steinbruche, die erst behauen werden müssen, teils gebrannte, sogenannte Backsteine. Auch Kalk, Gips und Sand sind in großer Menge herbeigeschafft worden. Er hat einen Keller mit gewölbter Decke angelegt und die hohen Mauern nach dem Bleilote und der Setzwage aufgeführt. Dabei haben ihm rüstige Gesellen und flinke Handlanger geholfen.

Jetzt sind die Zimmerleute dabei, das Gebälk herzustellen und das Dach aufzurichten. Schon längst haben sie auf dem Zimmerplatze tannenes und eichenes Bauholz mit Axt, Beil, Meißel und Säge bearbeitet und es nach dem Bauplatze geschafft. Den ganzen Tag hört man sägen und hämmern, und in kurzer Zeit wird das Haus gerichtet werden. Dann prangt oben auf der Firste des Daches ein grüner, mit Tüchern und Bändern geschmückter Busch. Hernach bleibt dem Nachbar immer noch übrig, das Dach zu decken und das Innere des Hauses wohnlich einzurichten. Das kann noch viele Wochen dauern.

66. Sonntagsglocken.

(Hey.)

Glockenton, du ernster Klang,
schallst die ganze Stadt entlang,
rufest allen nah und fern:
„Hört, heut' ist der Tag des Herrn,
ehrt ihn, kommt zur Kirche gern!"
Glockenton, wie lieb' ich dich,
freu' auf deine Stimme mich!

German pioneers found it important for their children to be educated. This copy of *Lesebuch fur Evangelische Schulen* was published in Missouri in 1887 and edited by the German Lutheran Snode von Nordamerika. The two selections were called "The Mason and the Carpenter" and "Sunday Bells." The book was written for the lower grades. (Courtesy of Donna Berg Betts.)

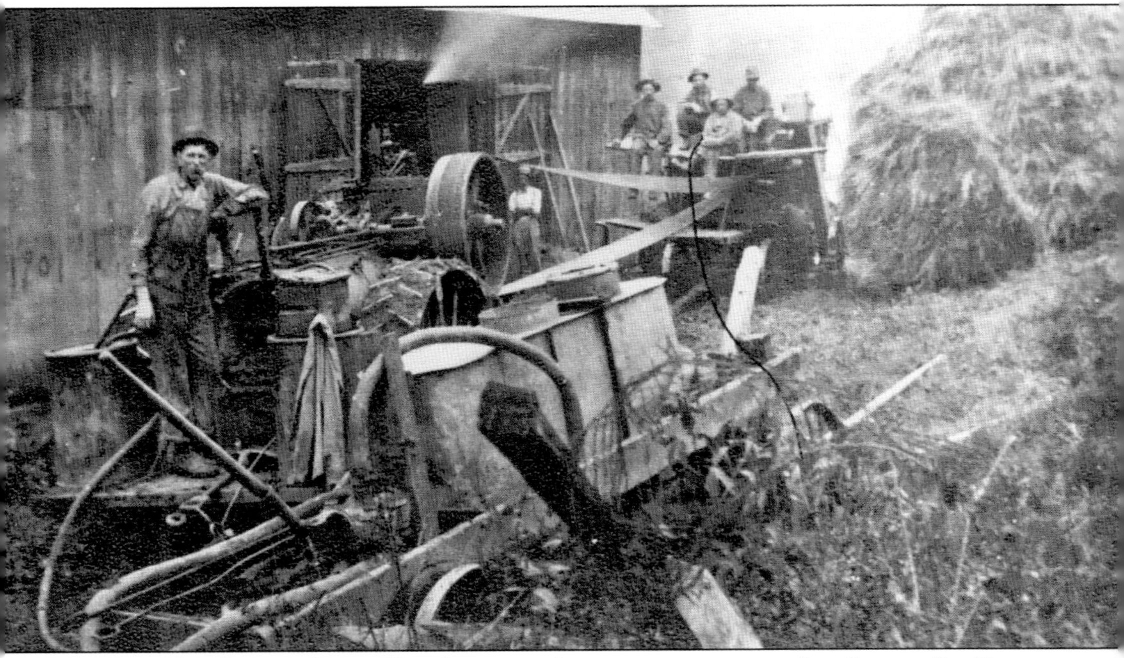

Barn raisings, thrashing circles, and butchering circles were common ways that German families would share the farmwork and have social gatherings. The photograph shows a "thrashing circle" at the Lou Pfaff farm. The machine separated the grain from the chaff. Straw is the stalk of small grains, such as rye, wheat, spelt, and oats. The thrashing machine would go from farm to farm to do the work in the community. It was owned by Lou Zimmer. Everyone was expected to participate in the work. These circles would also be an opportunity to socialize on Saturday nights. They would have square dances in barns, and individuals would play guitars, banjos, and fiddles. (Courtesy of Donna Berg Betts.)

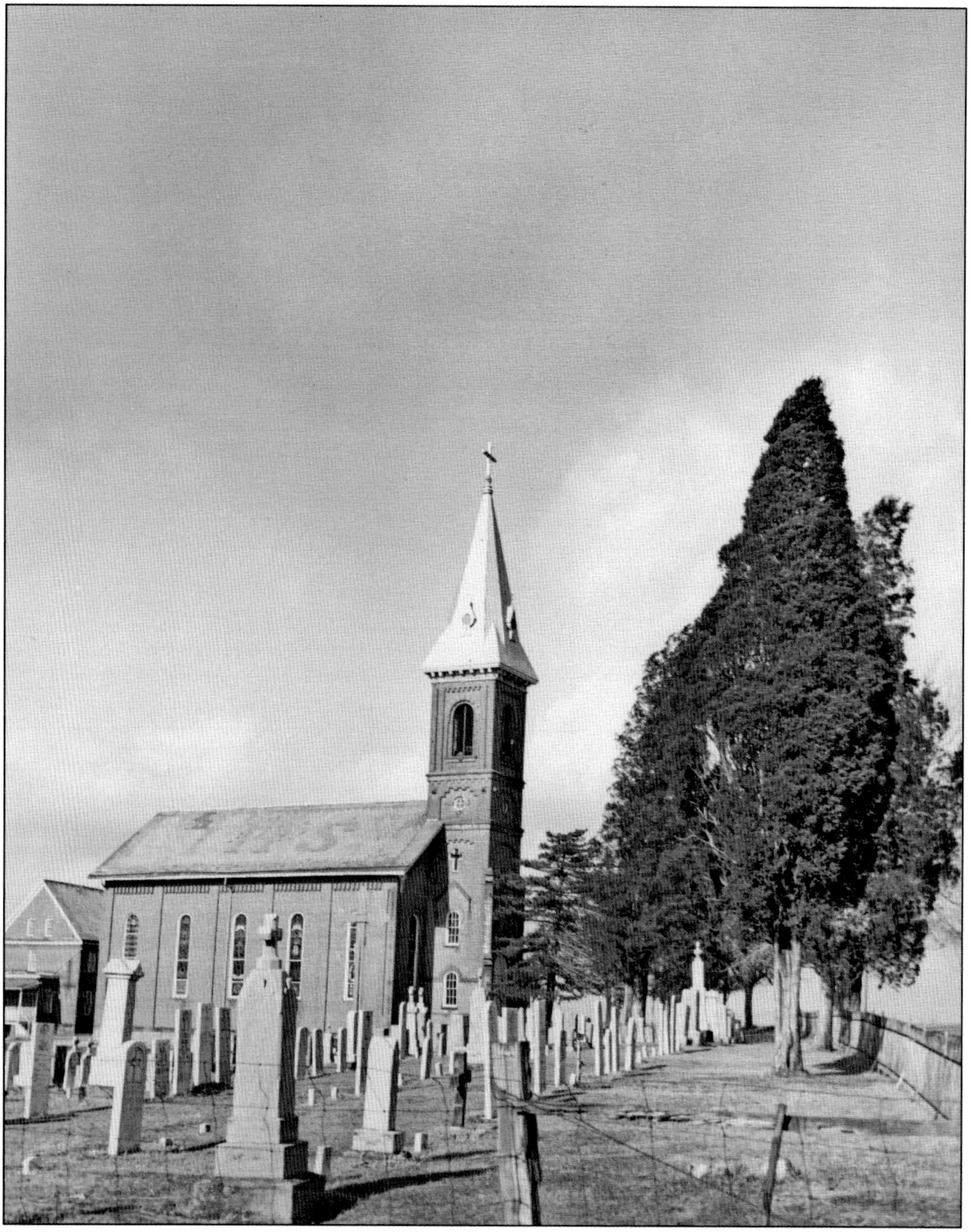

St. John the Baptist Church, as it sits on a ridge in Watertown Township, holds vigil over the rolling hills and highlands and valleys for as far as the eye can see. This beacon for the rural community of the unincorporated Churchtown has served its membership since 1841. After many years of sharing Mass in the homes of the congregation, the cornerstone of a church was laid in 1866 on land donated by a Mr. Jurden. The "town" once had a post office but no other stores. The Irish and German people were devoted farmers on these rolling hills. The cemetery next to the church has the German names of Thieman, Schwendeman, Offenberger, Tornes, Pottmeyer, Strahler, Rauch, and Schillings. (Courtesy of Marietta College.)

Ave Maria Church, set off on a lonely hill overlooking Rainbow Valley, was the center of worship for Catholic German farmers and carpenters who built it in 1866. Early leaders were Andrew Schwendeman, Joseph and Catherine Strahler, Louis and Mary Lang, Joseph Kerns, Theadore and Bernadine Huck, the Schilling family, and the Vonderau family. Services were held there for 50 years. German families enjoyed the choir singing "Stille Nacht" at Christmas Mass and the sun illuminating the stained-glass windows. Even the men singing a German dirge at funerals were a fond remembrance of the Fatherland. The stained-glass windows were manufactured in Dresden, Germany. Each window was engraved with the name of the donor; the names were Schwendeman, Kern, Vonderau, Lang, Meiser, Huck, Strahler, Schilling, and Eppink, the minister. In time, the remoteness of the church and cemetery was its demise, as the Bishop of the Columbus diocese closed it in 1919. Most of the congregation moved to a Lowell location. (Both, courtesy of Theresa R. Thomas.)

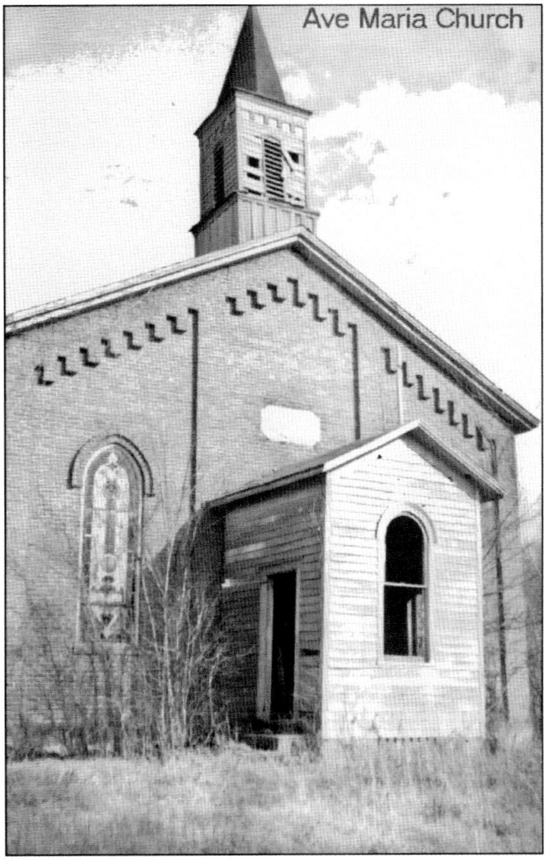

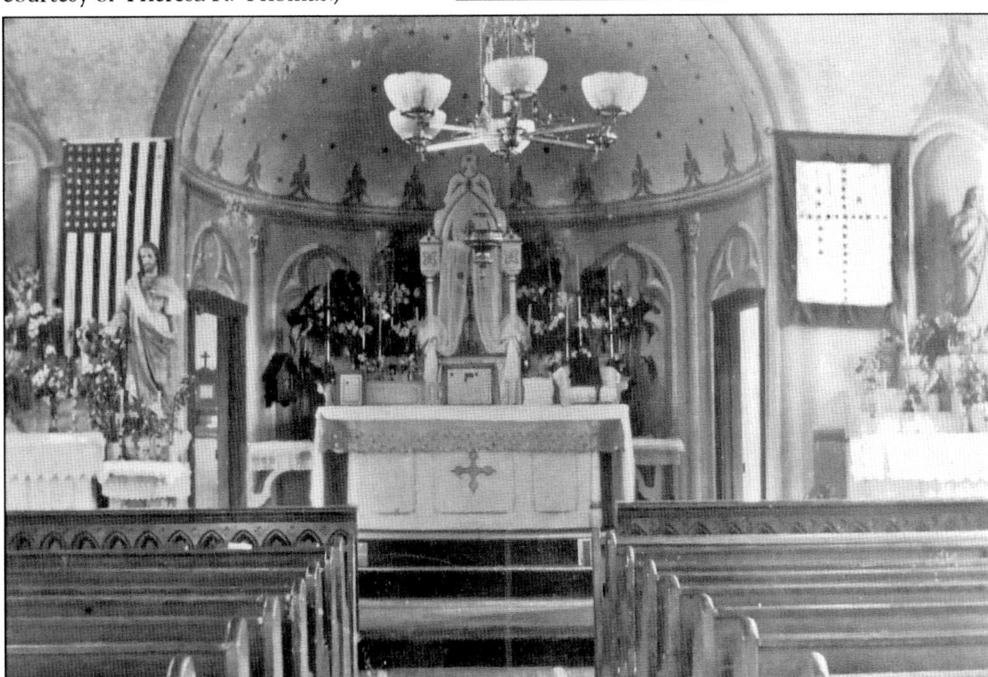

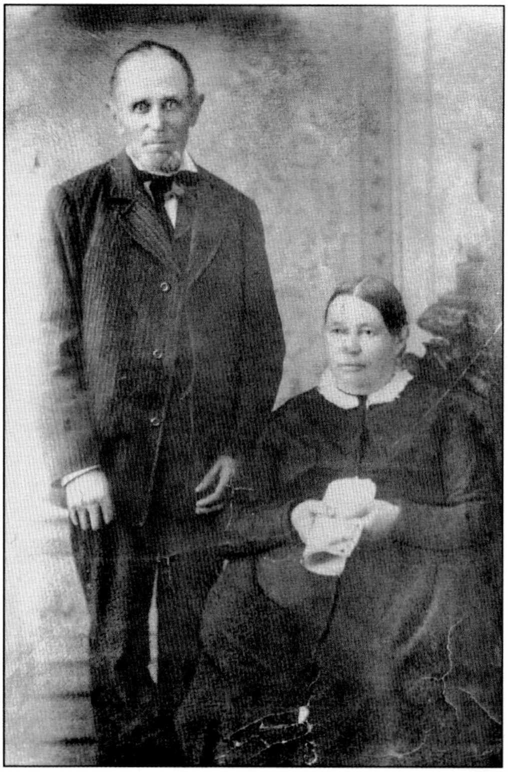

All of the local Strahlers descended from Joseph and Catherine Alt Strahler. They arrived in 1854 from Ettmannsdorf, Bavaria, and settled in Pennsylvania for a few years. Eventually, they settled in Watertown Township as farmers. Seven of their nine children, James, George, Mary, Franciska, Catherine, Landolin, and Justina settled here. (Courtesy of Theresa R. Thomas.)

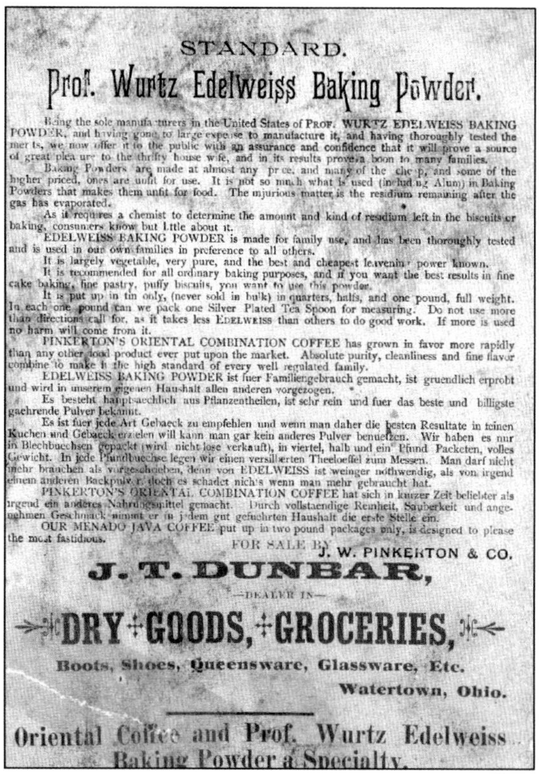

STANDARD.

Prof. Wurtz Edelweiss Baking Powder.

Being the sole manufacturers in the United States of PROF. WURTZ EDELWEISS BAKING POWDER, and having gone to large expense to manufacture it, and having thoroughly tested the merits, we now offer it to the public with an assurance and confidence that it will prove a source of great pleasure to the thrifty house wife, and in its results prove a boon to many families.

Baking Powders are made at almost any price, and many of the cheap, and some of the higher priced, ones are unfit for use. It is not so much what is used (including Alum) in Baking Powders that makes them unfit for food. The injurious matter is the residium remaining after the gas has evaporated.

As it requires a chemist to determine the amount and kind of residium left in the biscuits or baking, consumers know but little about it.

EDELWEISS BAKING POWDER is made for family use, and has been thoroughly tested and is used in our own families in preference to all others.

It is largely vegetable, very pure, and the best and cheapest leavening power known.

It is recommended for all ordinary baking purposes, and if you want the best results in fine cake baking, fine pastry, puffy biscuits, you want to use this powder.

It is put up in tin only, (never sold in bulk) in quarters, halfs, and one pound, full weight. In each one pound can we pack one Silver Plated Tea Spoon for measuring. Do not use more than directions call for, as it takes less EDELWEISS than others to do good work. If more is used no harm will come from it.

PINKERTON'S ORIENTAL COMBINATION COFFEE has grown in favor more rapidly than any other food product ever put upon the market. Absolute purity, cleanliness and fine flavor combine to make it the high standard of every well regulated family.

EDELWEISS BAKING POWDER ist fuer Familiengebrauch gemacht, ist gruendlich erprobt und wird in unserem eigenen Haushalt allen anderen vorgezogen.

Es besteht hauptsaechlich aus Pflanzentheilen, ist sehr rein und fuer das beste und billigste gaehrende Pulver bekannt.

Es ist fuer jede Art Gebaeck zu empfehlen und wenn man daher die besten Resultate in feinen Kuchen und Gebaeck erzielen will kann man gar kein anderes Pulver benuetzen. Wir haben es nur in Blechbuechsen gepackt (wird nicht lose verkauft), in viertel, halb und ein Pfund Packeten, volles Gewicht. In jede Pfundbuechse legen wir einen versilberten Theeloeffel zum Messen. Man darf nicht mehr brauchen als vorgeschrieben, denn von EDELWEISS ist weinger nothwendig, als von irgend einem anderen Backpulver, doch es schadet nichts wenn man mehr gebraucht hat.

PINKERTON'S ORIENTAL COMBINATION COFFEE hat sich in kurzer Zeit beliebter als irgend ein anderes Nahrungsmittel gemacht. Durch vollstaendige Reinheit, Sauberkeit und angenehmen Geschmack nimmt er in jedem gut gefuehrten Haushalt die erste Stelle ein.

OUR MENADO JAVA COFFEE put up in two pound packages only, is designed to please the most fastidious.

FOR SALE BY J. W. PINKERTON & CO.

J. T. DUNBAR,

—DEALER IN—

DRY GOODS, GROCERIES,

Boots, Shoes, Queensware, Glassware, Etc.

Watertown, Ohio.

Oriental Coffee and Prof. Wurtz Edelweiss Baking Powder a Specialty.

The J.T. Dunbar Dry Goods and Grocery Store advertised in English and German. The advertisement promoted the popular Prof. Wurtz Baking Powder and Pinkerton's Oriental Combination Coffee. The lengthy script described in detail why these products were the best to choose for one's family. (Courtesy of Steven Weber.)

One of the oldest German pioneers to the county was Conrad Bohl who settled in the Watertown Township. His son Conrad Bohl Jr., born in Bavaria, enlisted for service during the Civil War in the 77th Ohio Volunteer Infantry. He had the honor of being the color sergeant, the carrier of the flag, which was an elite and dangerous position since the flag bearer was often a target of the enemy. (Courtesy of Washington County Public Library.)

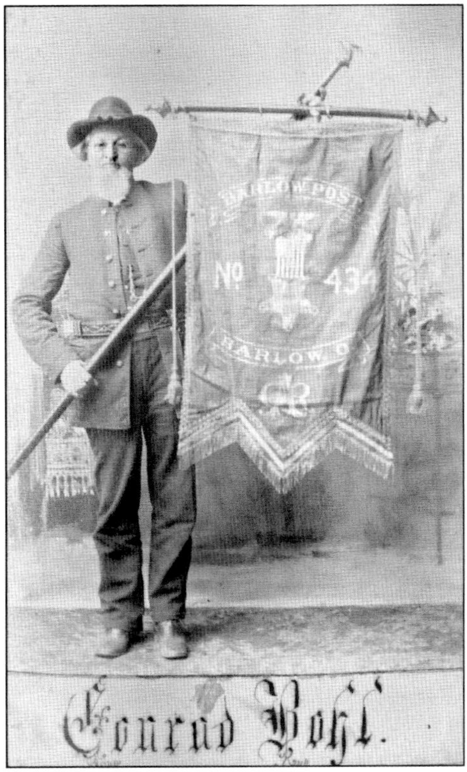

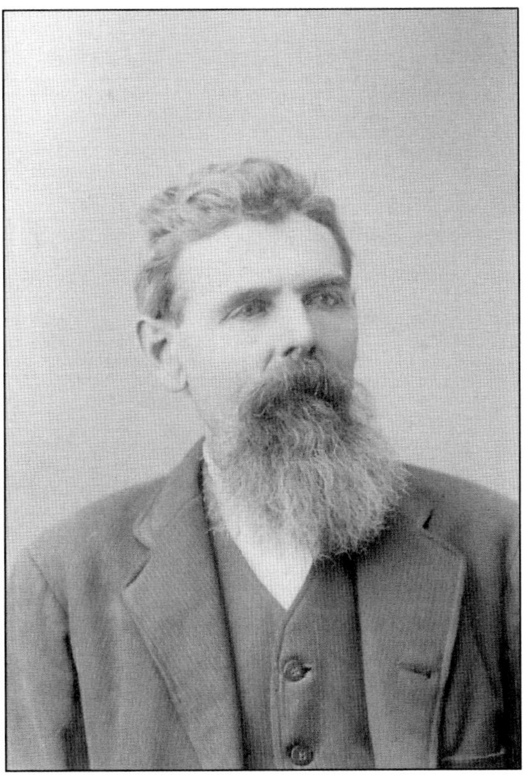

Jacob Steeber, born in 1836 in Bavaria, enlisted in Watertown in 1861 in the 1st West Virginia Artillery in Parkersburg, a group of almost all Marietta troops. He served as a teamster and wagoner. Steeber was discharged in 1865 in Wheeling. Sometimes his name was spelled Steber or Stuber. (Courtesy of Washington County Public Library.)

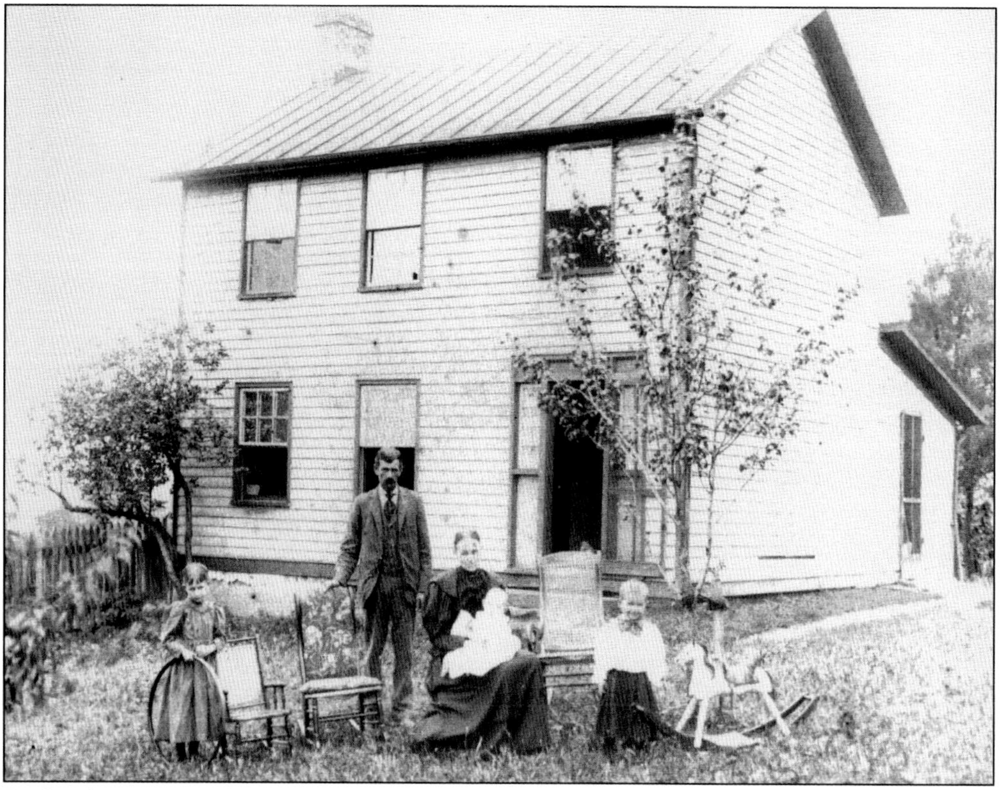

Fred and Anna Weimheimer Christy married in 1887 and moved to a farm in Warren Township where Washington County Career Center is today. Prior to marriage, Anna developed diphtheria, and while confined to her bed, she made a Victorian hair wreath that is presently on display at The Castle, a historic house museum in Marietta. Wreathes and hair flowers were made from the hair of her family. (Courtesy of Theresa R. Thomas.)

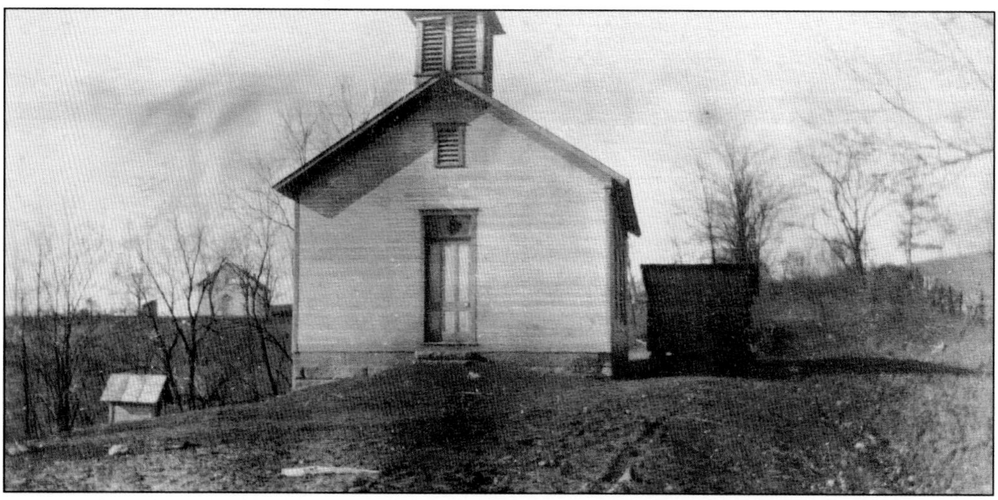

German farm families thought it important for children to be educated. Rural communities built one-room schoolhouses with a teacher found in the German community. Students were encouraged to learn English as well as proper German. Highland Ridge School served the children of one of the earliest German communities in Muskingum Township. (Courtesy of Steven Weber.)

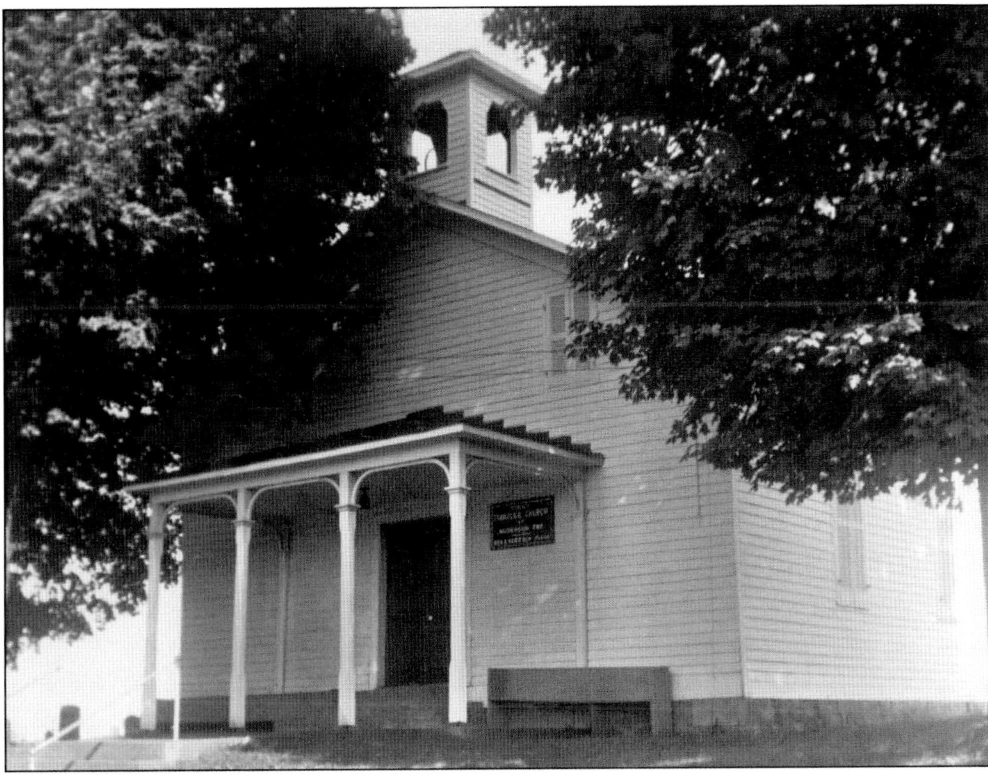

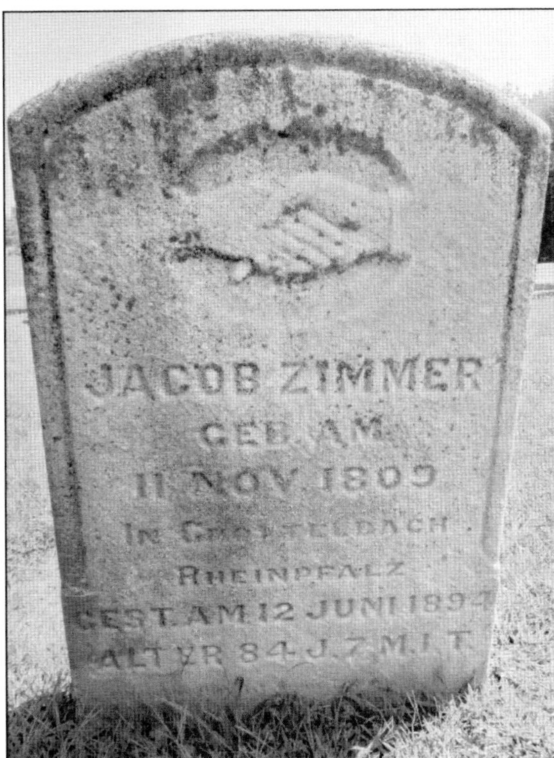

In 1833, a group of pioneers from the Bavarian Rhine Palatinate came to Highland Ridge to establish homes, farms, and a church. The German Protestant Evangelical Church was formed in 1835 with Theodore Schreiner as the first pastor. They met in homes and then in a hewed-log building. By 1849, a new frame church was built with the cemetery of German-language tombstones almost surrounding it. Rev. Sebastian Beach was minister here for 27 years. The first English service was held in 1913, but German was used for many years on occasion. Sunday services have almost continuously been held at this site since 1835 under of a variety of names. Highland Ridge Church and cemetery was the first and longest-running German community in Washington County. (Above, courtesy of Highland Ridge Community Church; right, courtesy of author's collection.)

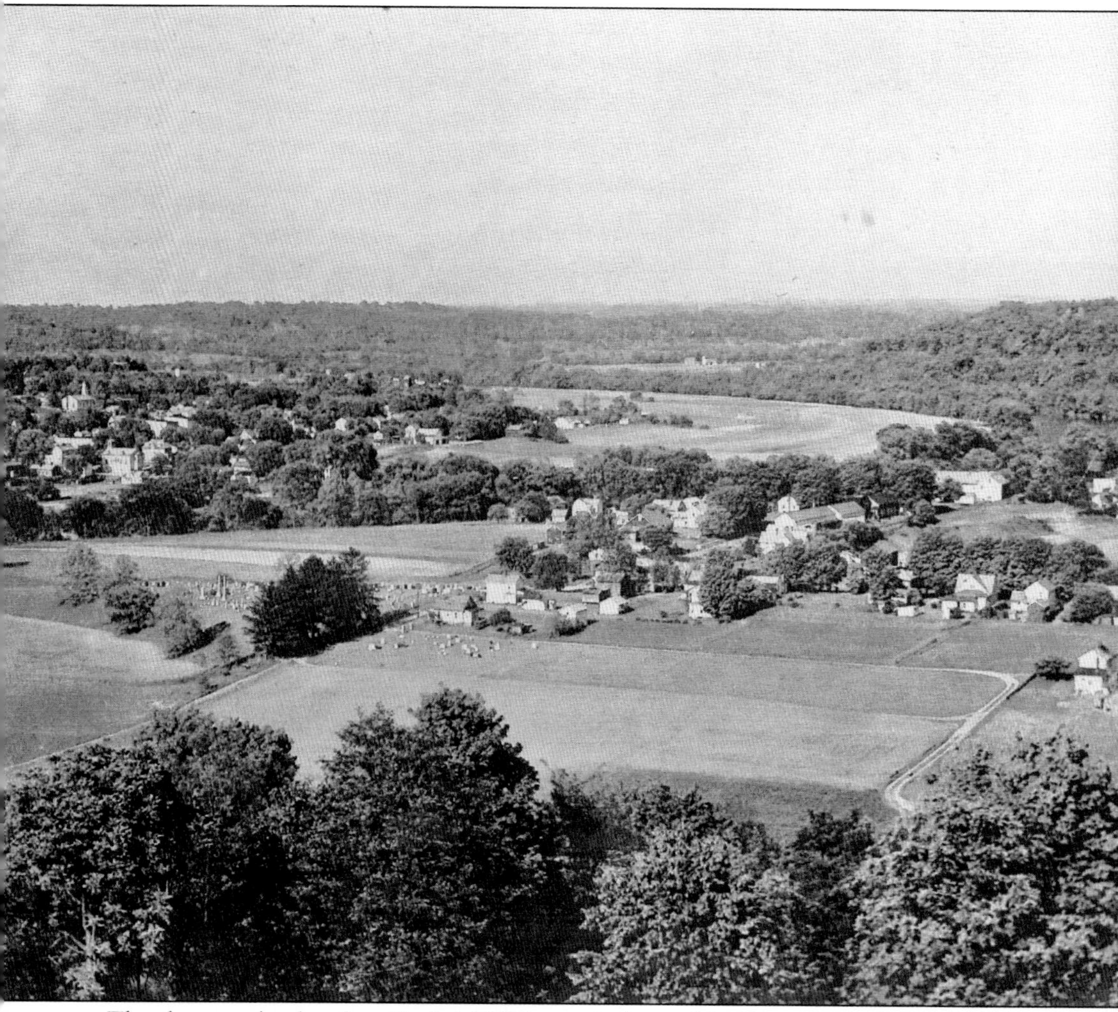

The photograph taken from Beebe's Hill shows the beautiful rolling plains of Waterford Township with the Muskingum River snaking through the towns of Beverly and Waterford. Beverly was formed from Waterford Township. Germans were not as plentiful in this northern township of Washington County, but there were a few merchants in town and farmers in the rural fertile soil of this township. Just south of this scene was the village of Watertown in Watertown Township with the same rolling plains of farmland. The township had a plentiful population of Germans who settled in the village and farmlands particularly after the Civil War. Common family names from the township were Arnold, Brooker, Bohl, Biedel, Bauerbach, Mindling, Pottmeyer, Schilling, Schaad, Schwendeman, Tornes, Theiman, and Schweikert. (Courtesy of Oliver Tucker Museum.)

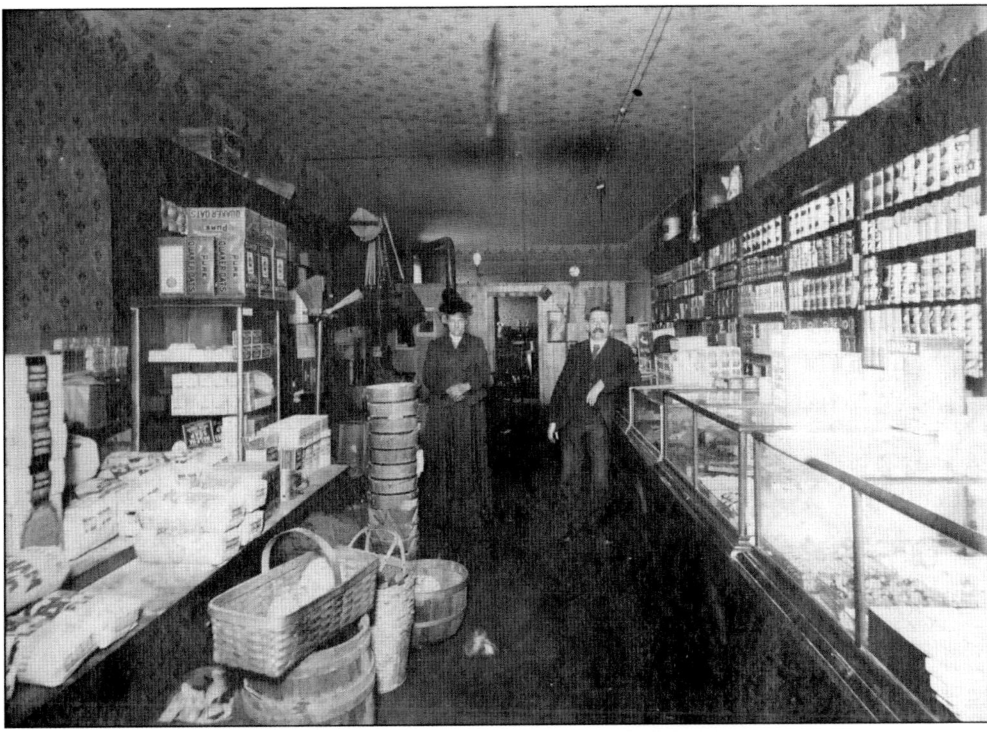

The Charles Langenberg Dry Goods Store in Beverly was located on Fifth Street. The general store contained groceries, clothing, and hardware. Charles, son of German immigrants, was active in the community as the township treasurer and councilman. After Charles died in 1915, his sons Henry and Edgar had the Langenberg Brothers and Company, selling wholesale meats and ice. (Courtesy of the Oliver Tucker Museum.)

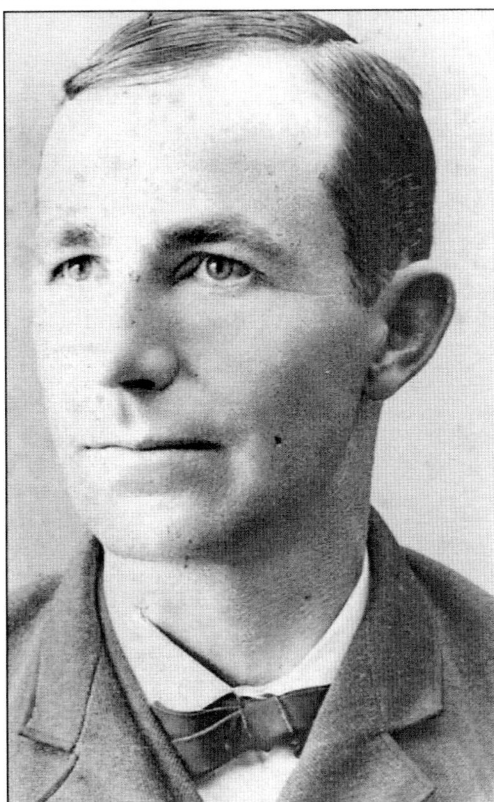

William H. Langenberg and his brother John were the proprietors of a flour mill in Beverly. Like their father, the brothers were tanners and took over his tannery until 1900, when they purchased the Hardin and Raney flouring mill. William H. Langenberg was part owner of the successful Beverly Milling Company. Langenberg served on the school board and town council and was postmaster. (Courtesy of the Oliver Tucker Museum.)

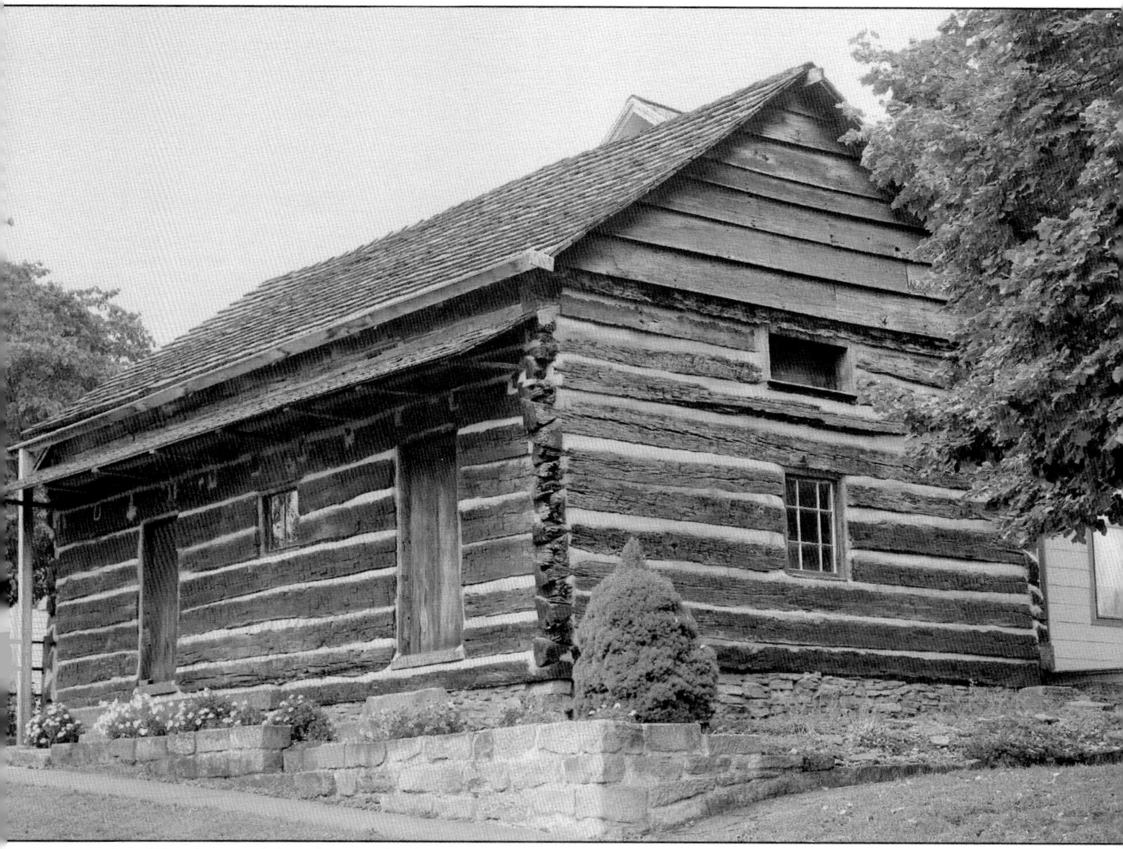

In 1798, Marvil Starlin Sr. built the hand-hewn log house near Waterford for his family of at least 21 children. Daniel Stollar purchased the farm in 1868. A few years later, Nicholas and Elizabeth Peters Mindling bought the property and raised their family of eight children in the log house. In 1893, the Mindlings built a larger house and used the log house as a milk house. The house was briefly a country store, but for over 80 years, it served as an old storage building. Incredibly, the log structure survived long enough to be moved to Beverly in 1974. Students and adults from Waterford, Beverly, and Marietta under the direction of Phillip Crane, restored the Old Log House as part of the Oliver Tucker Museum in 1974–1975. George W. Mindling, born in the log house, was the former head of the Ohio Weather Bureau. (Courtesy of Oliver Tucker Museum.)

Charles M. Grubb, engineer in the Civil War, was a well-known carpenter and bridge builder in the Beverly area. Grubb enlisted in 1861 and served for over three years in the Ohio Volunteer Infantry as a lieutenant. Charles Grubb was responsible for the building of the Beverly-Waterford Bridge over the Muskingum River, which was completed in 1881. (Courtesy of Washington County Public Library.)

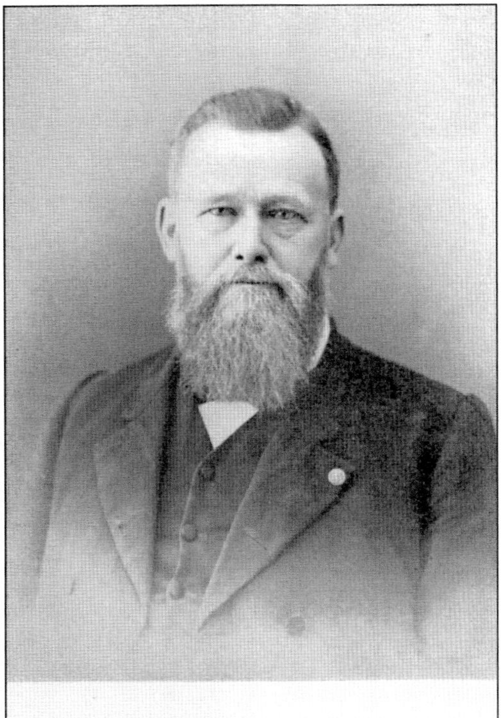

CHARLES M. GRUBB.

During the 1930s, Paul Cisler Dietz operated the Dietz Filling Station at the corner of Seventh and Putnam Streets in Marietta. After moving to Beverly, he owned the Dietz Insurance Agency and developed the Dietz Shopping Center. Dietz played a significant role in the foundation of the Oliver Tucker Museum and was the first president of the Lower Muskingum Historical Society. (Courtesy of the Oliver Tucker Museum.)

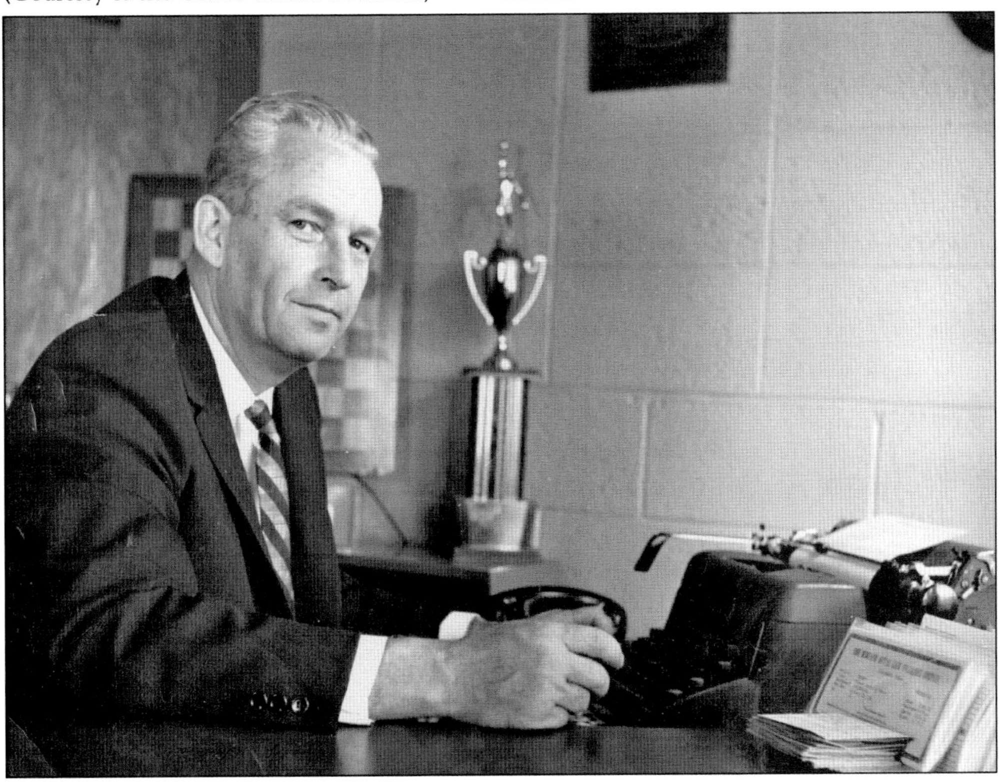

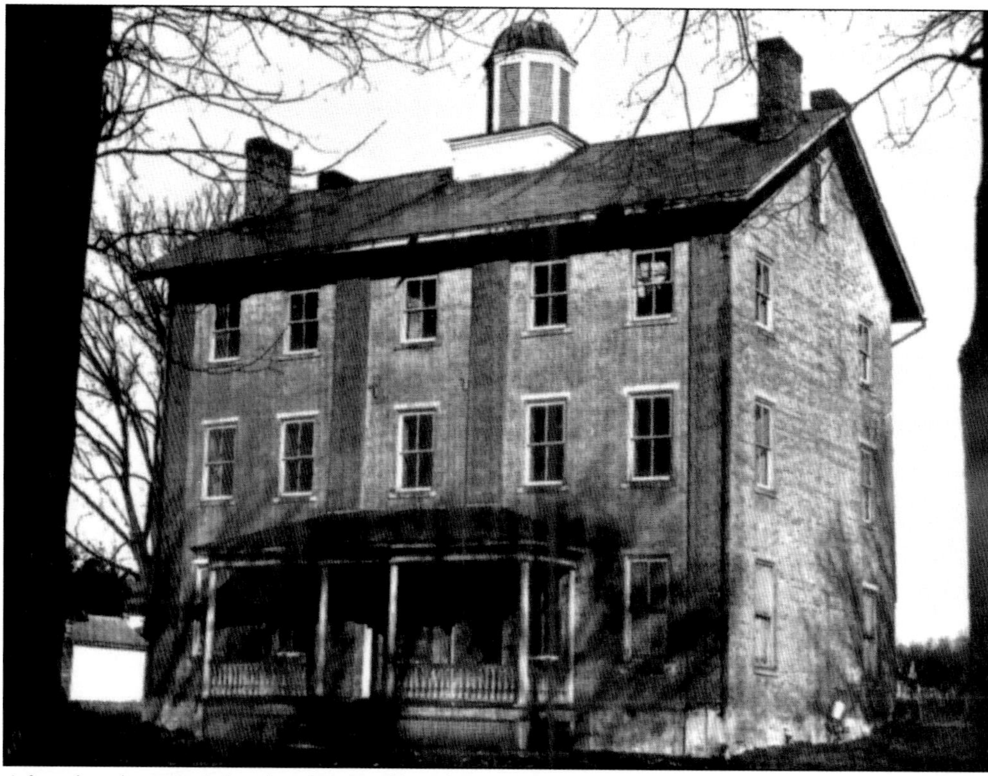

After the closing of the Ave Maria Church in Watertown Township, the old Beverly College building was purchased by the Catholic Diocese of Steubenville. German families and others attended the first Mass held there in 1919. In 1946, the parish had a full-time priest and explored erecting a new building. The new church was completed in 1953 directly behind the college building. (Courtesy of Theresa R. Thomas.)

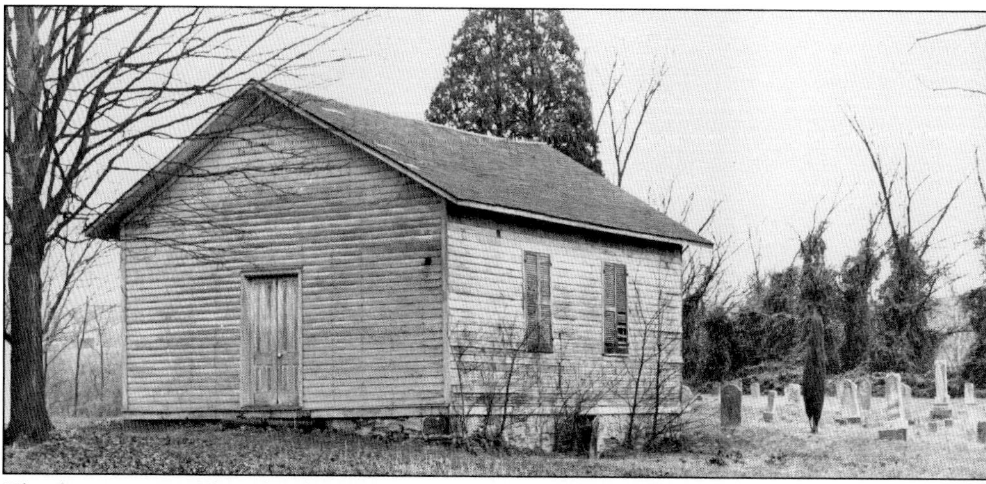

The first meeting place for the Evangelical Protestant Society of Lawrence Township was a German school. Sitka Church, built in the 1870s, is no longer used, but the structure and cemetery is maintained. Following the German tradition, the headstones are set in the order of death. Magdalena Spindler Jung was the first burial in 1853. (Courtesy of Washington County Historical Society.)

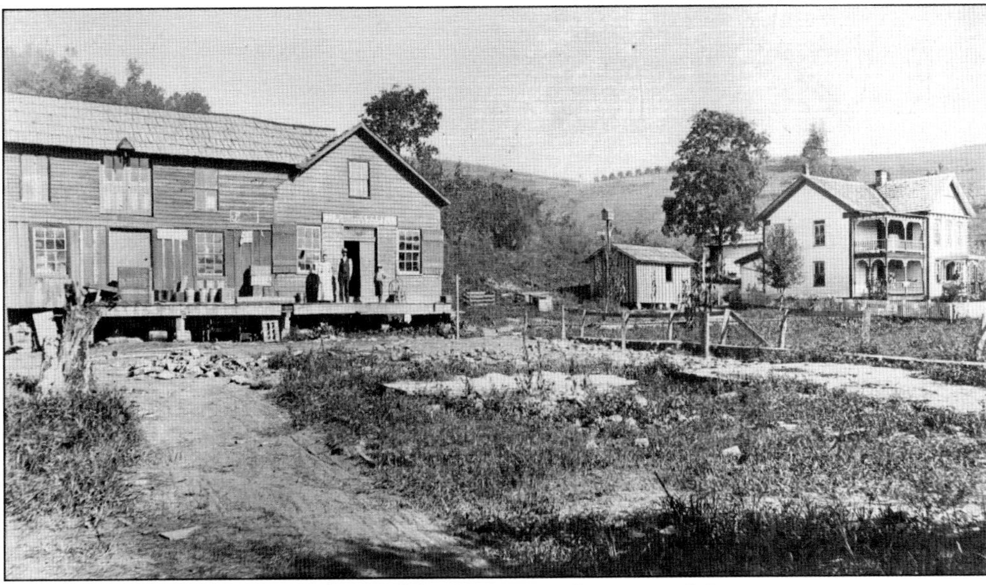

Alice Wallenfelsz Cline, a graduate of the Newspaper Institute of America, was no stranger to this Wingett Run Post Office in rural Ludlow Township. Cline was fluent in English, Spanish, German, and Italian. Her poetry was published in the *Marietta Times* and the *New Matamoras Enterprise* in the 1930s and 1940s. During that time, her brother Oscar owned the store and house. (Courtesy of Washington County Historical Society.)

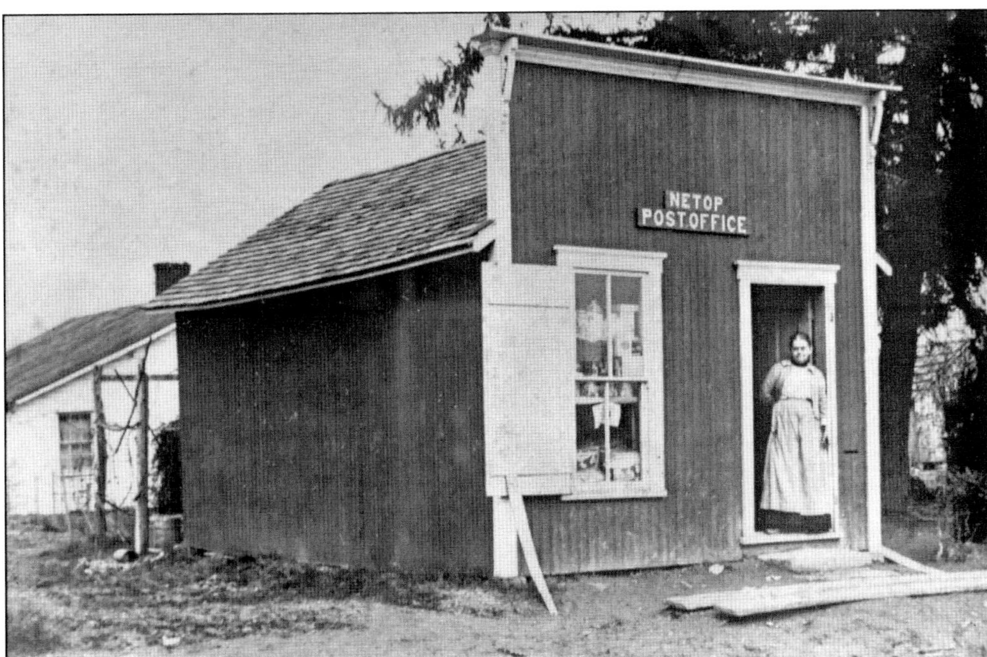

The Netop Post Office in Cornerville served Germans and others of Marietta Township for the years of 1897 to 1906. It was so named because of the knee-deep muddy roads of the area. The township held a population of farmers as well as people who worked in Marietta. (Courtesy of Marietta College.)

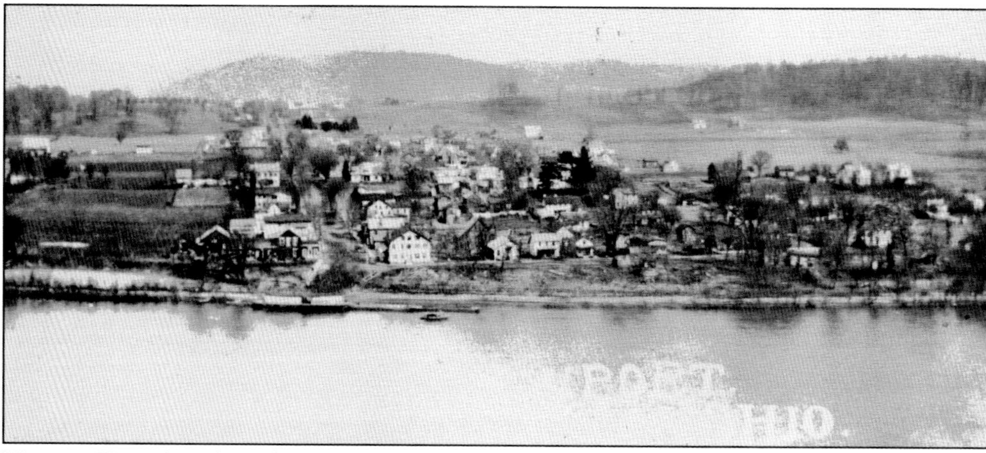

Newport Township along the Ohio River distinguished itself as a land of forested hills and valleys with plentiful farmland. Gordon Greene, a descendant of an early settler, and his wife, Mary Becker, daughter of a German immigrant, operated the Greene Line Steamships. Mary Becker Greene was the only female steamboat captain in Ohio. (Courtesy of Washington County Historical Society.)

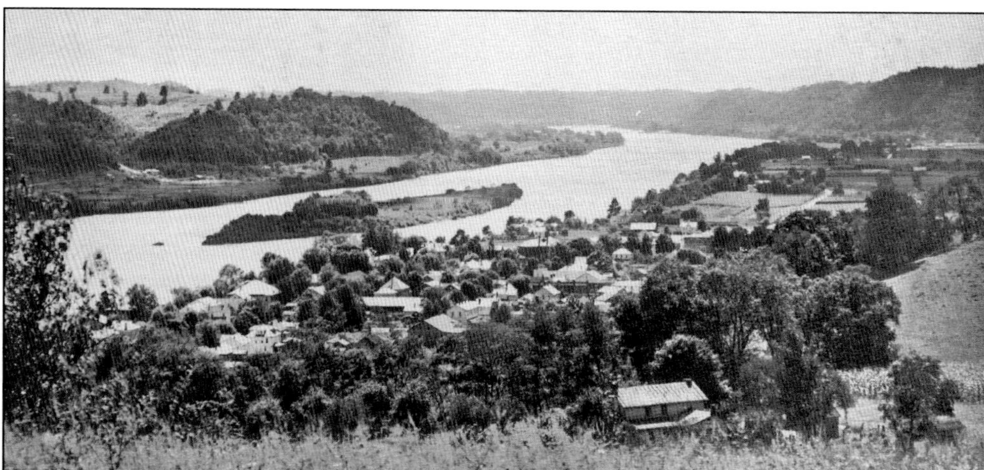

James Riggs and sons-in-law Martin and Anthony Sheets settled in the Matamoras area in 1797. It is possible that the Sheets brothers were of German descent. Grandview Township was established in 1803. The village was first platted in 1846 and received a post office in 1861 when the name became New Matamoras. It was once a thriving shipping community dependent on farming and oil. Decker Hardware and Hanshumacher stores were major businesses. (Courtesy of Matamoras Area Historical Society.)

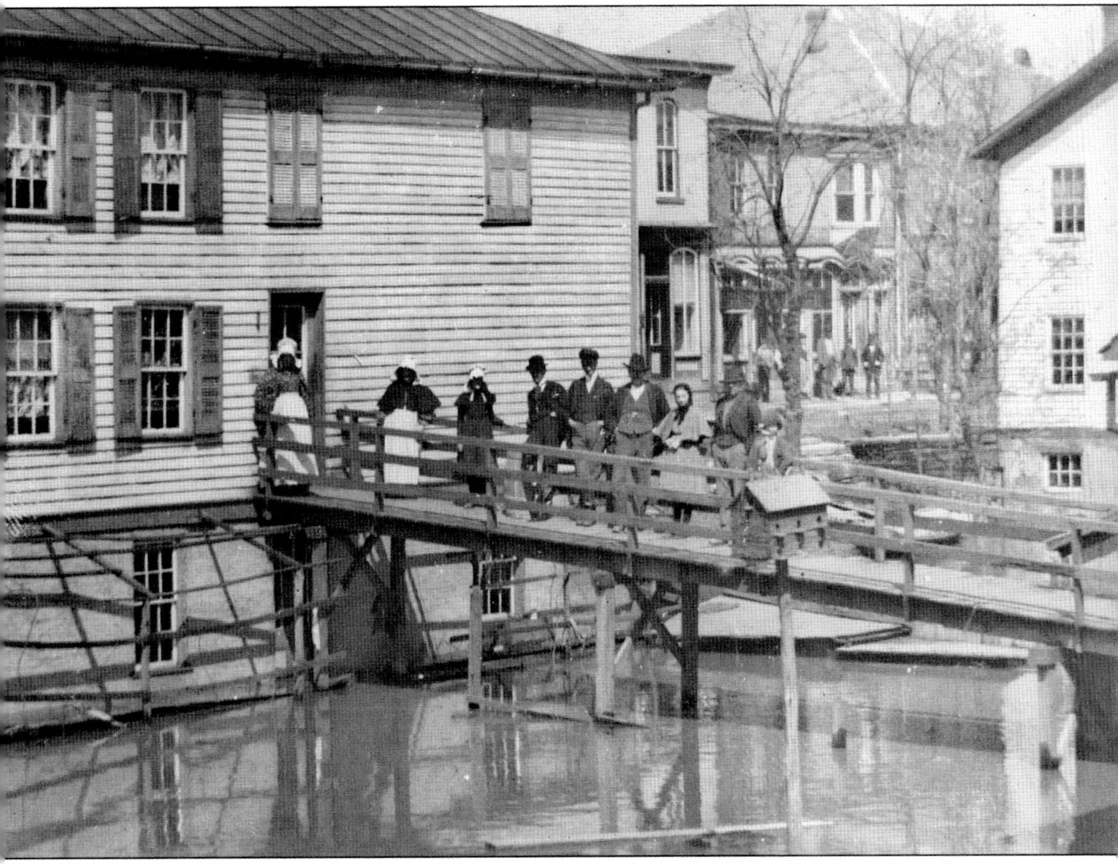

The Hanshumaker House, pictured here from the dock along the Ohio River, provided more than a general store in Matamoras. Since it was located at the ferry landing along the Ohio River and had the public well at its front door, people would gather to socialize and gossip. Philip Hanshumaker, born in Bavaria in 1840, went to Wheeling, Virginia, in 1845 and then worked in the rolling mills at Pittsburgh. He attended two terms at Duff College and became a bookkeeper. Hanshumaker went to Matamoras in 1863 and operated the popular store at the corner of Main and Front Streets. It carried a large inventory of goods including groceries, dry goods, and other household necessities. He married a local woman and was active in the community until his early death in 1888. His son Louis continued business and was well known for his grievances concerning sales tax. Only when the government threatened to close the store did he charge the fee. Louis Hanshumaker operated the store until the 1930s. (Courtesy of Washington County Historical Society.)

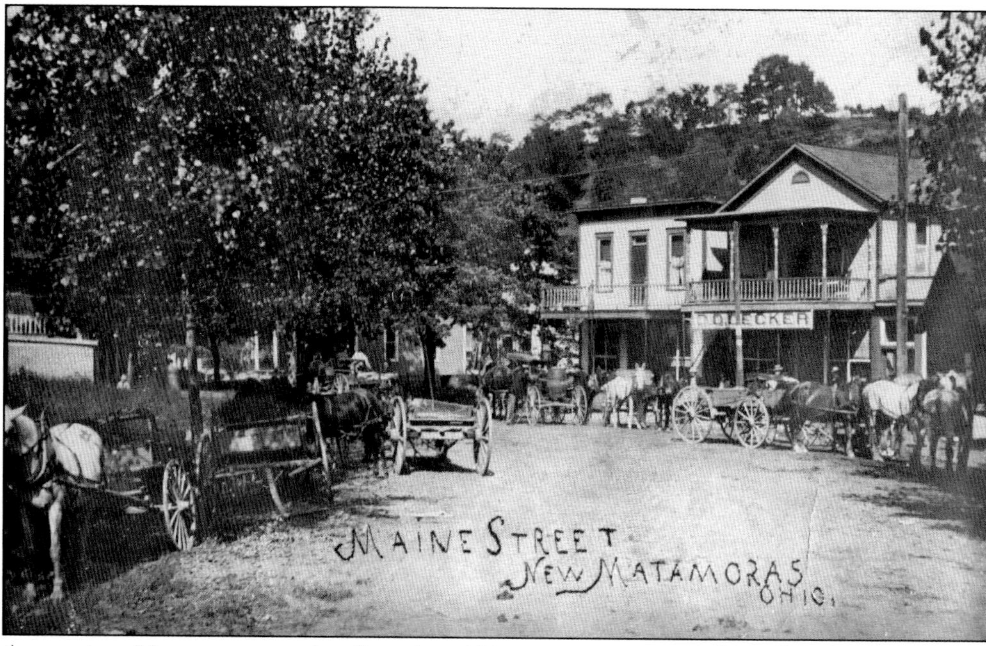

At one time, Matamoras was a bustling city with an active commerce along the Ohio River. Local farmers would bring tobacco and produce to the port to be shipped to other places, such as tobacco heading to Marietta. The Decker Hardware on Main Street would have been an important stop for German farmers. (Courtesy of Washington County Historical Society.)

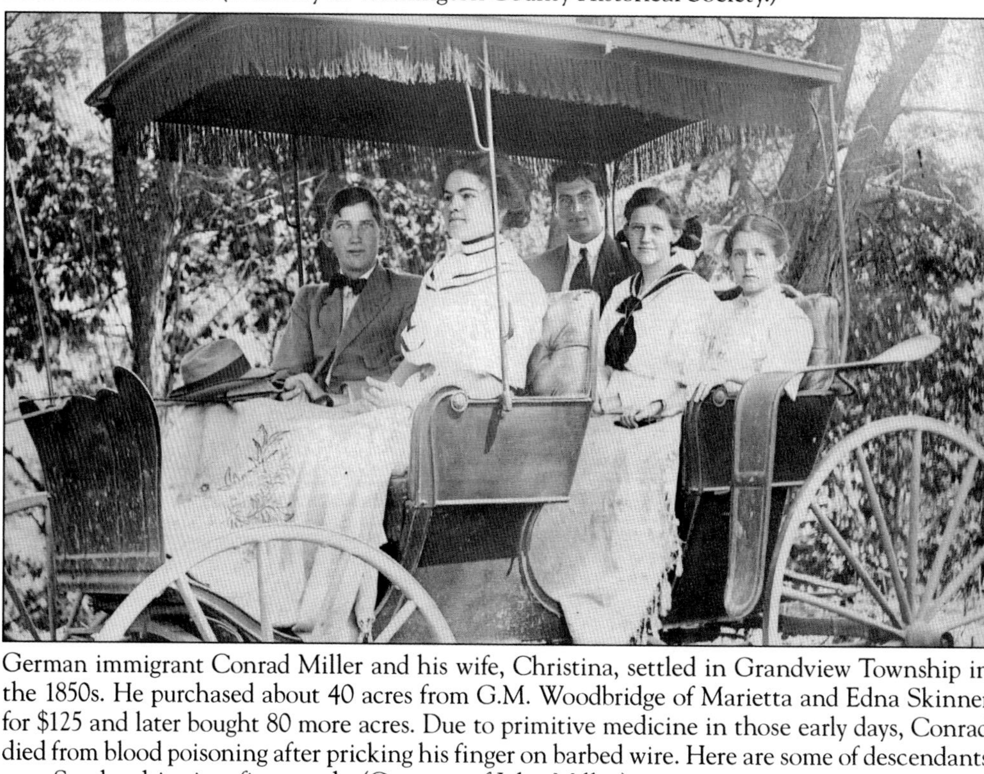

German immigrant Conrad Miller and his wife, Christina, settled in Grandview Township in the 1850s. He purchased about 40 acres from G.M. Woodbridge of Marietta and Edna Skinner for $125 and later bought 80 more acres. Due to primitive medicine in those early days, Conrad died from blood poisoning after pricking his finger on barbed wire. Here are some of descendants on a Sunday drive in a fine coach. (Courtesy of John Miller.)

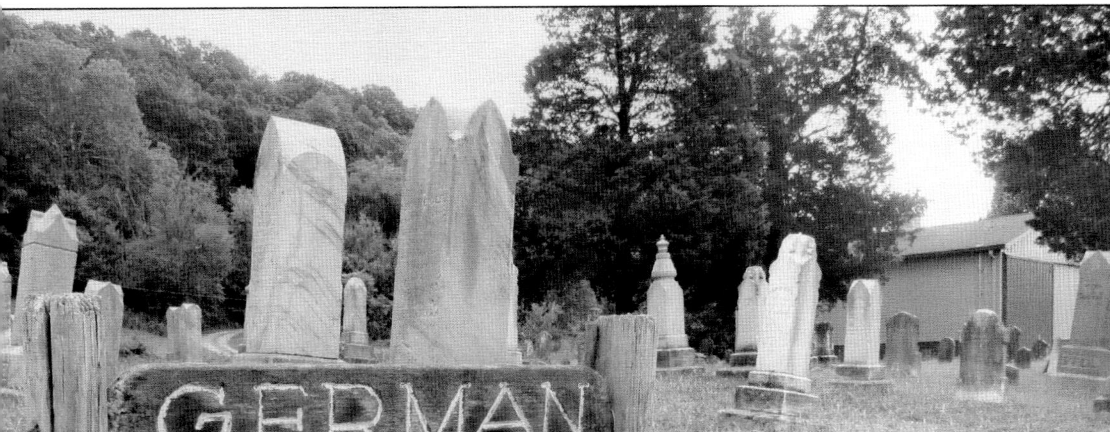

The German Cemetery, located just outside of Lowell, plainly honors the rich German heritage of the area. Only a few cemeteries in Washington County are named so simply. Ludlow, Grandview, and Salem Townships each have a cemetery labeled as German Cemetery. The German Lutheran Cemetery is in Independence Township, while Lawrence Township has a cemetery named the Old Dutch Cemetery. A person does not have to stroll far to see German names in many other cemeteries, such as Waxler, Berg, St. Jacob's, Highland Ridge, and the old Lutheran in Watertown. Townships with a German church and cemetery are mostly Adams, Fearing, Grandview, Lawrence, Liberty, Salem, Waterford, and Watertown. Washington County records suggest there are over 25 churches that had German-language services and German leadership. The headstones of German immigrants and their descendants are found in many cemeteries and give every succeeding generation an acknowledgement that an overwhelming number of German pioneers were a part of the history of Washington County. (Courtesy of author's collection.)